2000 YEARS OF
CLASSIC
CHRISTIAN
PRAYERS

✢

D0061449

2000 YEARS OF
CLASSIC
CHRISTIAN
PRAYERS

A COLLECTION FOR PUBLIC AND PERSONAL USE

EDITED BY

OWEN COLLINS

ORBIS BOOKS

Maryknoll, New York 10545

Second Printing, December 2000

The Catholic Foreign Mission Society of America (Maryknoll) recruits and trains people for overseas missionary service. Through Orbis Books, Maryknoll aims to foster the international dialogue that is essential to mission. The books published, however, reflect the opinions of their authors and are not meant to represent the official position of the society.

To obtain more information about Maryknoll and Orbis Books, please visit our website at www.maryknoll.org.

First published in Great Britain in 1999 by HarperCollins Publishers under the title *2000 Years of Classic Christian Prayers*.

Compilation © 1999 Owen Collins

Owen Collins asserts the moral right to be identified as the editor of this work.

Published in the United States of America in 2000 by Orbis Books, Maryknoll, NY 10545-0308.

All rights reserved.

No part of this publication may be reproduced or transmitted in any form or by any means, electronic or mechanical, including photocopying, recording, or any information storage or retrieval system, without prior permission in writing from the publisher.

Queries regarding rights and permissions should be addressed to: Orbis Books, P.O. Box 308, Maryknoll, NY 10545-0308.

Manufactured in the United States of America

ORBIS/ISBN 1-57075-306-7

CONTENTS

───────── ✢ ─────────

Chapter One

PRAYER AND PRAISE

I will bless the lord at all times;
  his praise shall continually be in my mouth

Psalm 34:1 NRSV

My spirit is dry within me because it forgets to feed on you.

John of the Cross

──────── ✠ ────────

For God Himself

O give thanks to the Lord, for he is good;
  his steadfast love endures for ever!
... I was pushed hard, so that I was falling,
  but the Lord helped me.
... You are my God, and I will give thanks to you;
  you are my God, I will extol you.   Psalm 118:1, 13, 28 NRSV

The God of love my shepherd is,
  And he that doth me feed:
While he is mine, and I am His,
  What can I want or need?

He leads me to the tender grass,
  Where I both feed and rest;
Then to the streams that gently pass:
  In both I have the best.

Or if I stray, he doth convert,
  And bring my mind in frame:
And all this not for my desert,
  But for his holy name.

1

Yea, in death's shady, black abode
    Well may I walk, not fear:
For thou art with me, and thy rod
    To guide, thy staff to bear.

Nay, thou dost make me sit and dine,
    Even in my enemies' sight;
My head with oil, my cup with wine
    Runs over day and night.

Surely thy sweet and wondrous love
    Shall measure all my days;
And as it never shall remove,
    So neither shall my praise.

George Herbert, The Temple

Eternal God, the refuge of all your children,
in our weakness you are our strength,
in our darkness our light,
in our sorrow our comfort and peace.
May we always live in your presence,
and serve you in our daily lives;
through Jesus Christ our Lord.

Boniface

O Lord my God, most merciful, most secret, most present, most constant, yet changing all things, never new and never old, ever in action, yet ever quiet, creating, upholding, and perfecting all, who has anything but your gift? Or what can anyone say when he speaks about you? Yet, have mercy on us, O Lord, that we may speak to you, and praise your name.

Jeremy Taylor

We give you thanks, omnipotent, ever-living God of truth, eternal Father of our Lord Jesus Christ, Creator of heaven and earth, of people, and of all creatures, Sustainer of all things, Giver of all life, order and wisdom, unfailing Source of help: And to your Son our Lord Jesus Christ, your Word and eternal Image: and to your Holy Spirit, with whom you endowed the apostles at Pentecost. We give thanks to you, O God of holiness, and truth, wisdom and goodness, justice and mercy, purity and loving kindness, for with goodness and wisdom unmatched you revealed yourself to us, sending your Son into the world, destined to assume human nature and to become a sacrifice for us.

We give thanks to you, O God, for gathering your eternal church, for guarding the ministry of your Word, for granting your Holy Spirit, and for giving everlasting life. We thank you, O God, because you gave us all good things, because you alleviated and removed the chastisement we justly deserve, because you bestowed on us all the blessings of soul and body. To you be all glory, honour, praise, and thanksgiving, for ever and ever.   Philipp Melanchthon

You are holy, Lord, the only God,
and your deeds are wonderful.
You are strong.
You are great.
You are the most high.
You are almighty.
You, holy Father are King of heaven and earth.
You are three and one, Lord God, all Good.
You are Good, all Good, supreme Good,
Lord God, living and true.
You are love. You are wisdom.
You are humility. You are endurance.
You are rest. You are peace.
You are joy and gladness.
You are justice and moderation.
You are all our riches, and you suffice for us.
You are beauty.
You are gentleness.
You are our protector.
You are our guardian and defender.
You are our courage. You are our haven and our hope.
You are our faith, our great consolation.
You are our eternal life, great and wonderful Lord,
God almighty, merciful Saviour.   Francis of Assisi

We praise thee, O God : we acknowledge thee to be the Lord.
All the earth doth worship thee : the Father everlasting.
To thee all Angels cry aloud : the Heavens, and all the Powers therein.
To thee Cherubim and Seraphim : continually do cry,
Holy, Holy, Holy : Lord God of Sabaoth;
Heaven and earth are full of the Majesty : of thy glory.
The glorious company of the Apostles : praise thee.
The goodly fellowship of the Prophets : praise thee.
The noble army of Martyrs : praise thee.
The holy Church throughout all the world : doth acknowledge thee;
The Father : of an infinite Majesty;
Thine honourable, true : and only Son;
Also the Holy Ghost : the Comforter.
Thou art the King of Glory : O Christ.
Thou art the everlasting Son : of the Father.
When thou tookest upon thee to deliver man : thou didst not abhor
        the Virgin's womb.
When thou hadst overcome the sharpness of death : thou didst open
        the Kingdom of Heaven to all believers.
Thou sittest at the right hand of God : in the glory of the Father.
We believe that thou shalt come : to be our Judge.
We therefore pray thee, help thy servants : whom thou hast redeemed
        with thy precious blood.
Make them to be numbered with thy Saints : in glory everlasting.
O Lord, save thy people : and bless thine heritage.
Govern them : and lift them up for ever.
Day by day : we magnify thee;
And we worship thy Name : ever world without end.
Vouchsafe, O Lord : to keep us this day without sin.
O Lord, have mercy upon us : have mercy upon us.
O Lord, let thy mercy lighten upon us : as our trust is in thee.
O Lord, in thee have I trusted : let me never be confounded.

Te Deum Laudamus, fifth century, Book of Common Prayer

I rise today with the power of God to guide me,
the might of God to uphold me,
the wisdom of God to teach me,
the eye of God to watch over me,
the ear of God to hear me,
the word of God to give me speech,
the hand of God to protect me,
the path of God to lie before me,
the shield of God to shelter me,
the host of God to defend me
    against the snares of the devil and the temptations of the world,
    against every man who meditates injury to me,
    whether far or near.   Breastplate of St Patrick

Love bade me welcome: yet my soul drew back,
    Guilty of dust and sin.
But quick-ey'd Love, observing me grow slack
    From my first entrance in,
Drew nearer to me, sweetly questioning,
    If I lack'd any thing.

A guest, I answer'd, worthy to be here:
    Love said, You shall be he.
I the unkind, ungrateful? Ah my dear,
    I cannot look on thee.
Love took my hand, and smiling did reply,
    Who made the eyes but I?

Truth Lord, but I have marr'd them: let my shame
    Go where it doth deserve.
And know you not, says Love, who bore the blame?
    My dear, then I will serve.
You must sit down, says Love, and taste my meat:
    So I did sit and eat.   George Herbert

——————— ✣ ———————

For God's creation

I thank you, my Creator and Lord, that you have given me these joys in your creation, this ecstasy over the deeds of your hands. I have made known the glory of your deeds to people as far as my finite spirit was able to understand your infinity. If I have said anything wholly unworthy of you, or have aspired after my own glory, graciously forgive me.

Johannes Kepler

For the beauty of the earth,
For the beauty of the skies,
For the love which from our birth
Over and around us lies:
Christ, our God, to thee we raise
This our sacrifice of praise.

For the beauty of each hour
Of the day and of the night,
Hill and vale and tree and flower,
Sun and moon and stars of light:
Christ, our God, to thee we raise
This our sacrifice of praise.

F.S. Pierpoint

Glory be to God for dappled things –
For skies of couple-colour as a brinded cow;
For rose-moles in all stipple upon the trout that swim;
Fresh-firecoal chestnut-falls; finches' wings;
Landscape plotted and pieced - fold, fallow and plough;
And all trades, their gear and tackle and trim.
All things counter, original, spare, strange;
Whatever is fickle, freckled (who knows how?)
With swift, slow; sweet, sour; adazzle, dim;
He fathers-forth whose beauty is past change:
Praise him.

Gerard Manley Hopkins, 'Pied Beauty'

All good gifts around us
Are sent from heaven above;
Then thank the Lord, O thank the Lord,
For all his love.   Matthias Claudius, translated by J.M. Campbell

Lord God through the light of nature you have aroused in us a longing for the light of grace, so that we may be raised in the light of your majesty. To you I give thanks, Creator and Lord, that you have allowed me to rejoice in your deeds. Praise the Lord you heavenly harmonies, and you who know the revealed harmonies. For from him, through him and in him, all is, which is perceptible as well as spiritual; that which we know and that which we do not know, for there is still much to learn.

Johannes Kepler

O all ye Works of the Lord, bless ye the Lord : praise him, and magnify him for ever.

O ye Angels of the Lord, bless ye the Lord : praise him, and magnify him for ever.

O ye Heavens, bless ye the Lord : praise him, and magnify him for ever.

O ye Waters that be above the firmament, bless ye the Lord : praise him, and magnify him for ever.

O all ye Powers of the Lord, bless ye the Lord : praise him, and magnify him for ever.

O ye Sun and Moon, bless ye the Lord : praise him, and magnify him for ever.

O ye Stars of heaven, bless ye the Lord : praise him, and magnify him for ever.

O ye Showers and Dew, bless ye the Lord : praise him, and magnify him for ever.

O ye Winds of God, bless ye the Lord : praise him, and magnify him for ever.

O ye Fire and Heat, bless ye the Lord : praise him, and magnify him for ever.

O ye Winter and Summer, bless ye the Lord : praise him, and magnify him for ever.

O ye Dews and Frosts, bless ye the Lord : praise him, and magnify him for ever.

O ye Frost and Cold, bless ye the Lord : praise him, and magnify him for ever.

O ye Ice and Snow, bless ye the Lord : praise him, and magnify him for ever.

O ye Nights and Days, bless ye the Lord : praise him, and magnify him for ever.

O ye Light and Darkness, bless ye the Lord : praise him, and magnify him for ever.

O ye Lightnings and Clouds, bless ye the Lord : praise him, and magnify him for ever.

O let the Earth bless the Lord : yea, let it praise him, and magnify him for ever.

O ye Mountains and Hills, bless ye the Lord : praise him, and magnify him for ever.

O all ye Green Things upon the earth, bless ye the Lord : praise him, and magnify him for ever.

O ye Wells, bless ye the Lord : praise him, and magnify him for ever.

O ye Seas and Floods, bless ye the Lord : praise him, and magnify him for ever.

O ye Whales, and all that move in the waters, bless ye the Lord : praise him, and magnify him for ever.

O all ye Fowls of the air, bless ye the Lord : praise him, and magnify him for ever.

O all ye Beasts and Cattle, bless ye the Lord : praise him, and magnify him for ever.

O ye Children of Men, bless ye the Lord : praise him, and magnify him for ever.

O let Israel bless the Lord : praise him, and magnify him for ever.

O ye Priests of the Lord, bless ye the Lord : praise him, and magnify him for ever.

O ye Servants of the Lord, bless ye the Lord : praise him, and magnify him for ever.

O ye Spirits and Souls of the Righteous, bless ye the Lord : praise him, and magnify him for ever.

O ye holy and humble Men of heart, bless ye the Lord : praise him, and magnify him for ever.

O Ananias, Azarias, and Misael, bless ye the Lord : praise him, and magnify him for ever.

Glory be to the Father, and to the Son : and to the Holy Ghost;

As it was in the beginning, is now, and ever shall be : world without
end. Amen.   Benedicite, omnia opera, Book of Common Prayer

Lord, purge our eyes to see
Within the seed a tree,
Within the glowing egg a bird,
Within the shroud a butterfly.
Till, taught by such we see
Beyond all creatures, Thee.

Christina Rossetti

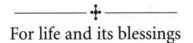

Artists

O God, who by thy Spirit in our hearts dost lead men to desire your perfection, to seek for truths and to rejoice in beauty: illuminate and
inspire, we beseech thee, all thinkers, writers, artists and craftsmen; that,
in whatsoever is true and pure and lovely, thy name may be hallowed
and thy kingdom come on earth; through Jesus Christ our Lord.

Prayer found in St Anselm's Chapel, Canterbury

For life and its blessings

O Lord, our Sovereign,
    how majestic is your name in all the earth!
...When I look at your heavens, the work of your fingers,
    the moon and the stars that you have established;
what are human beings that you are mindful of them,
    mortals that you care for them?
Yet you have made them a little lower than God,
    and crowned them with glory and honour.   Psalm 8:1,3–5 NRSV

I thank you, O Lord, my Lord,
for my being, my life, my gift of reason;
for my nurture, my preservation, by guidance;
for my education, my civil rights, my religious privileges;
for your gifts of grace, of nature, of this world;
for my redemption, my regeneration, in instruction in the Christian
        faith;
for my calling, my recalling, my manifold renewed recalling;
for your forbearance and long-suffering, your prolonged forbearance,
        many a time, and many a year;
for all the benefits I have received, and all the undertakings in which I
        have prospered;
for any good I may have done;
for the use of the blessings of this life.
... For all these and also for all other mercies, known and unknown,
        open and secret, remembered by me, or now forgotten,
        kindnesses received by me willingly, or even against my will,
        I praise you, I bless you, I thank you, all the days of my life.

Lancelot Andrewes

———— ✠ ————

For spiritual blessings

Bless the Lord, O my soul,
    and all that is within me,
    bless his holy name.
Bless the Lord, O my soul,
    and do not forget all his benefits –
who forgives all your iniquity,
    who heals all your diseases,
who redeems your life from the Pit,
    who crowns you with steadfast love and mercy,
who satisfies you with good as long as you live
    so that your youth is renewed like the eagle's.   *Psalm 103:1–5 NRSV*

O Lord, who art as the Shadow of a great Rock in a weary land, who beholdest thy weak creatures weary of labour, weary of pleasure, weary of hope deferred, weary of self; in thine abundant compassion, and unutterable tenderness, bring us, I pray thee, unto thy rest.

Christina Rossetti

Love divine, all loves excelling,
Joy of heaven to earth come down;
Fix in us thy humble dwelling;
All thy faithful mercies crown!
Jesus, Thou art all compassion,
Pure unbounded love Thou art;
Visit us with Thy salvation;
Enter every trembling heart.

Charles Wesley

How good is the God we adore,
Our faithful, unchangeable Friend!
His love is as great as his power,
And knows neither measure nor end!
'Tis Jesus, the First and the Last,
Whose Spirit shall guide us safe home:
We'll praise him for all that is past,
We'll trust him for all that's to come.

Joseph Hart

Almighty God, more generous than any father, we stand amazed at the
　　　　many gifts you shower upon us.
　　You give freely and willingly, always with regard to our ability to
　　　　receive.
　　You give daily gifts, teaching us to trust you for tomorrow.
　　You give us gifts through one another, so that we may learn to
　　　　share.
　　You give through our own effort, respecting our independence.
How thoughtfully you offer all your gifts!
　　So continue, Lord, of your goodness.

Author unknown

O God and Lord of the Powers, and Maker of all creation, who, because of Your clemency and incomparable mercy, didst send Thine Only-Begotten Son and our Lord Jesus Christ for the salvation of mankind, and with His venerable Cross didst tear asunder the record of our sins, and thereby didst conquer the rulers and powers of darkness; receive from us sinful people, O merciful Master, these prayers of gratitude and supplication, and deliver us from every destructive and gloomy transgression, and from all visible and invisible enemies who seek to injure us. Nail down our flesh with fear of Thee, and let not our hearts be inclined to words or thoughts of evil, but pierce our souls with Your love, that ever contemplating Thee, being enlightened by Thee, and discerning Thee, the unapproachable and everlasting Light, we may unceasingly render confession and gratitude to Thee: The eternal Father, with Thine Only-Begotten Son, and with Thine All-Holy, Gracious, and Life-Giving Spirit, now and ever, and unto ages of ages. Amen.

Basil the Great

Sometimes a light surprises
    The Christian while he sings:
It is the Lord who rises
    With healing in his wings;
When comforts are declining,
    He grants the soul again
A season of clear shining
    To cheer it after rain.

William Cowper

My spirit longs for Thee
Within my troubled breast,
Though I unworthy be
Of so divine a guest.

Of so divine a guest
Unworthy though I be,
Yet has my heart no rest
Unless it come from thee.

John Byrom

Amazing grace! how sweet the sound
That saved a wretch like me;
I once was lost, but now am found;
Was blind, but now I see.

'Twas grace that taught my heart to fear,
And grace my fear relieved;
How precious did that grace appear,
The hour I first believed!

Through many dangers, toils and snares
I have already come:
'Tis grace that brought me safe thus far,
And grace will lead me home.

The Lord has promised good to me,
His word my hope secures;
He will my shield and portion be
As long as life endures.

Yes, when this heart and flesh shall fail,
And mortal life shall cease,
I shall profess within the veil
A life of joy and peace.

When we've been there a thousand years,
Bright shining as the sun,
We've no less days to sing God's praise
Than when we first begun.   John Newton

Almighty God, Father of all mercies, we thine unworthy servants do give thee most humble and hearty thanks for all thy goodness and loving-kindness to us, and to all men; We bless thee for our creation, preservation, and all the blessings of this life; but above all, for thine inestimable love in the redemption of the world by our Lord Jesus Christ; for the means of grace, and for the hope of glory. And, we beseech thee, give us that due sense of all thy mercies, that our hearts may be unfeignedly thankful, and that we shew forth thy praise, not only with our lips, but in our lives; by giving up ourselves to thy service, and by walking before thee in holiness and righteousness all our days; through Jesus Christ our Lord, to whom with thee and the Holy Ghost be all honour and glory, world without end. Amen.

Edward Reynolds, Book of Common Prayer, Thanksgiving

Assurance

O happy day, that fixed my choice
On Thee, my Saviour and my God!
Well may this glowing heart rejoice,
And tell its raptures all abroad.

Refrain
Happy day, happy day, when Jesus washed my sins away!
He taught me how to watch and pray, and live rejoicing every day
Happy day, happy day, when Jesus washed my sins away.

O happy bond, that seals my vows
To Him Who merits all my love!
Let cheerful anthems fill His house,
While to that sacred shrine I move.
Refrain

It's done: the great transaction's done!
I am the Lord's and He is mine;
He drew me and I followed on;
Charmed to confess the voice divine.
Refrain

Now rest, my long divided heart,
Fixed on this blissful center, rest.
Here have I found a nobler part;
Here heavenly pleasures fill my breast.
Refrain

High heaven, that heard the solemn vow,
That vow renewed shall daily hear,
Till in life's latest hour I bow
And bless in death a bond so dear.
Refrain   Philip Doddridge

The second coming of Jesus Christ

Come, Almighty to deliver,
Let us all Thy life receive;
Suddenly return and never,
Never more Thy temples leave.
Thee we would be always blessing,
Serve Thee as Thy hosts above,
Pray and praise Thee without ceasing,
Glory in Thy perfect love.   Charles Wesley

——— ✝ ———

Prayers of worship and adoration

Let all mortal flesh keep silent, and with fear and trembling stand;
Ponder nothing earthly-minded, for with blessing in his hand,
Christ our God to earth descendeth, our full homage to command.
                                                    Liturgy of St James

Let all the world in every corner sing,
'My God and King!'
The heavens are not too high,
His praise may thither fly:
The earth is not too low,
His praises there may grow,
The church with psalms must shout,
No door can keep them out:
But, above all, the heart
Must bear the longest part.
Let all the world in every corner sing,
'My God and King!'   George Herbert

Worthy of praise from every mouth, of confession from every tongue, of
worship from every creature, is your glorious name, O Father, Son, and
Holy Spirit, who created the world by the word of your power, and in
love wonderfully redeemed it. Wherefore with angels, and archangels,
and all the company of heaven, we adore and magnify your holy name,
evermore praising you, and saying:

Holy, Holy, Holy Lord God of Hosts,
Heaven and earth are full of your glory:
Glory be to you, O Lord, most High.   Source unknown

In this hour of this day, fill us, O Lord, with your mercy, that rejoicing
throughout the whole day, we may take delight in your praise; through
Jesus Christ our Lord.   Sarum Missal

Most high, most great and good Lord, to you belong praises, glory and every blessing; to you alone do they belong, most high God.

May you be blessed, my Lord, for the gift of all your creatures and especially for our brother sun, but whom the day is enlightened. He is radiant and bright, of great splendour, bearing witness to you, O my God.

May you be blessed, my Lord, for our sister the moon and the stars; you have created them in the heavens, fair and clear.

May you be blessed, my Lord, for my brother the wind, for the air, for cloud and calm, for every kind of weather, for through them you sustain all creatures.

May you be blessed, my Lord, for our sister water, which is very useful, humble, pure and precious.

May you be blessed, my Lord, for our brother fire, bright, noble and beautiful, untamable and strong, by whom you illumine the night.

May you be blessed, my Lord, for our mother the earth, who sustains and nourishes us, who brings forth all kinds of fruit, herbs and brightly coloured flowers.

May you be blessed, my Lord, for those who pardon out of love for you, and who patiently bear illness and tribulation.

Happy are those who abide in peace, for through you, most high God, they will be crowned.

May you be blessed, my Lord, for our sister death of body, from whom no living person can escape. Woe to him who dies in a state of mortal sin. Happy are those who at the hour of death are found in obedience to your holy will, for the second death cannot hurt them.

Praise and bless, my Lord; give him thanks and serve him with great humility.   Francis of Assisi, 'Canticle of the Sun'

Let the eternal God be the portion of my soul;
let heaven be my inheritance and hope;
let Christ be my Head, and my promise of security;
let faith be my wisdom,
and love my very heart and will,
and patient persevering obedience be my life;
and then I can spare the wisdom of the world,
because I can spare the trifles that it seeks,
and all that they are like to get by it.   Richard Baxter

O good Lord Jesus Christ, I pray that you will open my mouth, so that I may praise you, and give you thanks for all your goodness towards me: and I beseech you to keep it from all vain talk, and from all other ways of offending you.   *Primer, 1557*

Fill Thou my life, O Lord my God,
In every part with praise,
That my whole being may proclaim
Thy being and Thy ways.
Not for the lip of praise alone,
Nor e'en the praising heart
I ask, but for a life made up
Of praise in every part!

Fill every part of me with praise;
Let all my being speak
Of Thee and of Thy love, O Lord,
Poor though I be, and weak.
So shalt Thou, Lord, from me, e'en me,
Receive the glory due;
And so shall I begin on earth
The song forever new.

So shall each fear, each fret, each care
Be turned into a song,
And every winding of the way
The echo shall prolong;
So shall no part of day or night
From sacredness be free;
But all my life, in every step
Be fellowship with Thee.   Horatius Bonar

Be thou my vision, O Lord of my heart;
Naught be all else to me, save that thou art,
Thou my best thought, by day or by night,
Waking or sleeping, thy presence my light.   Traditional Irish

Come, my Way, my Truth, my Life:
Such a Way as gives us breath:
Such a Truth as ends of strife:
Such a Life as killeth death.

Come, my Light, my Feast, my Strength:
Such a Light, as shows a feast:
Such a Feast, as mends in length:
Such a Strength, as makes his guest.

Come, my Joy, my Love, my Heart:
Such a Joy, as none can move:
Such a Love, as none can part:
Such a Heart, as joys in love.   George Herbert

Glorious things of thee are spoken,
    Zion, city of our God!
He, whose word cannot be broken,
    Formed thee for His own abode.
On the rock of ages founded,
    What can shake thy sure repose?
With salvation's walls surrounded,
    Thou may'st smile at all thy foes.

See! the streams of living waters,
    Springing from eternal love,
Well supply thy sons and daughters,
    And all fear of want remove.
Who can faint while such a river
    Ever flows their thirst t'assuage:
Grace which, like the Lord the giver,
    Never fails from age to age?

Round each habitation hov'ring,
    See the cloud and fire appear!
For a glory and a cov'ring,
    Showing that the Lord is near:
Thus deriving from their banner
    Light by night and shade by day,
Safe they feed upon the manna
    Which He gives them when they pray.

Blest inhabitants of Zion,
    Washed in the Redeemer's blood!
Jesus, whom their souls rely on,
    Makes them kings and priests to God:
'Tis His love His people raises
    Over self to reign as kings,
And as priests, His solemn praises
    Each for a thankoff'ring brings.

Saviour, if of Zion's city
    I through grace a member am,
Let the world deride or pity,
    I will glory in Thy name:
Fading is the worldling's pleasure,
    All his boasted pomp and show;
Solid joys and lasting treasure
    None but Zion's children know.

        John Newton

Grant, Lord God, that we may cleave to thee without parting,
worship thee without wearying,
serve thee without failing,
faithfully seek thee,
happily find thee,
and forever possess thee,
the one only God,
blessed for all eternity.

        Anselm

Praise to the Holiest in the height,
    And in the depth be praise;
In all his words most wonderful,
    Most sure in all his ways.

O loving wisdom of our God!
    When all was sin and shame,
A second Adam to the fight
    And to the rescue came.

O wisest love! that flesh and blood,
    Which did in Adam fail,
Should strive afresh against the foe,
    Should strive and should prevail.

And that a higher gift than grace
    Should flesh and blood refine,
God's presence and his very self,
    And essence all-divine.

O generous love! That he who smote
    In Man, for man, the foe,
The double agony in Man,
    For man, should undergo;

And in the garden secretly,
    And on the cross on high,
Should teach his brethren, and inspire
    To suffer and to die.

Praise to the Holiest in the height,
    And in the depth be praise;
In all his words most wonderful,
    Most sure in all his ways.

J.H. Newman

O for a closer walk with God,
    A calm and heavenly frame;
A light to shine upon the road
    That leads me to the Lamb!

Return, O holy Dove, return,
    Sweet messenger of rest;
I hate the sins that made thee mourn,
    And drove thee from my breast.

The dearest idol I have known,
    Whate'er that idol be,
Help me to tear it from thy throne,
    And worship only thee.

So shall my walk be close with God,
    Calm and serene my frame;
So purer light shall mark the road
    That leads me to the Lamb.

William Cowper

King of glory, King of peace,
    I will love thee:
And that love may never cease,
    I will move thee.

Thou hast granted my request,
    Thou has heard me:
Thou didst note my working breast,
    Thou has spared me.

Wherefore with my utmost art
    I will sing thee,
And the cream of all my heart
    I will bring thee.

Though my sins against me cried,
    Thou didst clear me;
And alone, when they replied,
    Thou didst hear me.

Seven whole days, not one in seven,
    I will praise thee.
In my heart, though not in heaven,
    I can raise thee.

Thou grew'st soft and most with tears,
    Thou relentedst.
And when Justice call'd for fears,
    Thou dissentedst.

Small it is, in this poor sort
    To enrol thee:
Even eternity's too short
    To extol thee.

George Herbert, *The Temple*

Praise, my soul, the King of heaven;
    To his feet thy tribute bring;
Ransomed, healed, restored, forgiven,
        Who like thee his praise should sing?
            Praise him, praise him,
        Praise the everlasting King.

Praise him for his grace and favour
    To our fathers in distress;
Praise him still the same for ever,
        Slow to chide, and swift to bless:
            Praise him, praise him,
        Glorious in his faithfulness.

Father-like he tends and spares us;
    Well our feeble frame he knows;
In his hands he gently bears us,
        Rescues us from all our foes:
            Praise him, praise him,
        Widely as his mercy flows.

Angels, help us to adore him,
    Ye behold him face to face;
Sun and moon, bow down before him;
        Dwellers all in time and space,
            Praise him, praise him.
        Praise with us the God of grace.

Henry Francis Lyte, based on Psalm 103

All people that on earth do dwell,
    Sing to the Lord with cheerful voice;
Him serve with mirth, his praise forth tell,
    Come ye before him, and rejoice.

The Lord, ye know, is God indeed;
    Without our aid he did us make;
We are his folk, he doth us feed,
    And for his sheep he doth us take.

Oh enter then his gates with praise,
    Approach with joy his courts unto;
Praise, laud, and bless his name always.
    For it is seemly so to do.

For why, the Lord our God is good;
    His mercy is for ever sure;
His truth at all times firmly stood,
    And shall from age to age endure.

William Kethe, based on Psalm 100

Almighty God, who hast given us grace at this time with one accord to make our common supplications unto thee; and dost promise, that when two or three are gathered together in thy Name thou wilt grant their requests; Fulfil now, O Lord, the desires and petitions of thy servants, as may be most expedient for them; granting us in this world knowledge of thy truth, and in the world to come life everlasting. Amen.

Chrysostom

'Holy, holy, holy, the Lord God the Almighty, who was and is and is to
    come' (Revelation 4:8).
'You are worthy, our Lord and God, to receive glory and honour and
    power, for your created all things, and by your will they exist-
    ed and were created' (Revelation 4:11).
'Worthy is the Lamb that was slaughtered to receive power and wealth
    and wisdom and might and honour and glory and blessing!'
    (Revelation 5:12).
Let us bless the Father, the Son and the Holy Spirit. Praise him and
    exult him above all for ever.
'Praise our God, all you his servants, and all who fear him, small and
    great' (Revelation 19:5).
Let 'every creature in heaven and on earth, and under the earth and in
    the sea, and that is them, [praise God] singing, "To the one
    seated on the throne and to the Lamb be blessing and honour
    and glory and might for ever and ever!"' (Revelation 5:13).

Glory be to the Father, and to the Son, and to the Holy Spirit. Praise
him and exalt him above all for ever. As it was in the
beginning, is now, and ever shall be, world without end.
Amen. Praise him and exalt him above all for ever.

Francis of Assisi used this collection of Bible verses to praise God. (NRSV)

Glory be to God in the highest,
Lord of heaven and earth,
who so loved the world
as to send his only Son
to redeem us from sin,
and to obtain for us everlasting life.
All praise be to you, most gracious God,
for your infinite mercies towards us in Jesus Christ our Lord.

Archbishop Hamilton

O Lord in whom all things live,
who commanded us to seek you,
who are always ready to be found:
to know you is life,
to serve you is freedom,
to praise you is our souls's delight.
We bless you and adore you,
we worship you and magnify you,
we give thanks to you for your great glory,
through Jesus Christ our Lord.   Augustine

Great, O Lord, is your kingdom, your power and your glory;
great also is your wisdom, your goodness, your justice, your mercy;
and for all these we bless you, and will magnify your name for ever
and ever.   George Wither

Chapter Two

PRAYERS ABOUT OUR RELATIONSHIP WITH GOD

So I tell you, whatever you ask for in prayer, believe that you have received it, and it will be yours.　　　Mark 11:24 NRSV

The first rule of right prayer is to have our heart and mind framed as becomes those who are entering into converse with God.　　　John Calvin

————— ✠ —————

God the Father

Eternal God,
the light of the minds that know thee,
the life of the souls that love thee,
the strength of the wills that serve thee;
help us so to know thee that we may truly love thee,
so to love thee that we may fully serve thee,
whom to serve is perfect freedom.

Gelasian Sacramentary, based on a prayer by Augustine

God be in my head,
and in my understanding;
God be in my eyes,
and in my looking;
God be in my mouth,
and in my speaking;
God be in my heart,
and in my thinking;
God be at my end,
and at my departing.   *Book of Hours,* 1514

O God, the Father of mercies, grant to us always to hold fast to the spirit of adoption, whereby we cry to you 'Father', and are called, and are, 'your children', through Jesus Christ, our Lord.   Roman Breviary

God guide me with your wisdom,
God help me with your mercy,
God protect me with your strength,
God fill me with your grace,
for the sake of your anointed Son.   Traditional Gaelic prayer

Grant, I thee pray, such heat into mine heart
That to this love of thine may be equal;
Grant me from Satan's service to astart,
With whom me rueth so long to have been thrall;
Grant me, good Lord and Creator all,
The flame to quench of all sinful desire
And in thy love set all mine heart afire.

That when the journey of this deadly life
My silly ghost hath finishèd, and thence
Departen must without his fleshly wife,
Alone into his Lordès high presènce,
He may thee find, O well of indulgènce,
In thy lordship not as a lord, but rather
As a very tender, loving father.   Thomas More

O Lord seek us, O Lord find us
In Thy patient care,
Be Thy love before, behind us,
Round us everywhere.
Lest the god of this world blind us,
Lest he bait a snare,
Lest he forge a chain to bind us,
Lest he speak us fair,
Turn not from us, call to mind us,
Find, embrace us, hear.
By Thy love before, behind us,
Round us everywhere.

Christina Rossetti

Wilt Thou forgive that sin where I begun,
    Which is my sin, though it were done before?
Wilt Thou forgive that sin through which I run,
    And do run still, though still I do deplore?
        When Thou hast done, Thou hast not done,
        For I have more.

Wilt Thou forgive that sin which I have won
    Others to sin? and made my sin their door?
Wilt Thou forgive that sin which I did shun
    A year or two, but wallowed in, a score?
        When Thou hast done, Thou hast not done,
        For I have more.

I have a sin of fear, that when I have spun
    My last thread, I shall perish on the shore;
Swear by Thyself, that at my death Thy Son
    Shall shine as He shines now and heretofore;
        And, having done that, Thou hast done,
        I fear no more.

John Donne

Hear me, O God!
    A broken heart
    Is my best part:
Use still thy rod,
    That I may prove
    Therein thy love.

If thou hadst not
    Been stern to me,
    But left me free,
I had forgot
    Myself and thee.

For sin's so sweet,
    As minds ill bent
    Rarely repent,
Until they meet
    Their punishment.

Who more can crave
    Than thou hast done?
    That gav'st a Son,
To free a slave
    First made of nought;
    With all since bought.

Sin, death, and hell
    His glorious name
    Quite overcame,
Yet I rebel,
    And slight the same.

But I'll come in,
    Before my loss
    Me farther toss,
As sure to win
    Under his cross.

Ben Jonson from 'The Underwood', *Poems of Devotion*

Lord, Thou art life, though I be dead,
Love's fire Thou art, however cold I be;
Nor heaven have I, nor place to lay my head,
Nor home, but thee.   Christina Rossetti

Almighty God, Father of our Lord Jesus Christ, establish and confirm us
in your truth by your Holy Spirit. Reveal to us what we do not know;
perfect in us what is lacking; strengthen us in what we know; and keep
us faultless in your service; through the same Jesus Christ our Lord.
                                                       Clement of Rome

Come, our Light, and illumine our darkness.
Come, our Life, and raise us from death.
Come, our Physician, and heal our wounds.
Come, Flame of divine Love, and burn up our sins.
Come, our King, sit upon the throne of our hearts and reign there.
For you alone are my King and my Lord   Dimitrii of Rostov

O good Shepherd, seek me, and bring me home to your fold again. I am
like the man on the road to Jericho who was attacked by robbers,
wounded and left half dead. You who are the Good Samaritan, lift me
up, and deal favourably with me according to your good pleasure, until
I may dwell in your house all the days of my life, and praise you for ever
and ever with those who are there.   Jerome

I pray to you, Lord God of Abraham, Isaac and Jacob, Father of our Lord
Jesus Christ. You are infinite in mercy, and it is your will that we should
learn to know you. You created heaven and earth, you rule over all. You
are the true, the only God, and there is no other god above you. Grant,
through our Lord Jesus Christ and the working of the Holy Spirit, that
all may come to know you, for you alone are God. Let them draw
strength from you and be kept from all teaching that is heretical or
godless.   Irenaeus

O Father, give perfection to beginners,
intelligence to the little ones,
and aid to those who are running their course.
Give sorrow to the negligent,
fervour of spirit to the lukewarm,
and to those who have attained a good ending.   Irenaeus

In confidence of your goodness and great mercy, O Lord, I draw near to
you, as a sick person to the Healer, as one hungry and thirsty to the
Fountain of life, a creature to the Creator, a desolate soul to my own tender Comforter. Behold, in you is everything that I can or ought to desire.
You are my salvation and my redemption, my Helper and my strength.

Thomas à Kempis

Write your blessed name, O Lord, upon my heart, there to remain so
indelibly engraved, that no prosperity, no adversity shall ever move me
from your love. Be to me a strong tower of defence, a comforter in tribulation, a deliverer in distress, a very present help in trouble and a guide
to heaven through the many temptations and dangers of this life.

Thomas à Kempis

You are holy, Lord, the only God, and your deeds are wonderful.
You are strong, you are great, you are the most high, you are the
          almighty King.
You, holy father, are King of heaven and earth.
You are Three and One, God above all gods.
You are good, all good, supreme good, Lord God, living and true.
You are love,
you are wisdom,
you are humility,
you are endurance,
you are rest,
you are peace,
you are joy and gladness,
you are justice and moderation.
You are all our riches, and you suffice for us.

You are beauty, you are gentleness.
You are our protector, our guardian and defender.
You are courage, you are our haven and our hope.
You are our faith, our great consolation.
You are our eternal life, great and wonderful Lord,
God almighty, merciful Saviour.

Francis of Assisi

My God, I will put myself without reserve into your hands. What have I in heaven, and apart from you what do I want upon earth? My flesh and my heart fail, but God is the God of my heart, and my portion forever.

J.H. Newman

Lord, I believe in you – increase my faith.
I trust in you – strengthen my trust.
I love you – let me love you more and more.
I am sorry for my sins – deepen my sorrow.
I worship you as my first beginning, I long for you as my last end,
    I praise you as my constant helper, and call on you as my
    loving protector.
Guide me by your wisdom, correct me with your justice, comfort me
    with your mercy, protect me with your power.
I offer you, Lord, my thoughts – to be fixed on you; my words – to
    have you for their theme; my actions – to reflect my love for
    you; my sufferings – to be endured for your greater glory.
I want to do what you ask of me – in the way you ask, for as long as
    you ask, because you ask it.
Lord, enlighten my understanding, strengthen my will, purify my
    heart, and make me holy.
Help me to repent of my past sins and to resist temptation in the
    future. Help me rise above my human weaknesses and to
    grow stronger as a Christian.
Let me love you, my Lord and my God, and see myself as I really am –
    a pilgrim in this world, a Christian called to respect and to
    love all whose lives I touch, those in authority over me or
    those under my authority, my friends and my enemies.

Help me to conquer anger with gentleness, greed with generosity,
apathy by fervour. Help me to forget myself and reach out to
others.
Make me prudent in planning, courageous in taking risks. Make me
patient in suffering, unassuming in prosperity.
Keep me, Lord, attentive at prayer, temperate in food and drink,
diligent in my work, firm in my good intentions.
Let my conscience be clear, my conduct without fault, my speech
blameless, and my life well-ordered.
Teach me to realize that this world is passing, that my true future is the
happiness of heaven, that life on earth is short, and the life to
come eternal.
Help me prepare for death with a proper fear of judgment, and a
greater trust in your goodness.
Lead me safely through death to the endless joy of heaven.
Grant this through Christ our Lord. Amen

The Universal Prayer, attributed to Pope Clement XI

---------- ✠ ----------

God the Son

Soul of Christ, sanctify me.
Body of Christ, save me.
Blood of Christ, inebriate me.
Water from the side of Christ, wash me.
Passion of Christ, strengthen me.
O good Jesus, hear me.
Hide me within your wounds
and never allow me to be separated from you.
From the wicked enemy defend me.
In the hour of my death call me,
and bid me come to you,
so that with your saints I may praise you
for ever and ever.

Anima Christi, fourteenth century

Lord Jesus Christ, you said that you are the Way, the Truth, and the
    Life.
Help us not to stray from you, for you are the Way;
nor to distrust you, for you are the Truth;
nor to rest on any other than you, as you are the Life.
You have taught us what to believe, what to do, what to hope, and
    where to take our rest.
Give us grace to follow you, the Way, to learn from you, the Truth, and
    live in you, the Life.   Desiderius Erasmus

Be thou a light to my eyes, music to my ears, sweetness to my taste, and
full contentment to my heart. Be thou my sunshine in the day, my food
at table, my repose in the night, my clothing in nakedness, and my succour in all necessities. Lord Jesu, I give thee my body, my soul, my substance, my fame, my friends, my liberty and my life. Dispose of me and
all that is mine as it may seem best to thee and to the glory of thy blessed
name.   John Cosin

Jesus, lover of my soul, let me to Thy bosom fly,
While the nearer waters roll, while the tempest still is high.
Hide me, O my Savior, hide, till the storm of life is past;
Safe into the haven guide; O receive my soul at last.

Other refuge have I none, hangs my helpless soul on Thee;
Leave, ah! leave me not alone, still support and comfort me.
All my trust on Thee is stayed, all my help from Thee I bring;
Cover my defenseless head with the shadow of Thy wing.

Wilt Thou not regard my call? Wilt Thou not accept my prayer?
Lo! I sink, I faint, I fall – Lo! on Thee I cast my care;
Reach me out Thy gracious hand! While I of Thy strength receive,
Hoping against hope I stand, dying, and behold, I live.

Thou, O Christ, art all I want, more than all in Thee I find;
Raise the fallen, cheer the faint, heal the sick, and lead the blind.
Just and holy is Thy Name, I am all unrighteousness;
False and full of sin I am; Thou art full of truth and grace.

Plenteous grace with Thee is found, grace to cover all my sin;
Let the healing streams abound; make and keep me pure within.
Thou of life the fountain art, freely let me take of Thee;
Spring Thou up within my heart; rise to all eternity.   Charles Wesley

Thank you, Lord Jesus, that you will be our hiding place whatever
          happens.   Corrie ten Boom

Lord Jesus, make yourself to me
A living, bright reality.
More present to faith's vision keen
Than any outward object seen.   Hudson Taylor

How sweet the name of Jesus sounds
In a believer's ear!
It soothes his sorrows, heals his wounds,
And drives away his fear.

It makes the wounded spirit whole,
And calms the troubled breast;
'Tis manna to the hungry soul,
And to the weary rest.   John Newton

If ask'd, what of Jesus I think?
Though still my best thoughts are but poor,
I say, He's my meat and my drink,
My life, and my strength, and my store;
My shepherd, my husband, my friend,
My Saviour from sin and from thrall;
My hope from beginning to end,
My portion, my Lord, and my all.   John Newton

Lord Jesus Christ, pierce my soul with your love so that I may always long for you alone, who are the bread of angels and the fulfilment of the soul's deepest desires. May my heart always hunger and feed on you, so that my soul may be filled with the sweetness of your presence. May my soul thirst for you, who are the source of life, wisdom, knowledge, light and all the riches of God our Father. May I always seek and find you, think about you, speak to you and do everything for the honour and glory of your holy name. Be always my hope, my peace, my refuge and my help in whom my heart is rooted so that I may never be separated from you.   Bonaventure

Jesus, the very thought of thee
With sweetness fills the breast;
But sweeter far thy face to see,
And in thy presence rest.

                        Bernard of Clairvaux, translated by Edward Caswell

May the mind of Christ my Saviour
Live in me from day to day,
By his love and power controlling
All I do and say.

May the word of God dwell richly
In my heart from hour to hour,
So that all may see I triumph
Only through his power.

May the love of Jesus fill me
As the waters fill the sea;
Him exalting, self abasing,
This is victory.   K. B. Wilkinson

Lord, keep me always near to you.
Let nothing separate me from you, let nothing keep me back from you.
If I fall, bring me back quickly to you, and make me hope in you, trust
in you, and love you for ever.   E.B. Pusey

Jesus, as a mother you gather your people to you:
You are gentle with us as a mother with her children;
Often you weep over our sins and our pride:
tenderly you draw us from hatred and judgement.
You comfort us in sorrow and bind up our wounds:
in sickness you nurse us,
and with pure milk you feed us.
Jesus, by your dying we are born to new life:
by your anguish and labour we come forth in joy.
Despair turns to hope through your sweet goodness:
through your gentleness we find comfort in fear.
Your warmth gives life to the dead:
your touch makes sinners righteous.
Lord Jesus, in your mercy heal us:
in your love and tenderness remake us.
In your compassion bring grace and forgiveness:
for the beauty of heaven may your love prepare us.   Anselm

Christ be with me, Christ within me,
Christ behind me, Christ before me,
Christ beside me, Christ to win me,
Christ to comfort and restore me,
Christ beneath me, Christ above me,
Christ in quiet, Christ in danger,
Christ in hearts of all that love me,
Christ in mouth of friend and stranger.   Breastplate of St Patrick

———————— ✛ ————————

God the Holy Spirit

O Holy Spirit of God, who with your holy breath cleanses the hearts
    and minds of people,
  comforting them when they are in sorrow,
  leading them when they are out of the way,
  kindling them when they are cold,
  knitting them together when they are at variance,
  and enriching them with many gifts;
    by whose working all things live:
We beseech you to maintain and daily increase the gifts which you
    have given us;
  that with your light before us and within us we may pass through
    this world without stumbling and without straying;
  who lives and reigns with the Father and the Son, for ever.

Desiderius Erasmus

O Lord God almighty, we thank you with all our hearts, for feeding our
souls with the body and blood of your most dear Son. We beseech you
to so illumine our minds with your Holy Spirit, that we may daily
increase in faith in you, in certainty of hope in your promises, and fer-
vency of love to you and our neighbour, to the glory and praise of your
holy name.

Miles Coverdale

Litany to the Holy Spirit
In the hour of my distress,
When temptations me oppress,
And when I my sins confess,
　　Sweet Spirit comfort me!

When I lie within my bed,
Sick in heart and sick in head,
And with doubts discomforted,
　　Sweet Spirit comfort me!

When the house doth sigh and weep,
And the world is drowned in sleep,
Yet mine eyes the watch do keep,
　　Sweet Spirit comfort me!

When the artless Doctor sees
No one hope but of his fees,
And his skill runs on the lees,
　　Sweet Spirit comfort me!

When the Tempter me pursu'th
With the sins of all my youth,
And half damns me with untruth,
　　Sweet Spirit comfort me!

When the passing bell doth toll,
And the furies in a shoel
Come to fright a parting soul,
　　Sweet Spirit, comfort me!

When the tapers now burn blue,
And the comforters are few,
And that number more than true,
　　Sweet Spirit, comfort me!...

When, God, knows, I'm tossed about,
Either with despair, or doubt;
Yet before the glass be out,
>Sweet Spirit, comfort me!...

When the judgment is revealed,
And that opened which was sealed,
When to thee I have appealed,
>Sweet Spirit comfort me!

Robert Herrick

Holy Spirit,
as the wind is thy symbol, so forward our goings,
as the dove, so launch us heavenwards,
as water, so purify our spirits,
as a cloud, so abate our temptations,
as dew, so revive our languor,
as fire, so purge out our dross.

Christina Rossetti

O God the Holy Spirit, most loving Comforter, I pray that you will always turn what is evil in me into good and what is good into what is better; turn my mourning into joy, my wandering feet into the right path, my ignorance into knowledge of your truth, my lukewarmness into zeal, my fear into love, all my material good into a spiritual gift, all my earthly desires into heavenly desires, all that is transient into what lasts for ever, everything human into what is divine, everything created and finite into that sovereign and immeasurable good, which you yourself are, O my God and Saviour.

Thomas à Kempis

O God, forasmuch as without thee we are not able to please thee; Mercifully grant, that thy Holy Spirit may in all things direct and rule our hearts; through Jesus Christ our Lord. Amen.

Book of Common Prayer, Collect for the Nineteenth Sunday after Trinity

Breathe on me, Breath of God;
Fill me with life anew,
That I may love what thou dost love,
And do what thou wouldst do.

Breath on me, Breath of God,
Till I am wholly thine,
Until this earthly part of me
Glows with thy fire divine.

Breath on me, Breath of God,
So shall I never die,
But live with thee the perfect life
Of thine eternity.   Edwin Hatch

Come, Holy Ghost, our souls inspire,
And lighten with celestial fire.
Thou the anointing Spirit art,
Who dost thy sevenfold gifts impart.

Thy blessed unction from above,
Is comfort, life, and fire of love.
Enable with perpetual light
The dullness of our blinded sight.

Anoint and cheer our soiled face
With the abundance of thy grace.
Keep far our foes, give peace at home;
Where thou art guide, no ill can come.

Teach us to know the Father, Son,
And thee, of both, to be but One;
That, through the ages all along,
This may be our endless song:
    Praise to thy eternal merit,
    Father, Son, and Holy Spirit.
        Book of Common Prayer, translated by Bishop John Cosin, The Ordinal

——————— ✟ ———————

The Trinity

Holy, holy, holy! Lord God Almighty!
Early in the morning our song shall rise to Thee;
Holy, holy, holy, merciful and mighty!
God in three Persons, blesséd Trinity!

Holy, holy, holy! All the saints adore Thee,
Casting down their golden crowns around the glassy sea;
Cherubim and seraphim falling down before Thee,
Who was, and is, and evermore shall be.

Holy, holy, holy! though the darkness hide Thee,
Though the eye of sinful man Thy glory may not see;
Only Thou art holy; there is none beside Thee,
Perfect in power, in love, and purity.

Holy, holy, holy! Lord God Almighty!
All Thy works shall praise Thy Name, in earth, and sky, and sea;
Holy, holy, holy; merciful and mighty!
God in three Persons, blesséd Trinity!

Reginald Heber

The Sacred Three
My fortress be
Encircling me
Come and be round
My hearth, my home.

Traditional Hebridean chant

Glory be to you, O Lord, my Creator.
Glory be to you, Jesus, my Redeemer.
Glory be to you, Holy Spirit, my Sanctifier, Guide and Comforter.
All love, all glory, be to the high and undivided Trinity, whose deeds
are inseparable, and whose worldwide rule is for ever; to you,
and to you alone, and to your Son, and to the Holy Spirit, be
glory for ever and ever.

Thomas Wilson

Glory be to you, O God, the Father, the Maker of the world:
Glory be to you, O God, the Son, the Redeemer of humankind:
Glory be to you, O God, the Holy Spirit, the Sanctifier of your people.

B.F. Westcott

We are enfolded in the Father, and we are enfolded in the Son, and we are enfolded in the Holy Spirit. And the Father is enfolded in us, and the Son is enfolded in us, and the Holy Spirit is enfolded in us: almightiness, all wisdom, all goodness: one God, one Lord.   Julian of Norwich

Holy Father, keep us in your truth;
holy Son, protect us under the wings of your cross;
holy Spirit, make us temples and dwelling places for your glory;
grant us your peace all the days of our lives, O Lord.

Office of Compline, Maronite Church

O Father, my hope
O Son, my refuge
O Holy Spirit, my protection.
Holy Trinity, glory to Thee.

Office of Compline, Eastern Orthodox Church

Batter my heart, three-person'd God, for you
As yet but knock, breathe, shine, and seek to mend.
That I may rise and stand, o'erthrow me, and bend
Your force to break, blow, burn, and make me new.
I, like an usurp'd town, to another due
Labour to admit you, but O, to no end!
Reason, your viceroy in me, me should defend,
But is captiv'd and proves weak or untrue.

Yet dearly I love you, and would be loved fain,
But am betrothed unto your enemy;
Divorce me, untie, or break that knot again,
Take me to you, imprison me, for I
Except you enthral me, never shall be free,
Nor ever chaste, except you ravish me.

John Donne

Blessing and honour, thanksgiving and praise
    more than we can utter,
    more than we can conceive,
be unto you, O most holy and glorious Trinity,
    Father, Son and Holy Spirit,
by all angels, all people, all creatures
    for ever and ever. Amen and Amen.

Lancelot Andrewes

I bind to myself the name,
the strong name of the Trinity;
by invocation of the same,
The Three in One, and One in Three.
Of whom all nature has creation;
eternal Father, Spirit, Word:
Praise to the Lord of my salvation,
Salvation is of Christ the Lord.

St Patrick

✛

Confessing sin and seeking God's forgiveness

O Lord, open our minds to see ourselves as you see us,
and from all unwillingness to know our weakness and our sin,
   Good Lord, deliver us.

From selfishness;
from wishing to be the centre of attention;
from seeking admiration;
from the desire to have our own way in all things;
from unwillingness to listen to others;
from resentment of criticism,
> *Good Lord, deliver us.*

From love of power; from jealousy;
from taking pleasure in the weakness of others,
> *Good Lord, deliver us.*

From the weakness of indecision; from fear of adventure;
from constant fear of what others are thinking of us; from fear of
speaking what we know is truth,
and doing what we know is right,
> *Good Lord, deliver us.*

From possessiveness about material things and people;
from carelessness about the needs of others;
from selfish use of time and money;
from all lack of generosity,
> *Good Lord, deliver us.*

From laziness of conscience;
from lack of self-discipline; from failure to persevere;
from depression in failure and disappointment,
> *Good Lord, deliver us.*

From failure to be truthful;
from pretence and acting a part; from hypocrisy;
from all dishonesty with ourselves and with others,
> *Good Lord, deliver us.*

From impurity in word, in thought, and in action;
from failure to respect the bodies and minds
of ourselves and others;
from any kind of addiction,
> *Good Lord, deliver us.*

From hatred and anger; from sarcasm;
from lack of sensitivity and division in our community;
from all failure to love and to forgive,
>   *Good Lord, deliver us.*

From failure to see our sin as an affront to God;
from failure to accept the forgiveness of others,
>   *Good Lord, deliver us.*

Peter Nott

Have mercy on me, O God,
>   according to your steadfast love;
according to your abundant mercy
>   blot out my transgressions.
Wash me thoroughly from my iniquity,
>   and cleanse me from my sin.
For I know my transgressions,
>   and my sin is ever before me.
Against you, you alone, have I sinned,
>   and done what is evil in your sight,
so that you are justified in your sentence
>   and blameless when you pass judgement.
... Create in me a clean heart, O God,
>   and put a new and right spirit within me.
Do not cast me away from your presence,
>   and do not take your holy spirit from me.
... O Lord, open my lips,
>   and my mouth will declare your praise.
For you have no delight in sacrifice;
>   if I were to give a burnt-offering, you would not be pleased.
The sacrifice acceptable to God is a broken spirit;
>   a broken and contrite heart, O God, you will not despise.

Psalm 51:1–4, 10–11, 15–17 NRSV

Oppressed with sin and woe,
A burdened heart I bear;
Oppressed by many a mighty foe,
Yet I will not despair.

With this polluted heart,
I dare to come to thee –
Holy and mighty as thou art –
For thou wilt pardon me.

I feel that I am weak,
And prone to every sin;
But thou, who giv'st to those who seek,
Wilt give me strength within.

I need not fear my foes;
I need not yield to care;
I need not sink beneath my woes,
For thou wilt answer prayer.

In my Redeemer's name,
I give myself to thee;
And, all unworthy as I am,
My God will cherish me.

Anne Brontë

O God, though our sins be seven, though our sins be seventy times seven, though our sins be more in number than the hairs of our head, yet give us grace in loving penitence to cast ourselves down into the depths of thy compassion.

Christina Rossetti

Lord, teach us how to pray aright,
With reverence and with fear;
Though dust and ashes in thy sight,
We may, we must draw near.

James Montgomery

O Good Shepherd, who laid down your life for the sheep, remember
us:
Be propitious, and have mercy on us.
O everlasting Power and Wisdom of the most high God, the Word of
the Father, remember us:
Be propitious, and have mercy on us.
O Maker of the world, the Life of all, the Lord of angels, remember us:
Be propitious, and have mercy on us.
O Lamb of God, who for us was led as a sheep to the slaughter,
remember us:
Be propitious, and have mercy on us.
You who was arrested, although innocent, mocked, given over to
robbers, remember us:
Be propitious, and have mercy on us.
You who alone has through your death overcome the death our guilt,
remember us:
Be propitious, and have mercy on us.   Mozarabic Breviary

May Christ the Lord, who brought back the lost sheep on his shoulders
to heaven, cleanse you from the stain of sin. Amen.
May he, who forgave the sins of the crucified robber, and restored him
to paradise, purify you from all sins, and enlighten you with
the presence of his brightness. Amen.
May he wipe away from you all guilt of sins, and place you in the
company of the blessed. Amen.
Through the mercy of our God, who is blessed and reigns, and governs
all things, world without end.   Mozarabic Breviary

Most great and glorious Lord God, accept my imperfect repentance, and
send your Spirit of adoption into my heart, that I may again be owned
by you, call you Father, and share in the blessings of your children.

John Wesley

O Lord God, eternal and almighty Father, we acknowledge and sincerely
confess before your holy majesty that we are miserable sinners,
conceived and born in iniquity and sin, prone to evil, and incapable of

any good work, and that in our depravity we make no end of breaking your holy commandments. We thus call down destruction on ourselves from your just judgments. Nevertheless, O Lord, we lament that we have offended you, and we condemn ourselves and our faults with true repentance, asking you to help us from wretchedness by your grace.

Deign, then, O most gracious and most merciful God and Father, to bestow your mercy on us in the name of Jesus Christ your Son our Lord. Effacing our faults, and all our sinfulness, daily increase on us the gifts of your Holy Spirit, that we from our inner hearts, acknowledging our sin, may be more and more displeasing to ourselves, and become truly repentant, and that your Holy Spirit may produce in us the fruits of righteousness and holiness, through Jesus Christ, our Saviour.

John Calvin

Jesus Christ, have mercy on me, as you are king of majesty; and forgive all my sins that I have committed, both great and small; and bring me, if it is your will to heaven to live always with you.   Richard Rolle

Almighty God, Father of our Lord Jesus Christ, Maker of all things, judge of all men; We acknowledge and bewail our manifold sins and wickedness, Which we, from time to time, most grievously have committed, By thought, word, and deed, Against thy Divine Majesty, Provoking most justly thy wrath and indignation against us. We do earnestly repent, And are heartily sorry for these our misdoings; The remembrance of them is grievous unto us; The burden of them is intolerable. Have mercy upon us, Have mercy upon us, most merciful Father; For thy Son our Lord Jesus Christ's sake, Forgive us all that is past; And grant that we may ever hereafter Serve and please thee In newness of life, To the honour and glory of thy Name; Through Jesus Christ our Lord. Amen.   Book of Common Prayer, The Lord's Supper

O God, the Father of our Saviour Jesus Christ, whose name is great, whose nature is blissful, whose goodness is inexhaustible, God and Ruler of all things, who are blessed for ever; before whom stand thousands and thousands, and ten thousand times ten thousand, the hosts of holy angels and archangels; sanctify, O Lord, our souls and bodies and spirits, search our consciences, and cast out from us every evil thought, every base desire, all envy and pride, all wrath and anger, and all that is contrary to your holy will. And grant us, O Lord, Lover of men and women, with a pure heart and contrite soul to call on thee, our holy God and Father who art in heaven.

Syrian Rite

Forgive them all, O Lord:
our sins of omission and our sins of commission;
the sins of our youth and the sins of our riper years;
the sins of our souls and the sins of our bodies;
our secret and our more open sins;
our sins of ignorance and surprise,
and our more deliberate and presumptuous sins;
the sins we have done to please ourselves,
and the sins we have done to please others;
the sins we know and remember,
and the sins we have forgotten;
the sins we have striven to hide from others
and the sins by which we have offended others;
forgive them, O Lord, forgive them all for his sake,
who died for our sins and rose for our justification,
and now stands at your right hand to make intercession for us,
Jesus Christ our Lord.

John Wesley

Almighty and merciful God, the fountain of all goodness, who knowest the thought of our hearts: we confess that we have sinned against Thee, and done evil in Thy sight. Wash us, we beseech Thee, from the stains of our past sins, and give us grace and power to put away all hurtful things; that, being delivered from the bondage of sin, we may bring forth fruits worthy of repentance, and at last enter into thy promised joy; through the mercy of Thy blessed Son, Jesus Christ our Lord.

Alcuin

A Litany

Drop, drop, slow tears,
    And bathe those beauteous feet
Which brought from Heaven
    The news and Prince of Peace:
Cease not, wet eyes,
    His mercy to entreat;
To cry for vengeance
    Sin doth never cease.
In your deep flood
    Drown all my faults and fears;
Nor let His eye
    See sin, but through my tears.

Phineas Fletcher

The hatred which divides nation from nation,
race from race, class from class,
Father, forgive.

The covetous desires of men and nations
to possess what is not their own,
Father, forgive.

The greed which exploits the labours of men,
and lays waste the earth,
Father, forgive.

Our envy of the welfare and happiness of others,
Father, forgive.

Our indifference to the plight of the homeless and the refugee,
Father, forgive.

The lust which uses for ignoble ends
the bodies of men and women,
Father, forgive.

The pride which leads to trust in ourselves
and not in God,
Father, forgive.

Prayer on a plaque on the altar of Coventry Cathedral, written in 1964

O Lord, heal our infirmities, pardon our offences, lighten our burdens,
enrich our poverty; through Christ our Lord.

Christopher Sutton

Forgive me my sins, O Lord; the sins of my present and the sins of my
past, the sins of my soul and the sins of my body, the sins which I have
done to please myself and the sins which I have done to please others.
Forgive me my casual sins and my deliberate sins, and those which I have
tried to hide so that I have hidden them even from myself. Forgive me
them, O Lord, forgive them all; for Jesus Christ's sake.

Bishop Thomas Wilson

Almighty and most merciful Father, we have erred and strayed from thy
ways like lost sheep, we have followed too much the devices and desires
of our own hearts, we have offended against thy holy laws. We have left
undone those things which we ought to have done, and we have done
those things which we ought not to have done, and there is no health in
us. But thou, O Lord, have mercy upon us miserable offenders; spare
thou them, O God, which confess their faults; restore thou them that are
penitent, according to thy promises declared unto mankind in Christ
Jesus our Lord. And grant, O most merciful Father, for his sake, that we
may hereafter live a godly, righteous, and sober life, to the glory of thy
holy Name.   Book of Common Prayer, 1552, Morning and Evening Prayer

Forgive me my sins, O Lord; forgive me the sins of my youth and the sins
of mine age, the sins of my soul and the sins of by body, my secret and
my whispering sins, my presumptuous and my crying sins, the sins that
I have done to please myself and the sins that I have done to please others. Forgive me those sins that I know and those sins which I know not;
forgive them, O Lord, forgive them all of your great goodness.

Private Devotions

We beseech thee, good Lord, that it may please thee to give us true repentance; to forgive us all our sins, negligences, and ignorances; and to endue us with the grace of thy Holy Spirit, to amend our lives according to thy holy word.   Thomas Cranmer, from *The Litany*, 1544

Lord, for thy tender mercies' sake, lay not our sins to our charge, but forgive that is past and give us grace to amend our lives; to decline from sin and incline to virtue, that we may walk with a perfect heart before thee, now and evermore.   Sixteenth century

Forgive me, Lord, my sins
    the sins of my youth,
    the sins of the present;
    the sins I laid upon myself in an ill pleasure,
    the sins I cast upon others in an ill example;
    the sins which are manifest to all the world,
    the sins which I have laboured to hide from mine acquaintance,
      from mine own conscience,
      and even from my memory;
    my crying sins and my whispering sins,
    my ignorant sins and my wilful;
    sins against my superiors, equals, servants,
      against my lovers and benefactors,
    sins against myself, mine own body, mine own soul,
    sins against thee, O heavenly Father, O merciful Son,
      O blessed Spirit of God.   Source unknown

Grant, we beseech thee, merciful Lord, to thy faithful people pardon and peace, that they may be cleansed from all their sins, and serve thee with a quiet mind; through Jesus Christ our Lord. Amen.

Book of Common Prayer, Collect for the Twenty-first Sunday after Trinity

Forgive me, O Lord, through the merits of thine Anointed, my Saviour,
    Jesus Christ.   John Donne

O most merciful Father, you forgive the sins of those who truly repent: we come before your throne in the name of Jesus Christ, that for his sake alone you will have compassion on us, and not allow our sin to be a cloud between you and us.   John Colet

O holy God, whose mercy and compassion made you come from the high throne down into this world for our salvation: mercifully forgive us all the sins we have done and thought and said. Send us cleanness of heart and purity of soul; restore us with your Holy Spirit, that we may from now on live virtuously and love you with all our hearts; through Jesus Christ your Son.   Richard Rolle

---

✢ Forgiving others

O Lord, remember not only the men and women of good will, but also those of ill will. But do not remember all the suffering they have inflicted on us; remember the fruits we have brought, thanks to this suffering – our comradeship, our loyalty, our courage, our generosity, the greatness of heart which has grown out of all this, and when they come to judgment let all the fruits which we have borne be their forgiveness.

Prayer found near the body of a dead child in the
Ravensbruck concentration camp

O Lord Jesus, because, being surrounded with infirmities we often sin and have to ask pardon, help us to forgive as we would be forgiven; neither mentioning old offences committed against us, nor dwelling upon them in thought, nor being influenced by them in heart; but loving our brother freely, as you freely loved us. For your name's sake.

Christina Rossetti

———— ✛ ————

Seeking God

Father,
give us wisdom to perceive you,
intellect to understand you,
diligence to seek you,
patience to wait for you,
eyes to behold you,
a heart to meditate on you
and a life to proclaim you,
through the power of the Spirit
of our Lord Jesus Christ.

Benedict

Give us, O Lord, a steadfast heart, which no unworthy affection may drag downwards; an unconquered heart, which no tribulation can wear out; give us an upright heart, which no unworthy purpose may tempt aside. Bestow on us also, O Lord, understanding to know you, diligence to seek you, wisdom to find you and a faithfulness that may finally embrace you; through Jesus Christ our Lord.   Thomas Aquinas

Lord, my heart is before you. I try, but by myself I can do nothing; do what I cannot. Admit me into the inner room of your love. I ask, I seek, I knock. You have made me seek, make me receive; you have enabled me to seek, enable me to find. You have taught me to knock, open to my knock. ...

I faint with hunger for your love; refresh me with it. Let me be filled with your love, rich in your affection, completely held in your care. Take me and possess me wholly, who with the Father and the Holy Spirit are alone blessed from age to age.

Anselm, *Meditation on Human Redemption*

Look on us, O Lord, and let all the darkness of our souls disappear before the beams of your brightness. Fill us with your holy love, and open to us the treasures of your wisdom. You know all our desire, so bring to perfection what you have started, and what your Spirit has awakened us to ask in prayer. We seek your face, turn your face to us and show us your glory. Then our longing will be satisfied and our peace will be perfect. Augustine

Come, Lord,
work on us,
set us on fire
and clasp us close,
be fragrant to us,
draw us to your love,
let us run to you. Augustine

Jesus, receive my heart,
and bring me to your love.
All my desire you are.
Kindle fire within me,
that I may receive your love,
and see your face in bliss
which will never cease,
in heaven with never an ending. Richard Rolle

Lord Jesus, I am not an eagle. All I have are the eyes and the heart of one. In spite of my littleness, I dare to gaze at the sun of love, and long to fly towards it. Thérèse of Lisieux

My God, I love you above all else and you I desire as my final goal. Always and in all things, with my whole heart, and strength I seek you. If you do not give yourself to me, you give nothing; if I do not find you, I find nothing. Grant me, therefore, most loving God, that I may always love you for yourself above all things, and seek you in all things in the present life, so that finally I may find you and keep you for ever in the world to come. Thomas Bradwardine

Almighty God, our heavenly Father, without whose help labour is useless, without whose light search in vain, invigorate my studies and direct my enquiries, that I may through due diligence and right discernment establish myself and others in your holy faith. Take not, O Lord, your Holy Spirit from me, let not evil thoughts have dominion in my mind. Let me not linger in ignorance and doubt, but enlighten and support me for the sake of Jesus Christ our Lord.   Dr Johnson

My stock lies dead, and no increase
Doth my dull husbandry improve:
O let thy graces without cease
          Drop from above!

If still the Sun should hide his face,
Thy house would but a dungeon prove,
Thy works night's captives: O let grace
          Drop from above!

The dew doth every morning fall;
And shall the dew outstrip thy Dove?
The dew, for which grass cannot call,
          Drop from above!

Death is still working like a mole,
And digs my grave at each remove:
Let grace work too, and on my soul
          Drop from above!

Sin is still hammering my heart
Unto a hardness, void of love:
Let suppling grace, to cross his art,
          Drop from above!

O come! for thou dost know the way.
Or if to me thou wilt not move,
Remove me where I need not say –
          Drop from above!   George Herbert, *The Temple*

Lord, teach me to seek you, and reveal yourself to me as I seek you. For I cannot seek you unless you first teach me and I cannot find you unless you first reveal yourself to me.   Ambrose of Milan

Unto Thee will I offer up an offering of praise.
Late have I loved you,
O Beauty ever old and ever new.
You were within and I without, and there I sought you.
You were with me when I was not with you.
You called and cried to me, and pierced my deafness.
You shone and glowed, and dispelled my blindness.
You touched me, and I burned for your peace.   Augustine, *Confessions*

O God, who wouldest not the death of a sinner, but that he should be converted and live: forgive the sins of us who turn to thee with all our heart, and grant us the grace of eternal life, through Jesus Christ our Lord.   Early Scottish prayer

O Lord, never allow us to think we can stand by ourselves and not
        need you, our greatest need.   John Donne

———————— ✛ ————————

Seeking salvation

Most bountiful and benign Lord God, we, your humble servants, freely redeemed and justified by the passion, death, and resurrection of our Saviour Jesus Christ, having our full trust of salvation therein, most humbly desire you so to strengthen our faith and illumine us with your grace, that we may walk and live in your favour; and after this life be partakers of your glory in the everlasting kingdom of heaven; through our Lord Jesus Christ.   York Minster, 1547

Let your mighty outstretched arm, O Lord God, be our defence; your mercy and loving kindness in Jesus Christ, your dear Son, our salvation; your true word our instruction; the grace of your life-giving Spirit our comfort and consolation, to the end and in the end; through the same Jesus Christ our Lord.   John Knox, Book of Common Order, 1564

Chapter Three

PRAYERS FOR GROWTH IN OUR WALK WITH GOD

The Spirit helps us in our weakness; for we do not know how to pray as we ought, but that very Spirit intercedes with sighs too deep for words. And God, who searches the heart, knows what is the mind of the Spirit, because the Spirit intercedes for the saints according to the will of God.

Romans 8:26–27 NRSV

The best prayers have more often groans than words.

John Bunyan

———— ✦ ————
Preparing to Pray

O Lord, who has mercy on all, take away from me my sins, and mercifully kindle in me the fire of your Holy Spirit. Take away from me the heart of stone, and give me a heart of flesh, a heart to love and adore you, a heart to delight in you, to follow and to enjoy you, for Christ's sake.

Ambrose

Prayer is the soul's sincere desire,
Uttered or unexpressed;
The motion of a hidden fire,
That trembles in the breast.

Prayer is the burden of a sigh,
The falling of a tear,
The upward glance of eye
Where none but God is near.

Prayer is the simplest form of speech
That infant lips can try;
Prayer the sublimest strains that reach
The majesty on high.

Prayer is the contrite sinner's voice
Returning from his ways,
While angels in their songs rejoice,
and cry, 'Behold, he prays!'

Prayer is the Christian's vital breath,
The Christian's native air,
His watchword at the gates of death:
He enters heaven with prayer.

James Montgomery

I need thee to teach me day by day, according to each day's opportunities and needs. Give me, O my Lord, that purity of conscience which alone can receive...

My ears are dull, so that I cannot hear thy voice.
My eyes are dim, so that I cannot see thy tokens.
Thou alone canst quicken my hearing, and purge my sight, and
    cleanse and renew my heart.
Teach me to sit at thy feet, and to hear thy word.

J.H. Newman

O my God, may I always keep myself in your love, by praying in the Holy Spirit. As your infinite love is always streaming in blessings on me, so let my soul be always breathing love to you.

Thomas Ken

Give to us the spirit of prayer, frequent and fervent, holy and persevering; an unreprovable faith, a just and humble hope, and a never-failing charity.

John Cosin

The prayers I make will then be sweet indeed
    If thou the spirit give by which I pray:
    My unassisted heart is barren clay,
That of its native self can nothing feed.

Michelangelo

Almighty God, from whom every good prayer comes, deliver us, when we draw close to you, from coldness of heart and wandering thoughts, that with steadfast thought and kindled desire we may worship you in the faith and spirit of Jesus Christ our Lord.

William Bright

Lift up our souls, O Lord, to the pure, serene light of your presence; that there we may breathe freely, there repose in your love, there may be at rest from ourselves, and from there return, arrayed in your peace, to do and bear what will please you; for your holy name's sake.

E.B. Pusey

O Lord, the Scripture says, 'There is a time for silence and a time for
        speech.'
Saviour, teach me the silence of humility,
the silence of wisdom,
the silence of love,
the silence of perfection,
the silence that speaks without words,
the silence of faith.
Lord, teach me to silence my own heart that I may listen to the gentle movement of the Holy Spirit within me and be aware of your depths.

Source unknown, 16th century

Dear Lord and Father of mankind,
Forgive our foolish ways!
Reclothe us in our rightful mind;
In purer lives your service find,
In deeper reverence, praise.

Breathe through the heats of our desire
Thy coolness and thy balm;
Let sense be dumb, let flesh retire;
Speak through the earthquake, wind, and fire,
O still small voice of calm!   J.G. Whittier

Give me grace, O my Father, to be utterly ashamed of my own reluctance to pray. Rouse me from sloth and coldness, and make me desire you with my whole heart. Teach me to love meditation, sacred reading, and prayer. Teach me to love what which must engage my mind for all eternity.

                                                                    J.H. Newman

O Lord, take away all coldness, all wanderings of thoughts, and fix our souls upon thee and thy love, O merciful Lord and Saviour, in this our hour of prayer.   E.W. Benson

O supreme Lord, most secret and most present, most beautiful and strong! What shall I say, my God, my life, my holy joy? What shall anyone say when he speaks to you?   Augustine

Save us, Lord, from being self-centred in our prayers, and teach us to remember to pray for others. May we be so caught up in love for those for whom we pray, that we may feel their needs as keenly as our own, and pray for them with imagination, sensitivity and knowledge. We ask this in Christ's name.   John Calvin

Lord, I know not what I ought to ask of you. You only know what I need. You know me better than I know myself. O Father, give to your child what he himself knows not how to as. Teach me to pray. Pray yourself in me.   F. Fénelon

Give us grace, almighty Father, to address you with all our hearts as
      well as with our lips.
You are present everywhere: from you no secrets can be hidden.
Teach us to fix our thoughts on you, reverently and with love, so that
      our prayers are not in vain, but are acceptable to you, now
      and always, through Jesus Christ our Lord.   Jane Austen

Holy Jesus, give me the gift and spirit of prayer.   Jeremy Taylor

O thou by whom we come to God,
The Life, the Truth, the Way,
The path of prayer thyself hast trod:
Lord, teach us how to pray.   James Montgomery

O almighty God, the searcher of all hearts, who has declared that who draw near to you with their lips when their hearts are far from you are an abomination to you: cleanse, we beseech you, the thoughts of our hearts by the inspiration of your Holy Spirit, that no wandering, vain, or idle thoughts may put out of our minds that reverence and godly fear that becomes all those who come into your presence.   Jonathan Swift

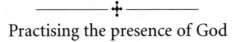

Practising the presence of God

Lord, we thy presence seek;
May ours this blessing be;
Give us a pure and lowly heart,
A temple meet for thee.

Author unknown, from *Hall's Psalms and Hymns*, 1836

Glory be to thee, O Lord,
for that thou didst create not only the visible light,
but the light invisible,
that which may be known of God, the law written in the heart;
give us a mind to perceive this light in
    the oracles of prophets,
    the melody of psalms,
    the prudence of proverbs,
    the experience of histories,
    and the life and love of our Lord Jesus Christ,
    for his sake.
                          Lancelot Andrewes

Teach us to pray often, that we may pray oftener.   *Jeremy Taylor*

More of thy presence, Lord, impart,
More of thine image let me bear;
Erect thy throne within my heart,
And reign without a rival there.   *John Newton*

O God, be present with us always, dwell within our heart. With your
light and your Spirit guide our souls, our thoughts, and all our actions,
that we may teach your Word, that your healing power may be in us and
in your worldwide church.   *Philipp Melanchthon*

Give me the lowest place: not that I dare
    Ask for that lowest place, but Thou hast died
That I might live and share
    Thy glory by Thy side.
Give me the lowest place: or if for me
    That lowest place too high, make one more low
Where I may sit and see
    My God and love Thee so.   *Christina Rossetti*

My words and thoughts do both express this notion,
That *Life* hath with the sun a double motion.
The first *Is* straight, and our diurnal friend;
The other *Hid*, and doth obliquely bend.
One life is wrapt *In* flesh, and tends to earth:
The other winds towards *Him*, whose happy birth
Taught me to live here so *That* still one eye
Should aim and shoot at that which *Is* on high;
Quitting with daily labour all *My* pleasure,
To gain at harvest an eternal *Treasure*.

George Herbert, *The Temple*, Colossians 3:3

O for a closer walk with God,
    A calm and heavenly frame;
A light to shine upon the road
    That leads me to the Lamb!

Return, O holy Dove, return,
    Sweet messenger of rest;
I hate the sins that made thee mourn,
    And drove thee from my breast.

The dearest idol I have known,
    Whate'er that idol be,
Help me to tear it from thy throne,
    And worship only thee.

So shall my walk be close with God,
    Calm and serene my frame;
So purer light shall mark the road
    That leads me to the Lamb.

William Cowper

O Lord our God, grant us grace to desire you with a whole heart, that so desiring you we may seek you and find you; and so finding you, may love you; and loving you, may hate those sins from which you have redeemed us, for Jesus Christ's sake.

Anselm

Clothe me, clothe me with yourself, eternal truth, so that I may live this earthly life with true obedience, and with the light of your most holy faith.   Catherine of Siena

Thanks be to you, my Lord Jesus Christ,
for all the benefits you have won for me.
For all the pains and insults you have borne for me.
O most merciful Redeemer, Friend, and Brother,
may I know you more clearly,
love you more dearly,
and follow you more nearly,
day by day.   Richard of Chichester

O Lord, thou knowest how busy I must be this day. If I forget thee, do not thou forget me.

General Lord Astley, before the battle of Edgehill

God, of your goodness, give me yourself,
for you are sufficient for me.
I may not correctly ask for anything less,
to be worthy of you.
If I were to ask anything less
I should always be in need,
for in you alone do I have all.   Julian of Norwich

———————— ✝ ————————

God's will

Discerning God's will

Father, I have sinned against heaven and before you; I am no longer
worthy to be called your son.   Luke 15:21 NRSV

Lord, who has form'd me out of mud,
    And hast redeem'd me through they blood,
    And sanctifi'd me to do good;

Purge all my sins done heretofore:
    For I confess my heavy score,
    And I will strive to sin no more.

Enrich my heart, mouth, hands in me,
    With faith, with hope, with charitie;
    That I may run, rise, rest with thee.

                                      George Herbert

God almighty, eternal, righteous and merciful, may we poor sinners, carry out your will and always do what pleases you. May we be so inwardly purified, enlightened and alight with the fire of the Holy Spirit that we follow in the footsteps of your well-beloved Son, our Lord Jesus Christ.
                                    Francis of Assisi

Eternal Light, shine into our hearts,
eternal Goodness, deliver us from evil,
eternal Power, be our support,
eternal Wisdom, scatter the darkness of our ignorance,
eternal Pity, have mercy upon us;
that with all our heart and mind and strength we may seek they face
        and be brought by your infinite mercy to your holy presence;
        through Jesus Christ our Lord.
                                      Alcuin

Obeying and following God's will

Happy are those
    who do not follow the advice of the wicked,
or take the path that sinners tread,
    or sit in the seat of scoffers;
but their delight is in the law of the Lord,
    and on his law they meditate day and night.
They are like trees
    planted by steams of water,
which yield their fruit in its season,
    and their leaves do not wither.
In all that they do, they prosper.   Psalm 1:1–3

Our Father, here I am, at your disposal, your child,
to use me to continue your loving the world,
by giving Jesus to me and through me,
to each other and to the world.
Let us pray for each other that we allow Jesus to love in us
and through us with the love with which his Father loves us.

Mother Teresa

Teach me, my Lord Jesus, instruct me, that I may learn from you what
I ought to teach about you.   William Laud

O Lord, I am yours. Do what seems good in your sight,
and give me complete resignation to your will.   David Livingstone

Deliver me, Lord God, from a slothful mind, from all lukewarmness, and
all dejection of spirit. I know these cannot but deaden my love for you;
mercifully free my heart from them, and give me a lively, zealous, active
and cheerful spirit; that I may vigorously perform whatever you command, thankfully suffer whatever you choose for me, and always be
ardent to obey in all things your holy love.   John Wesley

Thy way, not mine, O Lord,
However dark it be:
Lead me by thine own hand,
Choose out the path for me.

The kingdom that I seek
Is thine: so let the way
That leads to it be thine,
Else I must surely stray.

Take thou my cup, and it
With joy or sorrow fill,
As best to thee may seem;
Choose thou my good and ill.
Not mine, not mine the choice
In things or great or small;
By thou my guide, my strength,
My wisdom and my all.

Horatius Bonar

O Lord, we most humbly beseech you to give us grace not only to be hearers of the Word, but also doers of the Word; not only to love, but also to live your gospel; not only to profess, but also to practise your blessed commandments, for the honour of your holy name.

Thomas Becon

O thou who camest from above,
The pure celestial fire to impart,
Kindle a flame of sacred love
On the mean altar of my heart.

There let it for thy glory burn,
With inextinguishable blaze;
And trembling to its source return,
In humble love and fervent praise.

Jesus, confirm my heart's desire
To work, and speak, and thank for thee;
Still let me guard the holy fire,
And still stir up thy gift in me.

Ready for all thy perfect will,
My acts of faith and love repeat,
Till death thy endless mercies seal,
And make the sacrifice complete.   Charles Wesley

Guide me, O Lord, in all the changes and varieties of the world; that in all
things that shall happen, I may have an evenness and tranquillity of spirit; that my soul may be wholly resigned to thy divinest will and pleasure,
never murmuring at thy gentle chastisements and fatherly correction.

Jeremy Taylor

God of all goodness, grant us to desire ardently, to seek wisely, to know
surely, and to accomplish perfectly your holy will, for the glory of your
name.   Thomas Aquinas

Lord, lift up the light of your countenance on us, that in your light we
may see light; the light of your grace today, and the light of your glory
hereafter; through Jesus Christ our Lord.   Lancelot Andrewes

Govern all by your wisdom, O Lord, so that my soul may always be serving you according to your will, and now as I desire. Do not punish me,
I pray, by granting what I want and ask, if it offends your love, which
would always live in me. Let me die to myself, that I may serve you, let
me live to you, who in yourself are the true Life.   Teresa of Avila

Thank you, Lord Jesus, that you will be our hiding place whatever happens.
Corrie ten Boom

O Lord, to be turned from you is to fall, to be turned to you is to rise, and to stand in you is to abide for ever. Grant us in all our duties your help, in all our perplexities your guidance, in all our dangers your protection, and in all our sorrows your peace; through Jesus Christ our Lord.

Augustine

We beseech you, O Lord, to enlighten our minds and to strengthen our wills, that we may know what we ought to do, and be enabled to do it, through the grace of your most Holy Spirit, and for the merits of your Son, Jesus Christ our Lord.   William Bright

Save us, O Lord, from the snares of a double mind.
Deliver us from all cowardly neutralities.
Make us to go in the paths of your commandments,
and to trust for our defence in your mighty arm alone;
through Jesus Christ our Lord.   R. H. Froude

O give us patience and steadfastness in adversity, strengthen our weakness, comfort us in trouble and distress, help us to fight; grant to us that in true obedience and contention of mind we may give over our own will to you our Father in all things, according to the example of your beloved Son; that in adversity we grudge not, but offer up ourselves to you without contradiction. O give us a willing and cheerful mind, that we may gladly suffer and bear all things for your sake.

Miles Coverdale

O good Jesu, the word of the Father, the brightness of the Father's glory, whom angels desire to behold; teach me to do your will; that guided by your good spirit, I may come to that blessed city where there is everlasting day and all are of one spirit; where there is certain security and secure eternal tranquillity and quiet felicity and happy sweetness and sweet pleasantness; where you, with the Father and the Holy Spirit live and reign, world without end.   Gregory I

Speak, Lord, for thy servant heareth.
Grant us ears to hear,
eyes to see,
wills to obey,
hearts to love;
then declare what thou wilt,
reveal what thou wilt,
command what thou wilt,
demand what thou wilt.

Christina Rossetti

Open my eyes that I may see,
Incline my heart that I may desire,
Order my steps that I may follow
The way of your commandments.

Lancelot Andrewes

O Lord, you know what is best for me. Let this or that be done, as you wish. Give what you will, how much you will and when you will.

Thomas à Kempis

Send out your light and your truth, that I may live always near to you, my God. Let me feel your love, that I may be as it were already in heaven, that I may do my work as the angels do theirs; and let me be ready for every work, ready to go out or go in, to stay or depart, just as you direct.

Lord, let me have no will of my own, or consider my true happiness as depending in the smallest degree on anything that happens to me outwardly, but as consisting totally in conformity to your will.

Henry Martyn

Almighty God, in whom we live and move and have our being, you have made us for yourself and our hearts are restless until in you they find their rest. Grant us purity of heart and strength of purpose, that no selfish passion may hinder us from knowing your will, no weakness from doing it; but that in your light we may see light clearly, and in your service we may find our perfect freedom; through Jesus Christ our Lord.

Augustine

Grant me, I beseech thee, almighty and merciful God, fervently to desire, wisely to search out, truly to acknowledge, and perfectly to fulfil, all that is well-pleasing to thee. Order thou my worldly condition to the honour and glory of thy name; and of all that thou requirest me to do, grant me the knowledge, the desire, and the ability, that I may so fulfil it as I ought, and as is expedient for the welfare of my soul.   Thomas Aquinas

O Lord Jesus Christ, you have made me and redeemed me and brought me to where I now am: you know what you wish to do with me; do with me according to your will, for your tender mercies' sake.

King Henry VI

Take, Lord, and receive all my liberty,
my memory, my understanding,
and my whole will.
All that I have and call my own,
you have given to me.
I surrender it all to you
to be disposed of according to your will.
Give me only your love and your grace;
with these I will be rich enough,
and will desire nothing more.

Ignatius Loyola

Most high, glorious God,
enlighten the darkness of our minds.
Give us a right faith, a firm hope and perfect love,
so that we may always and in all things act according to your holy will.
    Amen.   Francis of Assisi

Open our hearts, O Lord, and enlighten our minds by the grace of your
Holy Spirit, that we may seek what is well-pleasing to your will; and so
order our doings after your commandments, that we may be found fit to
enter into your everlasting joy, through Jesus Christ our Lord.   Bede

———————— ✞ ————————

Dedication

Blessed be your name, Lord God, who has set before me life and death,
and has invited me to choose life. Now, Lord God, I choose life, with all
my heart. I choose you, my God, for you are my life.

Lord, make me completely holy, that all my spirit, soul and body
may be a temple for you. Live in me, and be my God and I will be your
servant.   Thomas Ken

O Lord Jesu, our only health and our everlasting life, I give myself
wholly unto thy will: being sure that the thing cannot perish which is
committed unto thy mercy.

Thou, merciful Lord, wast born for my sake: thou didst suffer both
hunger and thirst for my sake; thou didst preach and teach, didst pray
and fast, for my sake: and finally thou gavest thy most precious body to
die and thy blood to be shed on the cross, for my sake. Most merciful
Saviour, let all these things profit me which thou freely hast given me.
O Lord, into thy hands I commit my soul.   Primer, 1559

Give us, O Lord, we humbly pray, a wise, a sober, a patient, an understanding, a devout, a religious, a courageous heart; a soul full of devotion to serve you, and strength against all temptations; through Jesus
Christ our Lord.   William Laud

None other lamb, none other name,
    None other hope in heaven or earth or sea,
None other hiding-place from guilt and shame,
    None beside thee!

My faith burns low, my hope burns low;
    Only my heart's desire cries out in me,
By the deep thunder of its want and woe,
    Cries out to thee.

Lord, thou art life, though I be dead;
    Love's fire thou art, however cold I be:
Nor heaven have I, nor place to lay my head,
Nor home, but thee.

Christina Rossetti

Grant unto me
    to bruise the serpent's head,
    to remember the last things,
    to cut off occasions [for evil],
    to be sober,
    not to sit idle,
    to refuse the evil,
    to cleave to the good,
    to make a covenant touching the eyes,
    to bring the body into subjection,
    to give oneself to prayer,
    to withdraw to penitence.

Lancelot Andrewes

My Lord and my God, take me from all that keeps me from you.
My Lord and my God, grant me all that leads me to you.
My Lord and my God, take me from myself and give me completely
    to you.

Nicholas of Flue

Father, into your hands I give the heart
which left thee but to learn how good thou art.

George Macdonald

Use me, my Saviour, for whatever purpose and in what way you require. Here is my poor heart, any empty vessel: fill it with your grace. Here is my sinful and troubled soul: bring it to life and refresh it with your love. Take my heart for you to live in; my mouth to spread abroad the glory of your name; my love and all my powers for the advancement of your believing people; and never allow the steadfastness and confidence of my faith to abate.

D.L. Moody

Were earth a thousand times as fair,
Beset with gold and jewels rare,
    She yet wcre far too poor to be
    A narrow cradle, Lord, for thee.

Ah, dearest Jesus, holy child,
Make thee a bed, soft, undefiled,
    Within my heart, that it may be
    A quiet chamber kept for thee.

Martin Luther, translated by Catherine Winkworth

Lord, be thy word my rule,
In it may I rejoice;
Thy glory be my aim,
Thy holy will my choice.

Thy promises my hope;
Thy providence my guard;
Thine arm my strong support;
Thyself my great reward.

Christopher Wordsworth

Grant, O Lord,
that Christ himself may be formed in us,
that we may conform to his image;
for his name's sake.

Lancelot Andrewes

Lord Jesus, who would think that I am Thine?
   Ah, who would think
Who sees me ready to turn back or sink,
   That Thou art mine?

I cannot hold Thee fast tho' Thou art mine:
   Hold Thou me fast,
So earth shall know at last and heaven at last
   That I am Thine.
                        Christina Rossetti

Be Thou a light unto mine eyes,
   music to mine ears,
   sweetness to my taste,
   and a full contentment to my heart.
Be Thou my sunshine in the day,
   my food at the table,
   my repose in the night,
   my clothing in nakedness,
   and my succour in all necessities.
Lord Jesu, I give Thee my body, my substance, my fame, my friends,
   my liberty, and my life. Dispose of me and of all that is mine,
   as it seemeth best to Thee and to the glory of Thy Blessed
   Name.
             John Cosin, *A Collection of Private Devotions*

O Jesus, fill me with your love now, and I pray, accept me, and use me a
little for your glory. O do, do, I pray, accept me and my service, and take
all the glory.
             David Livingstone

Lord God Almighty, shaper and ruler of all creatures, we pray that by
your great mercy and by the token of the holy cross you will guide us to
your will. Make our minds steadfast, strengthen us against temptation,
and keep us from all unrighteousness. Shield us against our enemies,
seen and unseen. Teach us to inwardly love you before all things with a
clean mind and a clean body. For you are our Maker and Redeemer, our
help and comfort, our trust and hope, for ever.
     King Alfred the Great

O Lord, you are our Father, and we are only clay from the earth. You are our Creator, and we are the work of your hands. You are our Shepherd, we are your flock. You are our Redeemer, we are your people whom you have bought. You are our God, we are your heritage.　　　John Calvin

Teach us, dear Lord, frequently and attentively to consider this truth:
　　that if I gain the whole world and lose you, in the end I have lost
　　　　everything;
　　whereas if I lose the world and gain you, in the end I have lost
　　　　nothing.　　　　　　　　　　　　　　　J.H. Newman

Take my life, and let it be
Consecrated, Lord, to thee;
Take my moments and my days,
Let them flow in ceaseless praise.　　　　Frances Ridley Havergal

O Lord, take full possession of my heart, raise there your throne, and
　　　　command there as you do in heaven.
Being created by you, let me live for you;
being created for you, let me always act for your glory;
being redeemed by you, let me give to you what is yours;
and let my spirit cling to you alone, for your name's sake.　　John Wesley

Almighty and most merciful Father, look down on us your unworthy servants through the mediation and merits of Jesus Christ, in whom only are you well pleased. Purify our hearts by your Holy Spirit, and as you add days to our lives, so good Lord, add repentance to our days; that when we have passed this mortal life we may be partakers of your everlasting kingdom; through the merits of Jesus Christ our Lord.

King Charles I

My Lord, I have nothing to do in this world but to seek and serve you.
I have nothing to do with my heart and its affections but to breathe
after you.
I have nothing to do with my tongue and pen but to speak to you and
for you, and to make known your glory and your will.

Richard Baxter

Grant, O Lord, that I may be so ravished in the wonder of your love that I may forget myself and all things; may feel neither prosperity nor adversity; may not fear to suffer all the pain in the world rather than be parted from you.

O let me feel you more inwardly, and truly present with me than I am with myself, and make me most circumspect in your presence, my holy Lord.

Robert Leighton

Grant us, Lord, we beseech thee, not to mind earthly things, but to seek things heavenly; so that though we are set among scenes that pass away, our heart and affection may steadfastly cleave to the things that endure for ever; through Jesus Christ our Lord.

Leonine Sacramentary

Lord, almighty God, Father of your beloved and blessed Son Jesus Christ, through whom we have come to the knowledge of yourself, God of angels, of powers, of all creation, of all the saints who live in your sight, I bless you for judging me worthy of this day, this hour, so that in the company of the martyrs I may share the cup of Christ, your anointed one, and so rise again to eternal life in soul and body, immortal through the power of the Holy Spirit. May I be received among the martyrs in your presence today as a rich and pleasing sacrifice. God of truth, stranger to falsehood, you have prepared this and revealed it to me and now you have fulfilled your promise.

Polycarp, prayer he prayed as he was burned at the stake, c. 155

O love eternal,
my soul needs and chooses you eternally.
Oh, come Holy Spirit,
and inflame our hearts with your love.
To love – or to die.
To die – and to love.
To die to all other love
in order to live in Jesus' love,
so that we may not die eternally.
But that we may live in your eternal love,
O Saviour of our souls,
we eternally sing,
'Live, Jesus.
Jesus, I love.
Live, Jesus, whom I love.
Jesus, I love,
Jesus who lives and reigns forever and ever. Amen.'

Francis de Sales, concluding prayer in his book *Treatise on the Love of God*

Lord, I am yours,
and I must belong to no one but you.
My soul is yours,
and must live only through you.
My will is yours,
and must love only for you.
I must love you as my first cause,
since I am from you.
I must love you as my goal and rest,
since I am for you.
I must love you more than my own being,
since my being comes from you.
I must love you more than myself,
since I am all yours and all in you. Amen.

Francis de Sales

———— ✤ ————

Serving God

Keep me, O Lord, while I tarry on this earth, in a daily serious seeking after thee, and in a believing affectionate walking with thee; that, when thou comest, I may be found not hiding my talent, nor serving my flesh, nor yet asleep with my lamp unfurnished; but waiting and longing for my Lord, my glorious God, for ever and ever.   Richard Baxter

O Lord, who though you were rich yet for our sakes became poor, and has promised in your holy gospel that whatever is done for the least of your brethren you will receive as done to you: Give us grace, we humbly beseech you, to be always willing and ready to minister, as you enable us, to the needs of others, and to extend the blessings of your kingdom over all the world; to your praise and glory, who are God over all, blessed for ever.   Augustine

Almighty God, the Protector of all who trust in you, without whose grace nothing is strong, nothing is holy, increase and multiply on us your mercy, that through your holy inspiration we may think the things that are right and by your power may carry them out, through Jesus Christ our Lord.   Martin Luther

O Lord, the Author and Persuader of peace, love and goodwill, soften our hard and steely hearts, warm our frozen and icy hearts, that we may wish well to one another, and may be the true disciples of Jesus Christ. And give us grace even now to begin to show that heavenly life, where there is no hatred, but peace and love everywhere, towards one another.   Ludovicus Vives

Make us, O Lord, to flourish like pure lilies in the courts of your house, and to show forth to the faithful the fragrance of your good deeds, and the example of a godly life, through your mercy and grace.   Mozarabic Liturgy

Make us worthy, Lord,
To serve our fellow-men
Throughout the world
Who live and die in poverty and hunger.
Give them, through our hands,
This day their daily bread;
And by our understanding love,
Give peace and joy.   Mother Teresa

Dearest Lord, teach me to be generous;
teach me to serve you as you deserve;
to give and not to count the cost,
to fight and not to heed the wounds,
to toil and not to seek for rest,
to labour and not to seek reward,
except to know that I do your will.   Ignatius Loyola

O thou who camest from above
The pure, celestial fire to impart,
Kindle a flame of sacred love
On the mean altar of my heart.

There let it for thy glory burn
With inextinguishable blaze,
And trembling to its source return
In humble prayer and fervent praise.

Jesus, confirm my heart's desire
To work, and speak, and think for thee.
Still let me guard the holy fire,
And still stir up thy gift in me.   Charles Wesley

Lord Jesus, may the fire of your Holy Spirit consume in us all that dis-
pleases you, and kindle in our hearts a burning zeal for the service of our
kingdom; through our Saviour Jesus Christ.   Ancient collect

O Lord Jesus Christ, who when on earth was always occupied by your Father's business: grant that we may not grow weary in well-doing. Give us grace to do all in your name.

Be our beginning and end of everything: the pattern whom we follow, the Redeemer in whom we trust, the Master whom we serve, the Friend to whom we look for sympathy.

May we never shrink from our duty through any fear of people; make us faithful until death; and bring us at last into the eternal presence, where with the Father and the Holy Spirit you live and reign for ever.

E.B. Pusey

Make me, O my God,
humble without pretence,
cheerful without levity,
serious without dejection,
grave without moroseness,
active without frivolity,
truthful without duplicity,
fearful of thee without despair,
trustful of thee without presumption,
chaste without depravity,
able to correct my neighbour without angry feeling,
and by word and example to edify him without pride,
obedient without gainsaying,
patient without murmuring.

Thomas Aquinas

O God, who has warned us that you will require much from those to whom much is given; grant that we, whose lot is cast in so goodly a heritage, may strive together the more abundantly, by prayer, by almsgiving, by fasting, and by all appointed means, to extend to those who do not know you what we so richly enjoy; and as we have entered into the labours of others so to labour that, others may enter into ours, to the fulfilment of your holy will and the salvation of all mankind; through Jesus Christ our Lord.

Augustine's Manual

Eternal God,
the light of the minds that know you,
the joy of the hearts that love you,
the strength of the wills that serve you;
May we know you that we may truly love you,
and so to love you that we may freely serve you,
to the glory of your holy name.   Gelasian Sacramentary

Remember, O Lord, what thou hast wrought in us, and not what we deserve; and as thou hast called us to thy service, make us worthy of our calling; through Jesus Christ our Lord.   Leonine Sacramentary

——————— ✠ ———————

Pilgrimage

O Lord God, from whom we come, in whom we are enfolded, to
          whom we shall return:
Bring us in our pilgrimage through life;
     with the power of the Father protecting,
     with the love of Jesus indwelling,
     and the light of the Spirit guiding,
until we come to our ending,
in life and love eternal.   Peter Nott

     Who would true valour see,
     Let him come hither;
     One here will constant be,
     Come wind, come weather
     There's no discouragement
     Shall make him once relent
     His first avow'd intent
     To be a pilgrim.

Whoso beset him round
With dismal stories,
Do but themselves confound;
His strength the more is.
No lion can him fright,
He'll with a giant fight,
But he will have a right
To be a pilgrim.

Hobgoblin nor foul fiend
Can daunt his spirit;
He knows he at the end
Shall life inherit.
Then fancies fly away,
He'll not fear what men say;
He'll labour night and day
To be a pilgrim.

John Bunyan, *Pilgrim's Progress*

The Passionate Man's Pilgrimage
Give me my scallop-shell of quiet,
My staff of faith to walk upon,
My scrip of joy, immortal diet,
My bottle of salvation,
My gown of glory, hope's true gage;
And thus I'll take my pilgrimage.

Blood must be my body's balmer;
No other balm will there be given;
Whilst my soul, like quiet palmer,
Travelleth towards the land of heaven;
    Over the silver mountains,
    Where spring the nectar fountains:
        There will I kiss
        The bowl of bliss,
And drink mine everlasting fill
Upon every milken hill.
My soul will be a-dry before;
But, after, it will thirst no more.

From thence to heaven's Bribeless hall
Where no corrupted voices brawl,
No Conscience molten into gold,
Nor forged accusers bought and sold,
No cause deferred, nor vain spent journey,
For there Christ is the King's Attorney:
Who pleads for all without degrees,
And he hath Angels, but no fees.

When the grand twelve million Jury,
Of our sins with dreadful fury,
'Gainst our souls black verdicts give,
Christ pleads his death, and then we live,
Be thou my speaker, taintless pleader,
Unblotted Lawyer, true proceeder,
Thou movest salvation even for alms:
Not with a bribed Lawyer's palms.

And this is my eternal plea,
To him that made Heaven, Earth and Sea,
Seeing my flesh must die so soon,
And want a head to dine next noon,
Just at the stroke when my veins start and spread
Set on my soul an everlasting head.
Then am I ready like a palmer fit,
To tread those blest paths which before I writ.

> Sir Walter Raleigh, written when he was a prisoner in the Tower of London, awaiting execution. The scallop-shell was a symbol of pilgrimage in the Middle Ages.

—————— ✛ ——————

Resisting temptation

Incline your ear, O Lord, and answer me,
    for I am poor and needy.
... Teach me your way, O Lord,
    that I may walk in your truth;
      give me an undivided heart to revere your name.

Psalm 86:1, 11 NRSV

Turn my heart to your decrees,
    and not to selfish gain.
Turn my eyes from looking at vanities;
    give me life in your ways.

Psalm 119:36–37 NRSV

Heavenly Father, whose blessed Son was revealed that he might destroy the works of the devil and make us the sons of God and heirs of eternal life: grant that we, having this hope, may purify ourselves even as he is pure; that when he shall appear in power and great glory we may be made like him in his eternal and glorious kingdom; where he is alive and reigns with you and the Holy Spirit, one God, now and for ever.

Alternative Service Book, Collect for Epiphany 6

O God, by thy mercy strengthen us who lie exposed to the rough storms of troubles and temptations. Help us against our own negligence and cowardice, and defend us from the treachery of our unfaithful hearts. Succour us, we beseech thee, and bring us to thy safe haven of peace and felicity.

Augustine

O God, our Father, we are exceedingly frail, and indisposed to every virtuous and noble undertaking: Strengthen our weakness, we beseech you, that we may be valiant in this spiritual war; help us against our own negligence and cowardice, and defend us from the treachery of our unfaithful hearts; for the sake of Jesus Christ our Lord.

Augustine

O Lord our God, grant us, we beseech thee, patience in troubles, humility in comforts, constancy in temptations, and victory over all our spiritual enemies. Grant us sorrow for our sins, thankfulness for your benefits, fear of your judgment, love of your mercies, and mindfulness of your presence; now and for evermore.

John Cosin

The dearest idol I have known,
Whate'er that idol be,
Help me to tear it from thy throne,
And worship only thee.

William Cowper

Blessed Lord, who was tempted in all things just as we are, have mercy on our frailty. Out of weakness give us strength. Grant us to reverence you, so that we may reverence you only. Support us in time of temptation. Make us bold in time of danger. Help us to do your work with courage, and to continue your faithful soldiers and servants to our life's end; through Jesus Christ our Lord.

B.F. Westcott

I asked the Lord, that I might grow
    In faith, and love, and every grace;
Might more of His salvation know,
    And seek more earnestly His face.

I hoped that in some favoured hour
    At once He'd answer my request,
And by His love's constraining power
    Subdue my sins, and give me rest.

Instead of this, He made me feel
    The hidden evils of my heart;
And let the angry powers of hell
    Assault my soul in every part.

Yea more, with His own hand He seemed
    Intent to aggravate my woe;
Crossed all the fair designs I schemed,
    Blasted my gourds, and laid me low.

'Lord, why is this?' I trembling cried,
    'Wilt thou pursue Thy worm to death?'
''Tis in this way,' the Lord replied,
    'I answer prayer for grace and faith.
These inward trials I employ
    From self and pride to set thee free;
And break thy schemes of earthly joy,
    That thou may'st seek thy all in me.'

John Newton

O heavenly Father, subdue in me whatever is contrary to Thy holy will.
Grant that I may ever study to know Thy will, that I may know how to
please Thee. Grant, O God, that I may never run into those temptations
which, in my prayers, I desire to avoid. Lord, never permit my trials to
be above my strength.

Thomas Wilson

————— ✢ —————

Battling against evil

O God, who for our redemption gave your only begotten Son to the death of the cross, and by his glorious resurrection has delivered us from the power of the enemy: Grant us to die daily to sin, that we may evermore live with him in the joy of his resurrection; through the same Jesus Christ our Lord. ⸱Gregorian Sacramentary

O teach us to despise all vanities, to fight the battles of the Lord manfully against the flesh, the world, and the devil, to spend our time religiously and usefully, to speak gracious words, to walk always in your presence, to preserve our souls and bodies in holiness, fit for the habitation of the Holy Spirit of God. John Cosin

From all blindness of heart; from pride, vainglory, and hypocrisy; from
　　　　envy, hatred, and malice, and all uncharitableness,
Spare us, good Lord.
From fornication, and all other deadly sin; and from all the deceits of
　　　　the world, the flesh, and the devil,
Spare us, good Lord.
From lightning and tempest; from earthquake, fire, and flood; from
　　　　plague, pestilence, and famine; from battle and murder, and
　　　　from sudden death,
Spare us, good Lord.
From all sedition, privy conspiracy, and rebellion; from all false doc-
　　　　trine, heresy, and schism; from hardness of heart, and con-
　　　　tempt of thy Word and Commandment,
Spare us, good Lord.
By the mystery of thy holy Incarnation; by thy holy Nativity and
　　　　Circumcision; by thy Baptism, Fasting, and Temptation,
Spare us, good Lord.
By thine Agony and Bloody Sweat; by thy Cross and Passion; by thy
　　　　precious Death and Burial; by thy glorious Resurrection and
　　　　Ascension, and by the Coming of the Holy Ghost,
Spare us, good Lord.

In all time of our tribulation; in all time of our prosperity; in the hour
of death, and in the day of judgment,
Spare us, good Lord. Book of Common Prayer, The Litany

Heavenly Father, the Father of all wisdom, understanding, and true
strength, we beseech thee look mercifully upon thy servants, and send
thy Holy Spirit into their hearts; that when they must join to fight in the
field for the glory of thy name, they may be defended with the strength
of thy right hand, and may manfully stand in the confession of thy faith,
and continue in the same unto their lives' end, through our Lord Jesus
Christ. Nicholas Ridley

Set a watch, O Lord, before my mouth, and keep the door of my lips.
Lord, keep my tongue from evil, and my lips that they speak no guile.
Treasury of Devotion

Help me now, O God, to do all things in your sight, who sees in secret.
Shut out, O God, from my heart everything that offends you.
By your mighty power, repress all my wandering thoughts, and tread
down Satan under my feet.
Treasury of Devotion

✢

Holiness

Let the remembrance of all the glory wherein I was created make me
more serious and humble, more deep and penitent, more pure and holy
before thee. Thomas Traherne

—————— ✢ ——————

Dependence on God

Grant, Lord God, that in the middle of all the discouragements, difficulties and dangers, distress and darkness of this mortal life, I may depend on your mercy, and on this build my hopes, as on a sure foundation. Let your infinite mercy in Christ Jesus deliver me from despair, both now and at the hour of death.   Thomas Wilson

Lord, I am a countryman coming from my country to yours. Teach me the laws of your country, its way of life and its spirit, so that I may feel at home there.   William of St Thierry

Our Father, you called us and saved us in order to make us like your Son, our Lord Jesus Christ. Day by day, change us by the work of your Holy Spirit so that we may grow more like him in all that we think and say and do, to his glory.   Søren Kierkegaard

O eternal God, who has made all things subject to mankind, and mankind for your glory; sanctify our souls and bodies, our thoughts and our intentions, our words and actions. Let our body be the servant of our spirit, and both body and spirit servants of Jesus; that doing all things for your glory here, we may be partakers of your glory hereafter, through Jesus Christ our Lord.   Jeremy Taylor

O Lord Jesus, who came down from heaven to redeem us from all iniquity, we beseech you to write your word in our hearts that we may know you, and the power of your resurrection, and express it in turning from our sins. Rule in our hearts by faith, that being dead to sin and living to righteousness, we may bear the fruit of holiness and grow in grace and in personal knowledge of you.   Henry Hammond

---✝---

Diligence

Almighty God, in whose hands are all the powers of men, grant that we may not lavish away the life which you have given us on useless trifles; but enable us by your Holy Spirit so to shun sloth and negligence that every day we may carry out the task which you have allotted us, and obtain such success as will most promote your glory; for the sake of Jesus Christ.
Dr Johnson

---✝---

Endurance

Merciful God, grant us feeble people endurance in adversity. May wicked roots of envy and malice not grow in us. Pull out the wicked root of covetousness from us. Save us from being brought into temptation by Satan. Grant us love towards friends and enemies, that we may follow in your ways, our Father, and the example of your only-begotten Son, Jesus Christ.
Miles Coverdale

Almighty God, our heavenly Father, who from your tender love towards us sinners has given us your Son, that believing in him we may have everlasting life; Grant us your Holy Spirit that we may continue steadfast in this faith to the end, and may come to everlasting life; through Jesus Christ, your Son, our Lord.
John Calvin

My dear Lord, though I am so very weak that I have not strength to ask you for suffering as a gift, at least I will beg from you grace to meet suffering well when you in your love and wisdom brings it on me. Let me bear pain, reproach, disappointment, slander, anxiety, suspense, as you want me to, O my Jesus, and as you by your own suffering have taught me, when it comes.
J.H. Newman

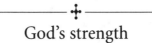

God's strength

Grant us, Lord, to know in weakness the strength of your incarnation:
in pain the triumph of your passion:
in poverty the riches of your Godhead:
in reproach the satisfaction of your sympathy:
in loneliness the comfort of your continual presence:
in difficulty the efficacy of your intercession:
in perplexity the guidance of your wisdom;
and by your glorious death and resurrection bring us at last to the joy
of seeing you face to face.   Author unknown

O King of Glory and Lord of Valours, our warrior and our peace, who
has said, 'Be of good cheer, I have overcome the world,' be victorious in
us your servants. Grant your compassion to go before us, your compassion to come behind us: before us in our undertaking, behind us in our
ending. And what will I now say, unless that your will be done, who wills
that all should be saved? Your will is our salvation, our glory our joy.

                                                                    Alcuin

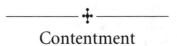

Contentment

Almighty God, who knows our necessities before we ask, and our ignorance in asking: Set free your servants from all anxious thoughts about
tomorrow; make us content with your good gifts; and confirm our faith
that as we seek your kingdom, you will not allow us to lack any good
thing; through Jesus Christ our Lord.   Augustine

Lord, I perceive my soul deeply guilty of envy. I would prefer your work
not done than done by someone else other than myself. Dispossess me,
Lord, of this bad spirit, and turn my envy into holy emulation; yes, make
other peoples' gifts to be mine, by making me thankful to you for them.

                                                            Thomas Fuller

He that is down needs fear no fall
He that is low, no pride:
He that is humble ever shall
Have God to be his guide.

I am content with what I have,
Little be it or much:
And, Lord, contentment still I crave,
Because thou savest such.

John Bunyan, Pilgrim's Progress

Grant me, most sweet and loving Jesus, to rest in you above every creature, above all health and beauty, above all glory and honour, above all power and dignity, above all skill and shrewdness, above all riches and talents, above all joy and exultation, above all fame and praise, above all hope and promise, above all merit and desire, above all gifts that you may shower on me, above all joy or tribulation that my mind may feel or receive. And grant me to rest in you above angels and archangels, above all the heavenly host, above all things visible and invisible, and above all that you are not, my God. For you, my God, are above all.

Thomas à Kempis

O Lord, whose way is perfect,
help us always to trust in thy goodness;
    that walking with thee
    and following thee in all simplicity,
we may possess quiet and contented minds,
    and may cast all our care on thee
    who carest for us;
for thy dear Son's sake, Jesus Christ.

Christina Rossetti

I asked God for strength, that I might achieve,
I was made weak, that I might learn humbly to obey.
I asked for health, that I might do greater things,
I was given infirmity, that I might do better things.
I asked for riches, that I might be happy,
I was given poverty, that I might be wise.

I asked for power, that I might have the praise of men,
I was given weakness, that I might feel the need of God.
I asked for all things, that I might enjoy life,
I was given life, that I might enjoy all things.
I got nothing that I asked for
but everything that I had hoped for,
almost despite myself, my unspoken prayers were answered.
I am among all men most richly blessed.

'A Soldier's Prayer', written by an anonymous confederate soldier in the US civil war

I asked for knowledge – power to control things;
I was granted understanding – to learn to love persons.
I asked for strength to be a great man;
I was make weak to become a better man.
I asked for wealth to make friends;
I became poor, to keep friends.
I asked for all things to enjoy life;
I was granted all life, to enjoy things.
I cried for pity; I was offered sympathy.
I craved for healing of my own disorders;
I received insight into another's suffering.
I prayed to God for safety – to tread the trodden path;
I was granted danger, to lost track and find the Way.
I got nothing that I prayed for;
I am among all men, richly blessed.   Author unknown

---------- ✠ ----------

Faith

Merciful God, be thou now unto me a strong tower of defence. Give me
grace to await thy leisure, and patiently to bear what you doest unto me,
nothing doubting or mistrusting thy goodness towards me. Therefore
do with me in all things as thou wilt: Only arm me, I beseech thee, with
thy armour, that I may stand fast; above all things taking to me the shield
of faith, praying always that I may refer myself wholly to thy will, being
assuredly persuaded that all thou doest cannot but be well. And unto
thee be all honour and glory.   Lady Jane Grey, before her execution

Lead, kindly Light, amid the encircling gloom,
 Lead Thou me on!
The night is dark, and I am far from home –
 Lead Thou me on!
Keep Thou my feet; I do not ask to see
The distant scene – one step enough for me.

I was not ever thus, nor pray'd that Thou
 Shouldst lead me on.
I loved to choose and see my path, but now
 Lead Thou me on!
I loved the garish day, and, spite of fears,
Pride ruled my will: remember not past years.

So long Thy power hath blest me, sure it still
 Will lead me on,
O'er moor and fen, o'er crag and torrent, till
 The night is gone;
And with the morn those angel faces smile
Which I have loved long since, and lost awhile.   J.H. Newman

O holy Jesus, meek Lamb of God; Bread that came down from heaven;
light and life of all holy souls: help me to a true and living faith in you.
Open yourself within me with all your holy nature and spirit, that I may
be born again by you, and in you be a new creation, brought alive and
revived, led and ruled by your Holy Spirit.   William Law

Just as I am, without one plea
But that thy blood was shed for me,
And that thou bidd'st me come to thee,
 O Lamb of God, I come.

Just as I am, though tossed about
With many a conflict, many a doubt,
Fightings within, and fears without,
 O Lamb of God, I come.

Just as I am, poor, wretched, blind;
Sight, riches, healing of the mind,
Yea all I need, in thee to find,
      O Lamb of God, I come.

Just as I am, thou wilt receive,
Wilt welcome, pardon, cleanse, relieve:
Because thy promise I believe,
      O Lamb of God, I come.

Just as I am (thy love unknown
Has broken every barrier down),
Now to be thine, yea thine alone,
      O Lamb of God, I come.

Just as I am, of that free love
The breadth, length, depth and height to prove,
Here for a season then above,
      O Lamb of God, I come.   Charlotte Elliott

O Saviour Christ, who leads to eternal blessedness those who commit
themselves to thee: grant that we, being weak, may not presume to trust
in ourselves, but may always have thee before our eyes to follow as our
guide; that thee, who alone knows the way, may lead us to our heavenly
desires. To thee, with the Father and the Holy Ghost, be glory for ever.

                                                Miles Coverdale

All will be well
All will be well, and all will be well, and all manner of things will be
      well.

                        Julian of Norwich, *Revelations of Divine Love*

I believe
    that thou didst create me:
        the workmanship of thy hands
            despise not.
    that I am after thine image and likeness:
        thy likeness
            suffer not to be blotted out.
    that thou didst redeem me in thy blood:
        the price of the ransom
            suffer not to perish.
    that thou didst make me a Christian after thine own name:
        thine own namesake
            think not scorn of.
    that thou didst hallow me in regeneration:
        thine own hallowed thing
            destroy not.
    that thou didst engraft me in the good olive tree:
        the member of the body mystical
            cut not off.
O think upon thy servant as concerning thy word,
    wherein thou hast caused me to put my trust.
My soul hath longed for thy salvation
    and I have a good hope because of thy word.
        Be thou my hope
            yet and yet again
        and my portion in the land of the living.

Lancelot Andrewes, translated by F.E. Brightman

Let nothing disturb you
nothing frighten you,
all things are passing;
patient endurance
attains all things.
One whom God possesses
lacks nothing,
for God alone suffices.

Teresa of Avila

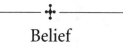

Belief

I acknowledge, Lord, and I give thanks that you have created your image in me, so that I may remember you, think of you, love you. But this image is so obliterated and worn away by wickedness, it is so obscured by the smoke of sins, that it cannot do what it was created to do, unless you renew and reform it. I am not attempting, O Lord, to penetrate your loftiness, for I cannot begin to match my understanding with it, but I desire in some measure to understand your truth, which my heart believes and loves. For I do not seek to understand in order that I may believe, but I believe in order to understand. For this too I believe, that 'unless I believe, I shall not understand.'

Anselm

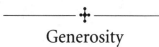

Generosity

O Lord Jesus Christ, who though you were rich became poor, grant that all our desire for and covetousness of earthly possessions may die in us, and that the desire of heavenly things may live and grow in us. Keep us from all idle and vain expenses that we may always have enough to give to him who is in need, and that we may not give grudgingly out of necessity, but cheerfully. Through your merits may we partake of the riches of your heavenly treasure.

Treasury of Devotion

Gratitude

And still, O Lord, to me impart
An innocent and grateful heart.

S.T. Coleridge

Thou that hast given so much to me,
give one thing more, a grateful heart.
Not thankful when it pleases me,
as if your blessings had spare days;
but such a heart whose very pulse
may be thy praise.   George Herbert

——————— ✝ ———————

Hope

I wait for the Lord, my soul waits,
    and in his word I hope;
my soul waits for the Lord
more than those who watch for the morning,
more than those who watch for the morning.   Psalm 130:5–6 NRSV

O Israel, hope in the Lord
    from this time on and for evermore.   Psalm 131:3 NRSV

The God and Father of our Lord Jesus Christ open all our eyes, that we
may see that blessed hope to which we are called; that we may altogether glorify the only true God and Jesus Christ, whom he hath sent down
to us from heaven; to whom with the Father and the Holy Ghost be ren-
dered all honour and glory to all eternity.   Bishop John Jewel

Teach us, gracious Lord, to begin our deeds with reverence, to go on with
obedience, and to finish them in love; and then to wait patiently in hope,
and with cheerful confidence to look up to you, whose promises are
faithful and rewards infinite; through Jesus Christ.   George Hickes

My God, I believe in you: increase my faith.

I hope in you: strengthen my hope.

I love you, and desire to love you more and more, and above all things, and above all others. Bring to life my love and make me completely yours.

Author unknown

Humility

Give us true humility, a meek and a quiet spirit, a loving and a friendly, a holy and a useful conversation, bearing the burdens of our neighbours, denying ourselves, and studying to benefit others, and to please thee in all things.

John Cosin

O God, who resists the proud, and gives grace to the humble: grant us the virtue of true humility, which your only-begotten Son himself gave us the perfect example; that we may never offend you by our pride, and be rejected by our self-assertion; through Jesus Christ our Lord.

Leonine Sacramentary

Incline us, O God, to think humbly on ourselves, to be saved only in the examination of our own conduct, to consider our fellow creatures with kindness, and to judge of all they say and do with the charity which we would desire from them ourselves.

Jane Austen

Eternal God, let this mind be in us which was also in Christ Jesus; that as he from his loftiness stooped to the death of the cross, so we in our lowliness may humble ourselves, believing, obeying, living and dying, for his name's sake.

Christina Rossetti

I am not worthy, Lord and Master, that you should come under the roof of my soul: nevertheless, since you desire, O lover of mankind, to dwell within me, I am bold to draw near. You invite me to open the door which you alone have made, that entering in there you may bring light into my darkened mind: I do believe that you will do this.

For you did not throw out the prostitute when she came with tears, neither did your reject the tax collector when he repented, nor did your reject the thief when he sought to enter your kingdom, nor did your reject the persecutor when he repented. But you treated all who came to you in penitence as your friends. You alone are to be blessed, now and for ever.   Chrysostom

Lord Jesus Christ, pattern of humility, who emptied yourself of your glory, and took on yourself the form of a servant, root out of us all pride of boasting in our hearts, that acknowledging that we are guilty sinners, we may willingly suffer contempt for your sake, and only glory in you. Not unto us, O Lord, but to your name be the praise, for your loving mercy and for your truth's sake.   *Treasury of Devotion*

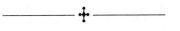

Light

Pour into our hearts, Almighty God, the pure serene light of your truth, that we may avoid the darkness of sin, who have come to know and fear you, the eternal Light; through Jesus Christ our Lord.

Ambrosian Manual

We beseech you, O Lord, in your loving-kindness, to pour your holy light into our souls; that we may always be devoted to you, by whose wisdom we were created, and by whose providence we are governed; through Jesus Christ our Lord.   **Gelasian Sacramentary**

Christ himself says to his Father, 'Your Word is truth.' May the almighty God, our heavenly Father, give us the love and light of truth to shine in our hearts through his Holy Spirit, through Jesus Christ, our Lord.

Nicholas Ridley

Jesus, your light is shining within us,
let not my doubts and my darkness speak to me;
Jesus, your light is shining within us,
let my heart always welcome your love. Brother Roger

Most loving Father, who has taught us to dread nothing except the loss
of you, preserve me from faithless fears and worldly anxieties, from cor-
rupting passions and unhallowed love of earthly treasures; and grant
that no clouds of this mortal life may hide me from the light of that love
which is immortal and which you have shown to us in your Son, Jesus
Christ our Lord. William Bright

O Light that followest all my way,
I yield my flickering torch to thee;
My heart restores its borrowed ray,
That in thy sunshine's blaze its day
May brighter, fairer be. George Matheson

Lord, I am blind and helpless, stupid and ignorant, cause me to hear;
cause me to know; teach me to do; lead me. Henry Martyn

Lord, give us weak eyes for things which are of no account and clear eyes
for all your truth. Søren Kierkegaard

Grant us your light, O Lord: that the darkness of our hearts being done
away, we may come to the true light, even Christ our Saviour.
Office of Compline, Sarum Missal

Open wide the window of our spirits, O Lord, and fill us full of light;
open wide the door of our hearts, that we may receive and entertain you
with all our powers of adoration and praise. Christina Rossetti

O God, who by your almighty word enlightens everyone who comes into the world, enlighten, we pray, the hearts of your servants, by the glory of your grace, that we may always think such things as are worthy and pleasing to your Majesty and love you with a perfect heart, through Jesus Christ our Lord.

Alcuin

———— ✢ ————

Purity

Blest are the pure in heart,
For they shall see our God:
The secret of the Lord is theirs;
Their soul is Christ's abode.

John Keble

Help me
    To live in purity;
    To speak in truth;
    To act in love
        All through today.
This I ask for Jesus' sake.

William Barclay

We beseech you, Christ Jesus, Son of God, crucified for us and risen again, have compassion on us. Intercede for us with the eternal Father. Purify us with your Holy Spirit.

Philipp Melanchthon

Lord Jesus, All-pure, purify us that we may behold thee.
All-holy, sanctify us that we may stand before thee.
All-gracious, mould us that we may please thee.
    Very love, suffer us not to set at naught thy love; suffer not devil, world, flesh, to destroy us; suffer not ourselves to destroy ourselves; us with whom thou strivest, who thou desirest, whom thou lovest.

Christina Rossetti

O eternal God, who has taught us in your holy Word that our bodies are temples of your Spirit: Keep us, we most humbly beseech you, temperate and holy in thought, word and deed, that at the last we, with all the pure in heart, may see you and be made like you in your heavenly kingdom; through Christ our Lord.

B.F. Westcott

O Son of God, Lord Jesus Christ, you shield and keep us, and love purity: through your Holy Spirit, pure and spotless, kindle purity in our hearts, and incline our rulers to true devotion. Quench the demonic forces and fires of impurity that rage in our hearts.

Philipp Melanchthon

——————— ✢ ———————

Wisdom

You desire truth in the inward being;
therefore teach me wisdom in my secret heart.   Psalm 51:6 NRSV

Almighty God, bestow on us the meaning of words, the light of understanding, the nobility of diction and the faith of the true nature. And grant that what we believe we may also speak.

Hilary

I beseech Thee, good Jesus, that as Thou hast graciously granted to me here on earth sweetly to partake of the words of Thy wisdom and knowledge, so Thou wilt vouchsafe that I may some time come to Thee, the fountain of all wisdom, and always appear before Thy face; who livest and reignest, world without end.

Bede

God, give us the serenity to accept what cannot be changed;
give us the courage to change what should be changed;
give us the wisdom to distinguish one from the other.

Attributed to Reinhold Niebuhr, also known as 'The Serenity Prayer'

———— ✠ ————

The fruit of the Spirit

The church floor
Mark you the floor? That square and speckled stone,
    Which looks so firm and strong,
        Is *Patience:*

And th' other black and grave, wherewith each one
    Is chequer'd all along,
        Humility:

The gentle rising, which on either hand
    Leads to the quire above,
        Is *Confidence:*

But the sweet cement, which in one sure band
    Ties the whole frame, is *Love*
        And *Charity.*

George Herbert, *The Temple*

O merciful God, fill our hearts, we pray, with the graces of your Holy
        Spirit; with love, joy, peace, patience, gentleness, goodness,
        faithfulness, humility and self-control.
O Lord, in confidence of your great mercy and goodness to all who
        truly repent and resolve to do better, I most humbly implore
        the grace and assistance of the Holy Spirit to enable me to
        become every day better.
Grant me the wisdom and understanding to know my duty, and the
        heart and will to do it.
Endue me, O Lord, with the true fear and love of you, and with a
        prudent zeal for your glory.
Increase in me the graces of charity and meekness, of truth and justice,
        of humility and patience, and a firmness of spirit to bear
        every condition with constancy of mind.   King William III

O Lord, give us more charity, more self-denial, more likeness to you. Teach us to sacrifice our comforts to others, and our preferences for the sake of doing good. Make us kindly in thought, gentle in word, generous in deed. Teach us that it is better to give than to receive, better to forget ourselves than to put ourselves forward, better to minister than to be ministered to. And to you, the God of love, be all glory and praise, now and for ever.   Henry Alford

Love

Love of God
Our hearts are cold; Lord, warm them with your selfless love.

Augustine

O Saviour, pour upon me thy Spirit of meekness and love,
annihilate the selfhood in me, be thou all my life.   William Blake

Lord God, the God of all goodness and grace, you are worthy of a greater love than we can give or understand: fill our hearts with such love towards you which overcomes laziness and fear, that nothing may seem too hard for us to do or to suffer as we obey you; and grant that in loving you we may become daily more like you, and may finally obtain the crown of life which you have promised to those who love you, through Jesus Christ our Lord.   Author unknown

My God, my Love: you are all mine, and I am all yours. Increase love in me, that with my inner heart I may taste how sweet it is to love. Let me love you more than myself, and myself only for you, and in you all that love you truly.   Thomas à Kempis

Lord Jesus Christ, draw our hearts to yourself; bind them together in inseparable love, that we may abide in you, and you in us, and that the everlasting covenant between us may remain certain for ever. O wound our hearts with the darts of fire of your piercing love. Let them pierce through all our sloth, that we may become whole and sound. Let us have no lover but you alone; let us seek no joy or comfort except in you.

Miles Coverdale

O God, who has taught us that love is the fulfilling of the law: Help us by your Holy Spirit so to love you that we may always seek to do your holy will; and so to love our neighbour that we may in all things do to others as we would that they should do to us; for the sake of him who loved us and gave himself for us, your Son Jesus Christ our Lord.

W.W. How

Most loving Lord, give me a childlike love of thee, which casts out all fear.

E.B. Pusey

Grant to your servants, O God,
to be set on fire with your love,
to be strengthened by your power,
to be illuminated by your Spirit,
to be filled with your grace,
and to go forward by your help;
through Jesus Christ our Lord.

Gallican Sacramentary

O my sweet Saviour Christ, who in your undeserved love towards humankind so kindly suffered the painful death of the cross, do not allow me to be cold or lukewarm in love again towards you.

Thomas More

O Love that wilt not let me go,
I rest my weary soul in thee;
I give thee back the life I owe,
That in thine ocean depths its flow
May richer, fuller be.

George Matheson

Set our hearts on fire with love to you, O Christ our God, that in its flame we may love you with all our heart, with all our mind, with all our soul and with all our strength and our neighbours as ourselves, so that, keeping your commandments, we may glorify you, the giver of all good gifts.

Eastern Orthodox Church

God, which has prepared to them that love thee, such good things as pass all man's understanding: Pour into our hearts such love toward thee, that we loving thee in all things, may obtain thy promises, which exceed all that we can desire: through Jesus Christ our Lord.

Book of Common Prayer, 1549, Collect for the Sixth Sunday
after Trinity Sunday

Lord of all power and might, who art author and giver of all good things: Graft in our hearts the love of thy Name, increase in us true religion, nourish us with all goodness, and of thy great mercy keep us in the same; through Jesus Christ our Lord.

Book of Common Prayer, Collect for the Seventh Sunday after Trinity

O Lord, give us, we beseech Thee, in the name of Jesus Christ Thy Son our Lord, that love which can never cease, that will kindle our lamps but not extinguish them, that they may burn in us and enlighten others.

Do Thou, O Christ, our dearest Saviour, Thyself kindle our lamps that they may evermore shine in Thy Temple and receive unquenchable light from Thee, that will enlighten our darkness and lessen the darkness of the world.

Columba

O Love, O God, you created me, in your love recreate me.

O Love, you redeemed me, fill up and redeem for yourself in me
whatever part of your love has fallen into neglect within me.

O Love, O God, you made me yours, as in the blood of your Christ
purchased me, in your truth sanctify me.

O Love, O God, you adopted me as a daughter, after your own heart
fashion and foster me.

O Love, you chose me as yours not another's, grant that I may cling to
you with my whole being.

O Love, O God, you loved me first, grant that with my whole heart,
and with my whole soul, and with my whole strength, I may
love you.

O Love, O God almighty, in your love confirm me.

O Love most wise, give me wisdom in the love of you.

O Love most sweet, give me sweetness in the taste of you.

O Love most dear, grant that I may live only for you.

O Love most faithful, in all my tribulations comfort and succour me.

O Love who is always with me, work all my works in me.

O Love most victorious, grant that I may persevere to the end in you.

Gertrude of Thüringen

O God, worthy of an infinite love, I have nothing which can adequately measure your dignity, but such is my desire towards you, that if I had all that you have, I would gladly and thankfully give all to you.

Gertrude of Thüringen

Lord, I pray, that the burning and delicious ardour of your love may detach my soul from all things which are under heaven, so that I may die for love of your love. For you are the One who for love of my love was prepared to die.
Francis of Assisi

Teach us, Lord, to fear thee without being afraid; to fear thee in love, that we may love without fear; through Jesus Christ our Lord.

Christina Rossetti

Lord Jesus Christ, fill us, we pray, with your light and life that we may show forth your wonderful glory. Grant that your love may so fill our lives that we may count nothing too small to do for you, nothing too much to give and nothing too hard to bear.   Ignatius Loyola

O God, who hast prepared for them that love thee such good things as pass man's understanding; Pour into our hearts such love toward thee, that we, loving thee above all things, may obtain thy promises, which exceed all that we can desire; through Jesus Christ our Lord. Amen.

Book of Common Prayer, Sixth Sunday after Trinity

O God, the God of all goodness and of all grace, who are worthy of a greater love than we can either give or understand: fill our hearts, we beseech you, with such love towards you that nothing may seem too hard for us to do or to suffer in obedience to your will; and grant that loving you, we may become daily more like you, and finally obtain the crown of life which you have promised to those who love you; through Jesus Christ our Lord.   B.F. Westcott

O Lord Jesus Christ, draw our hearts to yourself; join them together in inseparable love, that we may abide in you and you in us, and that the everlasting covenant between us may stand sure for ever. Let the fiery darts of your love pierce through all our slothful members and inner powers, that we, being happily wounded, may so become whole and sound. Let us have no lover but yourself alone; let us seek no joy or comfort except in you.   Miles Coverdale

Behold, Lord, an empty vessel that needs to be filled. My Lord, fill it. I am weak in the faith, strengthen me. I am cold in love; warm me and make me fervent that my love may go out to my neighbour. O Lord, help me. Strengthen my faith and trust in you.

With me, there is an abundance of sin; in you is the fullness of righteousness. Therefore I will remain with you, from whom I can receive, but to whom I may not give.   Martin Luther

Love of others
Lord, help us to be masters of ourselves, that we may be servants of
others.   Alexander Paterson

My Lord I love you
my God I am sorry
my God I believe in you
my God I trust you.
Help us to love one another
as you love us.   Mother Teresa

Love is kind and suffers long,
Love is meek and thinks no wrong,
Love than death itself more strong;
     Therefore give us love.

Faith will vanish into sight;
Hope be emptied in delight;
Love in heaven will shine more bright;
     Therefore give us love.   Christopher Wordsworth

O God, fountain of love, pour your love into our souls, that we may love
those whom you love with the love you give us, and think and speak
about them tenderly, meekly, lovingly; and so loving our brothers and
sisters for your sake, may grow in your love, and live in love and living
in love may live in you; for Jesus Christ's sake.   E.B. Pusey

I offer up unto you my prayers and intercessions, for those especially
who have in any way hurt, grieved, or found fault with me, or who have
done me any harm or displeasure.
     For all those also whom, at any time, I have annoyed, troubled, bur-
dened, and scandalized, by words or deeds, knowingly or in ignorance:
that you would grant us all equally pardon for our sins, and for our
offences against each other.

Take away from our hearts, O Lord, all suspiciousness, indignation, anger and contention, and whatever may harm charity, and lesson brotherly love. Have mercy, O Lord, have mercy on those who crave for your mercy, give grace to those who stand in need of your grace, and make us such that we may be worthy to receive your grace, and go forward to life eternal.   Thomas à Kempis

Bestow on me, Lord, a genial spirit and unwearied forbearance; a mild, loving patient heart; kindly looking, pleasant, friendly speech and manners in daily life; that I may give offence to no one, but as much as in me lies live in charity with all men.   Johann Arndt

Grant to us your servants: to our God – a heart of flame; to our fellow men – a heart of love; to ourselves – a heart of steel.   Augustine

O God, the well of love and Father of all, make us so to love that we know not but to love every man in Jesus Christ you our Lord.
                                                                        Collect, fourteenth century

Almighty and most merciful God, who hast given us a new commandment that we should love one another, give us also grace that we may fulfil it. Make us gentle, courteous, and forebearing. Direct our lives so that we may each look to the good of others in word and deed. And hallow all our friendships by the blessing of thy spirit; for his sake who loved us and gave himself for us, Jesus Christ our Lord.   B.F. Westcott

Grant, O Lord, that we may keep a constant guard on our thoughts and passions, that they may never lead us into sin; that we may live in perfect love with all humankind, in affection to those who love us, and in forgiveness to those, if any there are, who hate us. Give us good and virtuous friends. In the name of our blessed Lord and Saviour Jesus Christ.
                                                                        Warren Hastings

Make us always eager, Lord, to share the good things that we have. Grant us such a measure of your Spirit that we may find more joy in giving than in getting. Make us ready to give cheerfully without grudging, secretly without praise, and in sincerity without looking for gratitude, for Jesus Christ's sake.   John Hunter

O Lord, who hast taught us that all our doings without charity are nothing worth; Send thy Holy Ghost and pour into our hearts that most excellent gift of charity, the very bond of peace and of all virtues, without which whosoever liveth is counted dead before thee. Grant this for thine only Son Jesus Christ's sake. Amen.

Book of Common Prayer, Quinquagesima Sunday
(seven weeks before Easter)

Joy

Jesus, Risen Lord, you look at the heart, not at outward appearances. In the depths of our soul, sometimes we all you: Christ Jesus, I am not worthy of you, but only say a word and my soul will be calmed, healed. And you never create in us, Christ, either torment or anguish, but your continual presence comes to awaken the joy of living in you.

Brother Roger

O Joy that seekest me through pain,
I cannot close my heart to thee;
I trace the rainbow through the rain,
And feel the promise is not vain,
That morn shall tearless be.   George Matheson

As the hand is made for holding and the eye for seeing, you have created me for joy, O God.

Share with me in finding that joy everywhere: in the violet's beauty, in the lark's melody, in the child's face, in a mother's love, in the purity of Jesus.   Traditional Gaelic prayer

My God,
I pray that I may so know you and love you
that I may rejoice in you.
And if I may not do so fully in this life
let me go steadily on
to the day when I come to that fullness ...
Let me receive
That which you promised through your truth,
that my joy may be full

Anselm

Peace

To thee, O God, we turn for peace. Grant us the blessed assurance that nothing shall deprive us of that peace, neither ourselves, nor our foolish earthly desires, nor my wild longings, nor the anxious cravings of my heart.

Søren Kierkegaard

In these our days so perilous,
Lord, peace in mercy send us;
No God but thee can fight for us,
No God but thee defend us;
Thou our only God and Saviour.

Martin Luther

Set free, O Lord, the souls of your servants from all restlessness and anxiety. Give us that peace and power which flow from you. Keep us in all perplexity and distress, that upheld by your strength and stayed on the rock of your faithfulness we may abide in you now and evermore.

Francis Paget

Let us not seek *out* of thee, O Lord, what we can find only *in* thee: peace and joy and bliss. Lift up our souls above the weary round of harassing thoughts to the pure, serene atmosphere of your presence, that there we may breathe freely, there repose in your love, there be at rest from ourselves; and from there return arrayed with your peace, to do and bear what will best please you.   E.B. Pusey

Forgive me, Lord, for thy dear Son,
The ill that I this day have done,
That with the world, myself and thee,
I, ere I sleep, at peace may be.   Thomas Ken

O Lord, look mercifully on us, and grant that we may always choose
            the way of peace.   Sarum Missal

O God, who are peace everlasting, whose chosen reward is the gift of peace, and who has taught us that the peacemakers are your children: Pour your peace into our hearts, that everything discordant may utterly vanish, and that all that makes for peace be loved and sought by us always; through Jesus Christ our Lord.   Mozarabic Sacramentary

Shine from the cross to me, then all is peace;
Shine from the throne, then all my troubles cease;
Speak but the word, and sadness quits my soul;
Touch but my hand with thine, and I am whole.   Horatius Bonar

Almighty God, you have made us for yourself, and our hearts are restless until they find their rest in you. May we find peace in your service, and in the world to come, see you face to face; through Jesus Christ our Lord.
        Book of Alternative Services of The Anglican Church of Canada, 1985

Good Jesus, strength of the weary, rest of the restless, by the weariness and unrest of your sacred cross, come to me who am weary that I may rest in you.   E.B. Pusey

O Lord, calm the waves of this heart, calm its tempest!
Calm yourself, O my soul, so that the divine can act in you!
Calm yourself, O my soul, so that God is able to repose in you,
    so that his peace may cover you!
Yes, Father in heaven, often have we found that the world cannot give
       us peace, but make us feel that you are able to give us peace;
       let us know the truth of your promise: that the whole world
       may not be able to take away your peace.   Søren Kierkegaard

O God, make us children of quietness and heirs of peace.
                               Clement of Alexandria

Lord, you commanded peace:
    you gave peace.
You bequeathed peace;
    give us your peace from heaven.
Make this day peaceful,
    and the remaining days of our life.   Traditional Gaelic prayer

Lord, teach us to number our days, that we may apply our hearts to
       wisdom.
Lighten, if it is your will, the pressures of this world's cares.
Above all, reconcile us to your will, and give us a peace which the
       world cannot take away; through our Saviour Jesus Christ.
                               Thomas Chalmers

Almighty and everlasting God, who dost govern all things in heaven and
earth; Mercifully hear the supplications of thy people, and grant us thy
peace all the days of our life; through Jesus Christ our Lord. Amen.
      Book of Common Prayer, Second Sunday after the Epiphany

O Lord God, in whom we live and move and have our being, open our eyes that we may behold your fatherly presence always with us. Draw our hearts to you with the power of your love. Teach us to be anxious about nothing, and when we have done what you have given us to do, help us, O God our Saviour, to leave the issue to your wisdom. Take from us all doubt and mistrust. Lift our hearts up to you in heaven, and make us to know that all things are possible for us through your Son our Redeemer.

B.F. Westcott

Patience

Lord, here I am, do with me as seems best in Thine own eyes; only give me, I beseech Thee, a penitent and patient spirit to expect Thee. Make my service acceptable to Thee while I live, and my soul ready for Thee when I die.

William Laud

Give us, O Lord, purity of lips, clean and innocent hearts, and rectitude of action; give us humility, patience, self-wisdom and understanding, the spirit of counsel and strength, the spirit of knowledge and godliness, and of thy fear; make us ever to seek thy face with all our heart, all our soul, all our mind; grant us to have a contrite and humbled heart in thy presence, to prefer nothing to thy love. Have mercy upon us, we humbly beseech thee; through Jesus Christ our Lord.

Gallican Sacramentary

O Lord and Master of my life,
Grant that I may not have a spirit of idleness,
of discouragement,
of lust for power,
and of vain speaking.
But bestow on me, your servant,
the spirit of chastity,
of meekness,
of patience,
and of love.
Yes, O Lord and King,

grant that I may perceive
my own transgressions,
and judge not my brother,
For you are blessed from age to age. Ephraem

Take from us, O God, all tediousness of spirit, all impatience and
unquietness. Let us possess ourselves in patience, through
Jesus Christ our Lord. Jeremy Taylor

Lord, teach me the art of patience while I am well, and enable me to use
of it when I am sick. In that day either lighten my burden or strengthen
my back. Make me, who so often in my health have discovered my weakness in presuming on my own strength, to be strong in my sickness when
I solely rely on your assistance. Thomas Fuller

Kindness

Grant us, we beseech thee, O Lord, grace to follow thee whithersoever
thou goest.

In little daily duties to which thou callest us, bow down our wills to
simple obedience, patience under pain or provocation, strict
truthfulness of word or manner, humility and kindness.

In great acts of duty or perfection, if thou shouldst call us to them,
uplift us to sacrifice and heroic courage, that in all things, both small and
great, we may be imitators of thy dear Son, even Jesus Christ our Lord.

Christina Rossetti

Guide us, teach us, and strengthen us, O Lord, we beseech thee, until we
become such as thou wouldest have us be: pure, gentle, truthful, high-
minded, courteous, generous, able, dutiful and useful; for thy honour
and glory. Charles Kingsley

Goodness

Christ Jesus, you want nobody to experience inner distress. And you come to illuminate in us the profound mystery of human suffering. By it, we come close to an intimacy with God. Holy Spirit, Comforter, make us able to alleviate the pain of the innocent and to be attentive to those whose lives, place in situations of trial, are radiant with the holiness of Jesus Christ.   Brother Roger

Faithfulness

O Lord God, grant us always, whatever the world may say, to content ourselves with what you say, and to care only for your approval, which will outweigh all worlds; for Jesus Christ's sake.   General Charles Gordon

Grant, O Lord, that what we have said with our lips, we may believe in our hearts and practise in our lives; and of thy mercy keep us faithful unto the end; for Christ's sake.   John Hunter

Gentleness

God, the Father of our Lord Jesus Christ, increase in us faith and truth and gentleness, and grant us part and lot among his saints.

Polycarp

Take from us, O God, all pride and vanity, all boasting and self-assertiveness, and give us the true courage that shows itself by gentleness; the true wisdom that shows itself by simplicity; and the true power that shows itself by modesty; through Jesus Christ our Lord.

Charles Kingsley

Self-control

O eternal God, who has taught us in your holy Word that our bodies are temples of your Spirit: Keep us, we most humbly beseech you, temperate and holy in thought, word and deed, that at the last we, with all the pure in heart, may see you and be made like you in your heavenly kingdom; through Christ our Lord.   B.F. Westcott

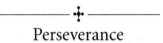

Perseverance

Strengthen me, O God, by the grace of your Holy Spirit; grant me to be strengthened with the might of the inner man, and to put away from my heart all useless anxiety and distress, and let me never be distracted by various longings, whether they are worthless or precious; but may I view all things as passing away, and myself as passing away with them.

Grant me prudently to avoid the one who flatters me, and patiently to bear with the one who contradicts me; for it is a mark of great wisdom not to be moved by every wind of words or to be influenced by wicked flattery; for thus we will go on securely in the course we have begun.   Thomas à Kempis

O Lord God, when Thou givest to Thy servants to endeavour any great matter, grant us also to know that it is not the beginning, but the continuing of the same to the end, until it be thoroughly finished, which yieldeth the true glory; through Him who for the finishing of Thy work laid down his life, our Redeemer, Jesus Christ.

Source unknown, based on a saying of Sir Francis Drake

Times of darkness

My spirit is dry within me because it forgets to feed on you.

John of the Cross

Almighty God, teach us by your holy Spirit, what to believe, what to do, and where to take our rest.   Desiderius Erasmus

Ah Lord, my prayers are dead, my affections dead, and my heart is dead: but you are a living God and I commit myself to you.   William Bridge

As pants the hart for cooling streams,
When heated in the chase,
So longs my soul, O God, for Thee
And Thy refreshing grace.

For Thee, my God, the living God,
My thirsty soul doth pine;
O, when shall I behold Thy face,
Thou majesty divine?

Why restless, why cast down, my soul?
Hope still; and thou shalt sing
The praise of Him Who is thy God,
Thy health's eternal spring.

To Father, Son, and Holy Ghost,
The God Whom we adore,
Be glory as it was, is now,
And shall be evermore.   Nahum Tate and Nicholas Brady, Psalm 42

O Lord, enlighten my heart, which evil desire has darkened. O Lord,
         help me to think about what is good.   Chrysostom

Chapter Four

DAILY PRAYERS

*I will do whatever you ask in my name, so that the Father may
be glorified in the Son. If in my name you ask me for anything,
I will do it.*

John 14:13–14

*Prayer, the Church's banquet, Angel's age,
God's breath in man returning to his birth,
The soul in paraphrase, the heart in pilgrimage,
The Christian plummet sounding heav'n and earth.*

George Herbert

———— ✛ ————

Prayers of ecstasy

O my Saviour, and my God, let it come. May the hour come when my
eyes are given the vision of what I already believe, and grasp what I now
hope for and greet from a distance. May my spirit embrace and kiss what
now with my whole might I yearn for, and be altogether absorbed in the
abyss of your love. But, meanwhile, bless, my soul, my Saviour, and
praise his name, which is holy and full of the holiest delights.

Anselm

O happy day, that fixed my choice
On Thee, my Saviour and my God!
Well may this glowing heart rejoice,
And tell its raptures all abroad.

Refrain
Happy day, happy day, when Jesus washed my sins away!
He taught me how to watch and pray, and live rejoicing every day
Happy day, happy day, when Jesus washed my sins away.

Philip Doddridge

———— ✛ ————

The Lord's Prayer

Our Father, which art in heaven, Hallowed be thy Name. Thy kingdom come. Thy will be done in earth, As it is in heaven. Give us this day our daily bread. And forgive us our trespasses, As we forgive them that trespass against us. And lead us not into temptation, But deliver us from evil. For thine is the kingdom, The power, and the glory, For ever and ever. Amen.   Book of Common Prayer

Our Father, which in Heaven art,
      We sanctify thy Name;
Thy Kingdom come, thy will be done,
      In Heaven and Earth the same.
Give us this day, our daily bread,
      And us forgive thou so,
As we on them that us offend,
      Forgiveness do bestow.
Into temptation lead us not,
      And us from evil free,
For thine the Kingdom, Power and Praise,
      Is and shall ever be.   George Wither

Our Father, who art in heaven
In whom we live, and move, and have our being; grant that I and all Christians may live worthy of this glorious relation, and that we may not sin, knowing that we are accounted as yours. We are yours by adoption; make us yours by the choice of our will.   Thomas Wilson

Hallowed be your name
O God, whose name is great, wonderful, and holy, grant that I and all your children may glorify you, not only with our lips but in our lives; that others, seeing our good works, may glorify our Father who is in heaven.   Thomas Wilson

Your kingdom come
May the kingdoms of the world become the kingdoms of our Lord and of his Christ. And may all that own you for their King, become your faithful subjects, and obey your laws. Dethrone, Lord God, and destroy Satan and his kingdom, and enlarge the kingdom of grace.

Thomas Wilson

Your will be done, in earth, as it is in heaven
We adore your goodness, Lord God, in making your will known to us in your holy Word. May this your Word be the rule of our will, of our desires, of our lives and actions. May we always sacrifice our will to yours, be pleased with all your choice for ourselves and others, and adore your providence in the government of the world.   Thomas Wilson

Give us this day our daily bread
Heavenly Father, who knows what we need, give us the necessities and comforts of this life with your blessing; but above all, give us the bread which nourishes us for eternal life. Lord God, who gives everyone life and breath and all things, give us grace to be generous to those in need, from what you have given us which is more than our daily bread.

Thomas Wilson

And forgive us our trespasses as we forgive those who trespass against us
Make us truly aware of your goodness and mercy and patience towards us, that we may from our hearts forgive everyone who has sinned against us. May my enemies always have a place in my prayers, and in your mercy.   Thomas Wilson

And lead us not into temptation
Support us, heavenly Father, through all our trials, and grant that they may bear the peaceful fruits of righteousness.   Thomas Wilson

But deliver us from evil
From all sin and wickedness, from our spiritual enemy, from the temptations and traps of the evil world, and from everlasting death, good Lord deliver us.

Thomas Wilson

O Lord God, *our Father in heaven*, we your unworthy children on earth pray that you will look on us in your mercy, and give us your grace; that *your holy name* may be sanctified among us and in all the world, through the pure and sincere teaching of the Word, and through earnest charity in our daily living and our conversation. Root out from us all false teaching and evil living, so that your name is not slandered.

Let *your kingdom come*, and be great. May all sinful, blind people who are in the devil's grip be brought to the knowledge of the true faith in Jesus Christ your Son.

Strengthen us, Lord, with your Spirit, to do and to suffer *your will* both in life and death, so that our will may always be broken, offered and put to death.

And *give us our daily bread*. Preserve us from covetous desire so that we may be assured of having the abundance of all good things.

Forgive us our trespasses, as we forgive those who offend us, that our heart may have a sure and glad conscience, and that we may never fear, or be afraid of any sin.

Lead us not into temptation, but help us through your Spirit to subdue the flesh, to despise the world with its vanities, and to overcome the devil with all his cunning attacks.

And finally, *deliver us from all evil*, physical and spiritual, temporal and eternal.

Miles Coverdale

---- ✤ ----

Daily prayers

Grant unto us, O Lord, this day
    to walk with you as Father,
    to trust in you as Saviour,
    to worship you as Lord;
    that all our works may praise you
    and our lives may give you glory.

Author unknown

And help us, this day and every day,
To live more nearly as we pray.

John Keble

O Lord, forgive what I have been, sanctify what I am, and order what I shall be.

Author unknown

Lift up our hearts, we beseech you, O Christ, above the false show of things, above fear, above laziness, above selfishness and covetousness, above custom and fashion, up to the everlasting truth and order that you are; that we may live joyfully and freely, in faithful trust that you are our Saviour, our example, and our friend, both now and for evermore.

Charles Kingsley

Help us, O God,
to serve thee devoutly
and the world busily.
May we do our work wisely,
give succour secretly,
go to our meat appetitely,
sit thereat discreetly,
arise temperately,
please our friend duly,
go to our bed merrily
and sleep surely,
for the joy of our Lord Jesus Christ.

After a translation by Sulpicius, printed by Wynkyn de Worde in 1500

Make me remember, O God, that every day is Thy gift and ought to be used according to Thy command, through Jesus Christ our Lord.

Dr Johnson

Inspire and strengthen us by your Holy Spirit, O Lord God, to seek your will and uphold your honour in all things:

> in the purity and joy of our homes,
> in the trust and fellowship of our common life,
> in daily service of the good,

after the pattern and in the power of your Son, our Lord and Saviour, Jesus Christ.

Jeremy Taylor

Lord, I hand over to your care, my soul and body, my prayers and my hopes, my health and my work, my life and my death, my parents and my family, my friends and my neighbours, my country and all people. Today and always.

Lancelot Andrewes

My faith looks up to thee,
Thou Lamb of Calvary,
> Saviour divine;

Now hear me while I pray,
Take all my guild away,
O let me from this day
> Be wholly thine.

Ray Palmer

O Lord, lift up the light of your countenance on us; let your peace rule in our hearts, and may it be our strength and our song in the house of our pilgrimage. We commit ourselves to your care and keeping; let your grace be mighty in us, and sufficient for us, in all the duties of the day. Keep us from sin. Give us the rule over our own spirits, and guard us from speaking unadvisedly with our lips. May we live together in holy love and peace, and under your blessing in this life and for evermore.

Matthew Henry

Prevent us O Lord, in all our doings with thy most gracious favour, and further us with thy continual help; that in all our works begun, continued, and ended in thee, we may glorify thy holy Name, and finally by thy mercy obtain everlasting life; through Jesus Christ our Lord. Amen.

Book of Common Prayer, the Lord's Supper, Post-Communion prayer

We commend to you, O Lord,
our souls and our bodies,
our minds and our thoughts,
our prayers and our hopes,
our health and our work,
our life and our death;
our parents and brothers and sisters,
our benefactors and friends,
our neighbours, our countrymen,
and all Christian people,
this day and always.

Lancelot Andrewes

Remember, Christian soul,
that thou hast this,
and every day of thy life,
God to glorify,
Jesus to imitate,
a soul to save,
a body to mortify,
sins to repent of,
virtues to acquire,
hell to avoid,
heaven to gain,
eternity to prepare for,
time to profit by,
neighbours to edify,
the world to despise,
devils to combat,
passions to subdue,
death, perhaps, to suffer,
judgment to undergo.

Christopher Smart

Be Lord, within me to strengthen me,
without me to preserve me,
over me to shelter me,
beneath me to support me,
before me to divert me,
behind me to bring me back,
and round about me to fortify me.

Lancelot Andrewes

O heavenly Father, in whom we live and move and have our being, we humbly pray thee so to guide and govern us by thy Holy Spirit, that in all the cares and occupations of our daily life we may never forget thee, but remember that we are ever walking in thy sight; for thine own name's sake.

An ancient Collect

O Lord, support us all the day long, until the shadows lengthen, and the evening comes, and the busy world is hushed, and the fever of life is over, and our work is done. Then, Lord, in your mercy grant us a safe lodging, and a holy rest, and peace at the last; through Jesus Christ our Lord.

Used by J.H. Newman, based on a sixteenth-century prayer

Ah, dearest Jesus, holy Child,
Make thee a bed, soft, undefiled,
Within my heart, that it may be
A quiet chamber kept for thee.

Martin Luther

The Elixir
Teach me, my God and King,
In all things thee to see,
And what I do in any thing,
To do it as for thee.

Not rudely, as a beast,
To run into an action;
But still to make thee prepossest,
And give it his perfection.

A man that looks on glass,
     On it may stay his eye;
Or if he pleaseth, through it pass,
     And then the heaven espy.

All may of thee partake:
     Nothing can be so mean,
Which with this tincture *(for thy sake)*
     Will not grow bright and clean.

A servant with this clause
     Makes drudgery divine:
Who sweeps a room, as for thy laws,
     Makes that and th' action fine.

This is the famous stone
     That turneth all to gold:
For that which God doth touch and own
     Cannot for less be told.
                                        George Herbert, *The Temple*

Grant us, we beseech thee, O Lord, grace to follow thee wheresoever
thou goest.

    In little daily duties to which thou callest us, bow down our
wills to simple obedience, patience under pain or provocation, strict
truthfulness in word or manner, humility and kindness.

    In great acts of duty or perfection, if thou shouldest call us to
them, uplift us to sacrfice and heroic courage; that in all things, both
small and great, we may be imitators of thy dear Son, even Jesus Christ
our Lord.
                                        Christina Rossetti

Almighty God, who hast promised to hear the petitions of them that ask
in thy Son's Name: we beseech thee mercifully to incline thine ears to us
that have now made our prayers and supplications unto thee; and grant
that those things, which we have faithfully asked according to thy will,
may effectually be obtained, to the relief of our necessity, and to the setting forth of thy glory; through Jesus Christ our Lord.
                        Book of Common Prayer, 1549, Post-Communion collect

Save us, O Lord, while waking, and guard us while sleeping: that awake
we may watch with Christ, and asleep we may rest in peace.

Office of Compline, Sarum Missal

Blessed are all your saints, our God and King, who have travelled over
life's tempestuous sea, and have arrived in the harbour of peace
and felicity. Watch over us who are still in our dangerous voyage; and
remember those who lie exposed to the rough storms of trouble
and temptations. Frail is our vessel, and the ocean is wide; but as in your
mercy you have set our course, so steer the vessel of our life toward the
everlasting shore of peace, and bring us at length to the quiet haven of
our heart's desire, where you, O our God, are blessed, and live and reign
for ever and ever.

Augustine

1. O Lord, deprive me not of your heavenly blessings;
2. O Lord, deliver me from eternal torment;
3. O Lord, if I have sinned in my mind or thought, in word or deed,
   forgive me.
4. O Lord, deliver me from every ignorance and inattention, from a
   petty soul and a stony, hard heart;
5. O Lord, deliver me from every temptation;
6. O Lord, lighten my heart darkened by evil desires;
7. O Lord, I, being a human being, have sinned; you, being God, forgive
   me in your loving kindness, for you know the weakness of my soul.
8. O Lord, send down your grace to help me, that I may glorify your
   holy name;
9. O Lord Jesus Christ, write me the name of your servant in the Book
   of Life, and grant me a blessed end;
10. O Lord my God, even if I have done nothing good in your sight, yet
    grant me, your grace, that I may make a start doing good.
11. O Lord, sprinkle on my heart the dew of your grace;
12. O Lord of heaven and earth, remember me, your sinful servant, with
    my cold and impure heart, in your kingdom.
13. O Lord, receive me in repentance;
14. O Lord, do not leave me;
15. O Lord, save me from temptation;
16. O Lord, grant me pure thoughts;

17. O Lord, grant me tears of repentance, remembrance of death, and the sense of peace;
18. O Lord, make me remember to confess my sins;
19. O Lord, grant me humility, love, and obedience;
20. O Lord, grant me tolerance, magnanimity, and gentleness;
21. O Lord, implant in me the root of all blessings: the reverence of you in my heart;
22. O Lord, grant that I may love you with all my heart and soul, and that I may obey your will in all things;
23. O Lord, shield me from evil people, devils and passions;
24. O Lord, you know your creation and what you have planned for it; may your will also be fulfilled in me, a sinner, for you are blessed for ever more. Amen.

Chrysostom, according to the hours of the day and night

My God, I give you this day.
I offer you, now,
all of the good that I shall do
and I promise to accept,
for love of you,
all of the difficulty that I shall meet.
Help me to conduct myself during this day
in a way that pleases you.

Francis de Sales

My dearest Lord,
be thou a bright flame before me,
be thou a guiding star above me,
be thou a smooth path beneath me,
be thou a kindly shepherd behind me,
today – tonight – and forever.

Columba

O God, the Father of lights, from whom comes down every good and perfect gift: mercifully look upon our frailty and infirmity, and grant us such health of body as you know is neeedful for us; that both in body and soul we may evermore serve you with all our strength; through Jesus Christ our Lord.

John Cosin

———————— ✦ ————————

Morning prayers

Let me hear of your steadfast love in the morning,
      for in you I put my trust.
Teach me the way I should go,
      for to you I lift up my soul.   Psalm 143:8, 10 NRSV

Most blessed Trinity, and one eternal God, as you have today woken me up from physical sleep, so wake up my soul from the sleep of sin; and as you have strengthened me through sleep, so after death give me life; for death to me is but to sleep with you; to whom be all glory, wisdom, majesty, dominion, and praise, now and always.   Henry Vaughan

O God, by whom the meek are guided in judgment, grant that the spirit of wisdom may guide me from all false choices, and that walking in your straight path I may not stumble or fall.   William Bright

We give thanks to you, heavenly Father, through Jesus Christ your dear Son, that you have protected us through the night from all danger and harm; and we beseech you to preserve and keep us, this day also, from all sin and evil; that in all our thoughts, words and deeds, we may serve and please you. In your hands we commend our bodies and souls, and all that is ours. Let your holy angel guard us, that the wicked one may have no power over us.   Martin Luther, his morning prayer

Blessed are thou, O Lord our God, the God of our fathers, who turnest the shadow of death into the morning; who hast lightened mine eyes that I sleep not in death.

     O Lord, blot out as a night-mist mine iniquities. Scatter my sins as a morning cloud. Grant that I may become a child of the light, and of the day. Vouchsafe to keep me this day without sin. Uphold me when I am falling, and lift me up when I am down. Preserve this day from any evil of mine, and me from the evils of the day. Let this day add some knowledge, or good deed, to yesterday.

Oh, let me hear thy loving-kindness in the morning, for in thee is my trust. Teach me to do the thing that pleaseth thee, for thou art my God. Let thy loving Spirit lead me forth into the land of righteousness.

Lancelot Andrewes

May the Lord Jesus Christ, who is the splendour of eternal Light, remove from your hearts the darkness of night. Amen.
May he drive far from you the snares of the crafty enemy, and always give to guard you the angel of light. Amen.
That you may rise to your morning praises, kept safe in him, in whom consists all the fulness of your salvation. Amen.   Mozarabic Psalter

Help us this day, O God, to serve thee devoutly, and the world busily. May we do our work wisely, give succour secretly, go to meat appetitely, sit thereat discreetly, arise temperately, please our friend duly, go to bed merrily, and sleep surely; for the joy of our Lord, Jesus Christ.

Traditional

Heavenly Father, I most heartily thank thee, that it has pleased thy fatherly goodness to take care of me this night past. I most entirely beseech thee, most merciful Father, to show the same kindness toward me this day, in preserving my body and soul; that I may neither think, breathe, speak, nor do anything that may be displeasing to thy fatherly goodness, dangerous to myself, or hurtful to my neighbour; but that all my doings may be agreeable to your most blessed will, which is always good; that they may advance thy glory, answer to my vocation, and profit my neighbour, whom I ought to love as myself; that, whenever thou callest me hence, I may be found the child not of darkness but of light; through Jesus Christ our Lord.

Thomas Becon

Lord God, you have sent out your light, created the morning, and have made the sun to rise on the good and the evil; enlighten the blindness of our minds with the knowledge of the truth. Pour out the light of your countenance on us, that in your light we may see light, and, at the last, see the light of your grace and the light of your glory.

Lancelot Andrewes

Strengthen, O Lord, our weakness in your compassion, and comfort and help the needs of our soul in your loving kindness. Waken our thoughts from sleep, and lighten the weight of our limbs; wash us and cleanse us from the filth of our sins.
Nestorian Liturgy

My Father, for another night
Of quiet sleep and rest,
For all the joy of morning light,
Your holy name be blest.
H.W. Baker

O Lord, who has brought us through the darkness of night to the light of the morning, and who by your Holy Spirit illumines the darkness of ignorance and sin: We beseech you, from your loving kindness, pour your holy light into our souls; that we may always be devoted to you, by whose wisdom we were created, by whose mercy we were redeemed, and by whose providence we are governed; to the honour and glory of your great name.
Book of Hours, 1864

New every morning is the love
Our wakening and uprising prove;
Through sleep and darkness safely brought,
Restored to live, and power, and thought.

New mercies, each returning day,
Hover around us while we pray;
New perils past, new sins forgiven,
New thoughts of God, new hopes of heaven.

If on our daily course our mind
Be set to hallow all we find,
New treasures still, of countless price,
God will provide for sacrifice.

The trivial round, the common task,
Would furnish all we ought to ask,
Room to deny ourselves, a road
To bring us daily nearer to God.

Only, O Lord, in thy dear love
Fit us for perfect rest above;
And help us this and every day
To live more nearly as we pray.

John Keble

O Lord, our heavenly Father, almighty and everliving God, which hast safely brought us to the beginning of this day: defend us in the same with thy mighty power; and grant that this day we fall into no sin, neither run into any kind of danger, but that all our doings may be ordered by thy governance, to do always that is righteous in thy sight: through Jesus Christ our Lord.

Book of Common Prayer, 1549, Matins, Collect for Grace

Enlighten the darkness of our minds, stretch forth your helping hand, confirm and give us strength; that we may arise and confess you and glorify you without ceasing all the days of our life, O Lord of all.

Nestorian Liturgy

Almighty, eternal God, Father of our Lord Jesus Christ, creator of heaven and earth and mankind, together with your Son, our Lord Jesus Christ, your Word and Image, and with your Holy Spirit: Have mercy on us, and forgive us all our sins for you Son's sake, whom you have made our Mediator. Guide and sanctify us by your Holy Spirit, who was poured out on the apostles. Grant that we may truly know and praise you throughout eternity. Philipp Melanchthon, his morning prayer

Matins

I cannot open mine eyes,
But thou art ready there to catch
My morning-soul and sacrifice:
Then we must needs for that day make a match.

My God, what is a heart?
Silver, or gold, or precious stone,
Or star, or rainbow, or a part
Of all these things, or all of them in one?

My God, what is a heart,
That thou shouldst it so eye, and woo,
Pouring upon it all thy art,
As if that thou hadst nothing else to do?

Indeed, man's whole estate
Amounts (and richly) to serve thee:
He did not heaven and earth create,
Yet studies them, not Him by whom they be.

Teach me thy love to know;
That this new light, which now I see,
May both the work and workman show:
Then by a Sunbeam I will climb to thee.

George Herbert, *The Temple*

Awake, my soul, and with the sun
Thy daily stage of duty run;
Shake off dull sloth, and early rise
To pay thy morning sacrifice.

Redeem thy misspent time that's past;
Live this day as if 'twere thy last;
T'improve thy talent take due care:
'Gainst the great day thyself prepare.

Let all thy converse be sincere,
Thy conscience as the noonday clear;
Think how all-seeing God thy ways
And all thy secret thoughts surveys.

Influenced by the light divine
Let thy own light in good works shine:
Reflect all heaven's propitious ways,
In ardent love and cheerful praise.

Wake, and lift up thyself, my heart,
And with the angels bear thy part,
Who all night long unwearied sing
Glory to the eternal king.

I wake, I wake, ye heavenly choir;
May your devotion me inspire,
That I like you my age may spend,
Like you may on my God attend.

May I like you in God delight,
Have all day long my God in sight,
Perform like you my Maker's will;
Oh may I never more do ill!

Had I your wings, to heaven I'd fly;
But God shall that defect supply,
And my soul, winged with warm desire,
Shall all day long to heaven aspire.

Glory to Thee who safe has kept,
And hath refreshed me whilst I slept.
Grant, Lord, when I from death shall wake,
I may of endless light partake.

I would not wake, nor rise again,
Even heaven itself I would disdain,
Wert not Thou there to be enjoyed,
And I in hymns to be employed.

Heaven is, dear Lord, where'er Thou art:
Oh never, then, from me depart;
For to my soul 'tis hell to be
But for one moment without Thee.

Lord, I my vows to Thee renew;
Disperse my sins as morning dew;
Guard my first springs of thought and will,
And with Thyself my spirit fill.

Direct, control, suggest, this day,
All I design, or do, or say,
That all my powers, with all their might,
In Thy sole glory may unite.

Thomas Ken

The day returns and brings us the petty round of irritating concerns and duties. Help us to play the man, help us to perform them with laughter and kind faces, let cheerfulness abound with industry. Give us to go blithely on our business all this day; bring us to our resting beds weary and content and undishonoured; and grant us in the end the gift of sleep.

R. L. Stevenson

My Heavenly Father, I thank you, through Jesus Christ, your beloved Son, that you kept me safe from all evil and danger last night. Save me, I pray, today as well, from every evil and sin, so that all I do and the way that I live will please you. I put myself in your care, body and soul and all that I have. Let your holy angels be with me, so that the evil enemy will not triumph over me. Amen.

Martin Luther, Morning Devotions, from Luther's Small Catechism

God Almighty bless us with his Holy Spirit this day;
guard us in our going out and coming in;
keep us always steadfast in his faith,
free from sin and safe from danger;
through Jesus Christ our Lord.

Author unknown

The Lord preserve my going out and my coming in: from this time forth for evermore.

O give your angels charge over me, to keep me in all my ways.

Order my steps according to your word, so shall no wickedness have dominion over me.   *Treasury of Devotion*

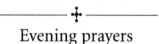

Evening prayers

We give you thanks, heavenly Father, through Jesus Christ, your dear Son, that you have today so graciously protected us, and we beseech you to forgive us all our sins, and the wrong which we have done, and through your great mercy defend us from all the perils and dangers of this night. Into your hands we commend our bodies and souls, and all that is ours. Let your holy angel guard us, that the wicked one may have no power over us.   Martin Luther, his evening prayer

Preserve me, Lord, while I am waking, and defend me while I am sleeping, that my soul may continually watch for you, and both body and soul may rest in your peace for ever.   John Cosin

Go with each of us to rest; if any awake, temper them the dark hours of watching; and when the day returns, return to us, our sun and comforter, and call us up with morning faces and with morning hearts, eager to labour, eager to be happy, if happiness should be our portion, and if the day be marked for sorrow, strong to endure it.

R.L. Stevenson, written on the eve of his unexpected death

Yours, O Lord, is the day, yours also is the night; cover our sins with your mercy as you cover the earth with darkness; and grant that the Sun of Righteousness may always shine in our hearts, to chase away the darkness of all evil thoughts; through Jesus Christ our Lord.

Author unknown

Into your hands, O Lord, we commend our souls and bodies, beseeching you to keep us this night under your protection and to strengthen us for your service tomorrow, for Christ's sake.   William Laud

I will both lie down and sleep in peace;
> for you alone, O Lord, make me like down in safety.

Psalm 4:8 NRSV

May the angels watch me
> As I lie down to sleep.
May angels guard me
> As I sleep alone.   Gaelic blessing

Abide with us, O Lord, for it is toward evening and the day is far spent; abide with us, and with your whole church. Abide with us in the evening of the day, in the evening of life, in the evening of the world. Abide with us and with all your faithful ones, O Lord, in time and eternity.

Lutheran Manual of Prayer

> *Glory to Thee, my God, this night*
> Forgive me, Lord, for thy dear Son,
> The ill that I this day have done,
> That with the world, myself, and thee,
> I, ere I sleep, at peace may be.
>
> Teach me to live, that I may dread
> The grave as little as my bed;
> Teach me to die, that so I may
> Rise glorious at the awful day.
>
> O may my soul on thee repose,
> And with sweet sleep mine eyelids close,
> Sleep that may me more vigorous make
> To serve my God when I awake.

When in the night I sleepless lie,
My soul with heavenly thoughts supply;
Let no ill dreams disturb my rest,
No powers of darkness me molest.

Thomas Ken

O God, from whom all holy desires, all good counsels, and all just works do proceed: Give unto thy servants that peace which the world cannot give; that both our hearts may be set to obey thy commandments, and also that by thee we, being defended from the fear of our enemies, may pass our time in rest and quietness; through the merits of Jesu Christ our Saviour.

Book of Common Prayer, 1549, Evensong, Second Collect

Lighten our darkness, we beseech thee, O Lord, and by thy great mercy, defend us from all perils and dangers of this night, for the love of thy only Son, our Saviour Jesus Christ.

Book of Common Prayer, 1549, Evensong, Collect for Aid against all Perils

Glory to thee, my God, this night
for all the blessings of the light;
keep me, O keep me, King of kings,
beneath thy own almighty wings.

Thomas Ken

Evensong
        Blest be the God of love,
Who gave me eyes, and light, and power this day,
        Both to be busy and to play.
        But much more blest be God above,

        Who gave me sight alone,
        Which to himself he did deny;
        For when he sees my ways, I die:
But I have got his Son, and he hath none.

What have I brought thee home
For this thy love? have I discharged the debt,
Which this day's favour did beget?
I ran; but all I brought, was foam.

Thy diet, care, and cost
Do end in bubbles, balls of wind;
Of wind to thee whom I have crost,
But balls of wild-fire to my troubled mind.

Yet still thou goest on,
And now with darkness closest weary eyes,
Saying to man, *It doth suffice:*
Henceforth repose; your work is done.

Thus in thy Ebony box
Thou dost enclose us, till the day
Put our amendment in our way,
And give new wheels to our disordered clocks.

I must, which shows more love,
The day or night: that is the gale, this th' harbour;
That is the walk, and this the arbour;
Or that the garden, this the grove.

My God, thou art all love.
Not one poor minute 'scapes thy breast,
But brings a favour from above;
And in this love, more than in bed, I rest.

George Herbert, *The Temple*

Holy Lord, almighty and eternal Father, thank you for your mercy that has protected me throughout this day. Let me pass through this night peacefully and with a pure mind and body, that rising with purity in the morning, I may serve you gratefully.   Alcuin

Into your hands, O Lord, I commend my spirit, for you have redeemed me, O Lord, the God of truth. I will lay down in peace, and take my rest, for it is you Lord only who make me live in safety.

Treasury of Devotion

My Heavenly Father, I thank you, through Jesus Christ, your beloved Son, that you have protected me, by your grace. Forgive, I pray, all my sins and the evil I have done. Protect me, by your grace, tonight. I put myself in your care, body and soul and all that I have. Let your holy angels be with me, so that the evil enemy may not triumph over me. Amen.   Martin Luther.

Evening Devotions, from Luther's Small Catechism

Visit, we beseech thee, O Lord, this place, and drive from it all the snares of the enemy; let your holy angels dwell here to preserve us in peace; and may your blessing be on us evermore; through Jesus Christ our Lord.

Office of Compline, Roman Breviary

Look down, O Lord, from your heavenly throne, illuminate the darkness of this night with your celestial brightness, and from the sons of light banish the deeds of darkness; through Jesus Christ our Lord.

Office of Compline, Roman Breviary

Be present, O merciful God, and protect us through the silent hours of this night, so that we who are wearied by the changes and chances of this fleeting world, may repose on your eternal changelessness; through Jesus Christ our Lord.   Office of Compline, Roman Breviary

Save us, Lord, while waking, and guard us while sleeping, that awake we may watch with Christ, and asleep we may rest in peace.

Office of Compline, Roman Breviary

✠

Prayers for meals

Lord God, Heavenly Father, bless us and these your gifts, which we receive from your generous hand, through Jesus Christ, our Lord. Amen.

Martin Luther

For health and strength and daily food,
We praise your name, O Lord.

Author unknown

Come, Lord Jesus, be our guest,
And may our meal by you be blest. Amen.

Attributed to Martin Luther

Bless me, O Lord, and let my food strengthen me to serve you, for Jesus Christ's sake.

Isaac Watts

Bless, O Lord, this food to our use and us in your service, and keep us mindful of the needs of others; for Christ's sake.

Traditional

Blessèd are you, Lord God of creation.
Generously you give us of the fruits of the earth to delight and nourish us.
Bless this meal and strengthen us in your service; through Christ our Lord.

Traditional

For what we are about to receive may the Lord make us truly thankful.

Traditional

Be present at our table, Lord,
Be here and everywhere ador'd,
These creatures bless and grant that we
May feast in paradise with thee.

> Josiah Wedgwood gave a teapot with these words on it to John Wesley.
> This grace was often used by Methodists.

Give me a good digestion, Lord,
And also something to digest;
But when and how that something comes
I leave to thee, who knowest best.

Give me a healthy body, Lord;
Give me the sense to keep it so;
And a heart that is not bored
Whatever work I have to do.

Give me a healthy mind, good Lord;
That finds the good that dodges sight;
And seeing sin, is not appalled,
But seeks a way to put it right.

Give me a point of view, good Lord,
Let me know that it is, and why,
Don't let me worry overmuch
About the thing that's known as 'I'.

Give me a sense of humour, Lord,
Give me the power to see a joke,
To get some happiness from life,
And pass it on to other folk.

> Refectory Grace, Chester Cathedral. Written by Thomas Henry Basil Webb
> while a schoolboy at Winchester College. He was killed in 1917 on the
> Somme, aged 19.

Prayer after a meal
We thank you, O Christ our God, that you have satisfied us with your earthly gifts; deprive us not of your heavenly kingdom, but as you came among your disciples, O Saviour, and gave them peace, come to us and save us.   Eastern Orthodox Church

———————— ✠ ————————

Prayers for reading the Bible

Father of mercies, in thy word
What endless glory shines!
For ever be thy name adored
For these celestial lines.

O may these heavenly page be
My ever dear delight,
And still new beauties may I see,
And still increasing light.

Divine instructor, gracious Lord,
Be thou for ever near;
Teach me to love thy sacred word,
And view my Saviour here.   Anne Steele

Lord, thy word abideth,
And our footsteps guideth,
Who its truth believeth
Light and joy receiveth.

O that we discerning
Its most holy learning,
Lord, may love and fear thee,
Evermore be near thee.   H.W. Baker

Take away, O Lord, the veil of my heart
while I read the scriptures.

Lancelot Andrewes

Most gracious God, our heavenly Father, in whom alone dwells all the
fullness of light and wisdom, enlighten our minds by your Holy Spirit to
truly understand your Word. Give us grace to receive it reverently and
humbly. May it lead us to put our whole trust in you alone, and so to
serve and honour you that we may glory your holy name and encourage
others by setting a good example.

John Calvin

O Lord, you have given us your Word as a light to shine on our path;
grant that we may so meditate on that Word, and follow its teaching,
that we may find in it the light that shines more and more until the perfect day; through Jesus Christ our Lord.

Jerome

O Lord Jesus, let not your word become a judgment on us, lest we hear
it and do not do it, or believe it and do not obey it.

Thomas à Kempis

Grant us, merciful God, knowledge and true understanding of your
word, that we may know what your will is, and also may show in our
lives those things that we do know; so that we may not only be knowers
of your word, but also doers of your word, through our Lord and
Saviour Jesus Christ.

Author unknown, King Henry VIII's Primer

Gracious God and most merciful Father, who has given us the rich and
precious jewel of your holy word: assist us with your Spirit so that your
word may be written in our heart for our everlasting comfort, to reform
us, to renew us to be like your own image, to build us up in the perfect
heavenly virtues. Grant this, heavenly Father, for the sake of Jesus Christ.

Geneva Bible, attributed to King Edward VI

Blessed Lord, who hast caused all holy Scriptures to be written for our learning: grant that we may in such wise hear them, read, mark, learn, and inwardly digest them, that by patience and comfort of thy holy Word, we may embrace and ever hold fast the blessed hope of everlasting life, which thou hast given us in our Saviour Jesus Christ.

Book of Common Prayer, 1549, Collect, Second Sunday in Advent

May the Lord grant that we may engage in contemplating the mysteries of his heavenly wisdom with really increasing devotion, to his glory and to our edification. Amen.

John Calvin. Calvin often used this prayer at the beginning of his lectures, which now form the basis of his Bible commentaries.

Chapter Five

PRAYERS FOR GOD'S WORLDWIDE CHURCH

Far be it from me that I should sin against the Lord by ceasing to pray for you.

1 Samuel 12:23 NRSV

I urge upon you communion with Christ, a growing communion.

Samuel Rutherford

Church's spiritual welfare

Most gracious Father, we most humbly beseech thee for thy Holy Catholic [universal] Church. Fill it with all truth; in all truth with all peace. Where it is corrupt, purge it; where it is in error, direct it; where anything is amiss, reform it; where it is right, strengthen and confirm it; where it is in need, furnish it; where it is divided and torn apart, make up its breaches, O holy One of Israel.   William Laud

Unity

O almighty God, who has built your church on the foundations of the apostles and prophets, Jesus Christ himself being the head cornerstone: grant us to be so joined together in unity of spirit by their teaching that we may be made into a holy temple, acceptable to you, through Jesus Christ our Lord.   English reformers, 1549

O Lord, grant all who contend for the faith, never to injure it by clamour and impatience; but, speaking thy precious truth in love, so to present it that it may be loved, and that men may see in it thy goodness and beauty.   William Bright

O God of peace, good beyond all that is good, in whom is calmness and concord: Heal the dissensions which divide us from one another, and bring us to unity of love in you; through Jesus Christ our Lord.

Liturgy of St Dionysius

Father, we pray for your Church throughout the world, that it may share to the full in the work of your Son, revealing you to men and reconciling men to you and to one another; that we and all Christian people may learn to love one another as you have loved us, and your Church may more and more reflect the unity which is your will and your gift, in Jesus Christ our Lord.   Chapel of Unity, Coventry Cathedral

May the almighty Son of God, Jesus Christ, who prayed in deepest anguish to his eternal Father that we in him might be one, mercifully unite us all.   Philipp Melanchthon

O God the Father of our Lord Jesus Christ, our only Saviour, the Prince of Peace: Give us grace seriously to lay to heart the great dangers we are in by our unhappy divisions. Take away all hatred and prejudice, and whatsoever else may hinder us from godly union and concord: that, as there is but one Body, and one Spirit, and one hope of our calling, one Lord, one faith, one baptism, one God and Father of us all; so we may henceforth be all of one heart, and of one soul, united in one holy bond of truth and peace, of faith and charity, and with one mind and one mouth glorify thee; through Jesus Christ our Lord. Amen.

Book of Common Prayer, Accession Service, 1715

———————— ✝ ————————

Mission

Dear Jesus,
Help us to spread your fragrance everywhere we go.
Flood our souls with your Spirit and life.
Penetrate and possess our whole being so utterly
that our lives may only be a radiance of yours.
Shine through us
and be so in us
that every soul we come in contact with
may feel your presence in our soul.
Let them look up and see no longer us
but only Jesus.
Stay with us
and then we shall begin to shine as you shine,
so to shine as to be light to others.
The light, O Jesus, will be all from you.
None of it will be ours.
It will be your shining on others through us.
Let us thus praise you in the way you love best
by shining on those around us.
Let us preach you without preaching
not by words, but by our example
by the catching force
the sympathetic influence of what we do
the evident fullness of the love our hearts bear to you.   Mother Teresa

God has created me to do for him some definite service; he has committed some work to me which he has not committed to another. I have my mission. ... I am a link in a chain, a connection between people. God has not created me for nothing. I shall do good, I shall do his work; I shall be a preacher of truth in my own place, while not intending it, if I do but keep his commandments and serve him in my calling.

J.H. Newman

O Lord, who has warned us that you will require much from those to whom much is given: Grant that we, whose lot is cast in so goodly a heritage, may strive together the more abundantly, by our prayers, our labours and our gifts, to extend to those who do not know what we so richly enjoy; and as we have entered into the labours of others, so to labour that others may enter into ours, to the fulfilment of your holy will and the salvation of all humankind; through Jesus Christ our Lord.

Author unknown, fifth century

O God of all the nations of the earth, remember the multitudes of the heathen, who, though created in thine image, have not known thee, nor the dying of thy Son their Saviour Jesus Christ; and grant that by the prayers and labours of thy holy church they may be delivered from all superstition and unbelief and brought to worship thee; through him whom thou hast sent to be the resurrection and the life to all men, the same thy Son Jesus Christ our Lord.

Francis Xavier

———————— ✞ ————————

Christian workers and church leaders

Almighty God, our Heavenly Father, Who hast purchased to Thyself an Universal Church by the precious Blood of Thy dear Son, Mercifully look upon the same, and at this time so guide and govern the minds of Thy servants, the Bishops and Pastors of Thy flock, that they may lay hands suddenly on no man, but faithfully and wisely make choice of fit persons to serve in the sacred Ministry of thy Church. And to those which shall be ordained to any holy function give Thy grace and Heavenly benediction; that both by their life and doctrine they may set forth Thy glory and set forward the salvation of all men; through Jesus Christ our Lord. Amen.

Book of Common Prayer, first Ember Collect, attributed to John Cosin

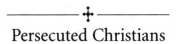

Revival

O Lord, convert the world – and begin with me.

Chinese student's prayer

Persecuted Christians

O God of all power, you called from death the great pastor of the sheep, our Lord Jesus: comfort and defend the flock which he has redeemed through the blood of the everlasting covenant. Increase the number of true preachers; enlighten the hearts of the ignorant; relieve the pain of the afflicted, especially of those who suffer for the testimony of the truth; by the power of our Lord Jesus Christ.

John Knox

---------- ✛ *Chapter Six* ✛ ----------

PRAYERS FOR
GOD'S WORLD

*First of all, then, I urge that supplications, prayers, intercessions
and thanksgivings should be made for everyone, for kings and
all who are in high positions, so that we may lead a quiet and
peaceable life in all godliness and dignity.*

1 Timothy 2:1–2 NRSV

*Prayer is the ascent of the mind to God. It is an abstract and
summary of Christian religion. Prayer is an act of religion
and divine worship, confessing His power and His mercy; it
celebrates His attributes, and confesses His glories, and reveres
His Person, and implores His aid, and gives thanks for His
blessings; it is an act of humility, condescension, and
dependence, expressed in the prostration of our bodies and
humiliation of our spirits; it is an act of charity, when we pray
for others; it is an act of repentance, when it is confesses and
begs pardon for our sins, and exercises every grace according
to the design of the man, and the matter of the prayer.*

Jeremy Taylor

Lord God, graciously comfort and care for all who are imprisoned,
hungry, thirsty, naked, and miserable; also all widows, orphans, sick, and
sorrowing. In brief, give us our daily bread, so that Christ may abide in
us and we in him for ever, and that with him we may worthily bear the
name of *Christian*.

Martin Luther

Blessed Lord, who for our sakes was content to bear sorrow, and want,
and death, grant to us such a measure of your Spirit that we may follow
you in all self-denial and tenderness of soul. Help us, by your great love,
to support the afflicted, to relieve the needy and destitute, to comfort the
feeble-minded, to share the burdens of the heavy laden, and always to see
you in all who are poor and destitute.

B.F. Westcott

O Lord, baptize our hearts into a sense of the needs and conditions of
all.   George Fox

We beg you, Lord, to help and defend us.
Deliver the oppressed,
have compassion on the despised,
raise the fallen,
reveal yourself to the needy,
heal the sick,
bring back those who have strayed from you,
feed the hungry,
lift up the weak,
remove the prisoners' chains.
May every nation come to know that you are God alone,
that Jesus is your Son,
that we are your people, the sheep of your pasture.   Clement of Rome

Relieve and comfort, O Lord, all the persecuted and afflicted; speak
peace to troubled consciences; strengthen the weak; confirm the strong;
instruct the ignorant; deliver the oppressed; relieve the needy; and bring
us all, by the waters of comfort and in the ways of righteousness, to the
kingdom of rest and glory, through Jesus Christ our Lord.
                                                                   Jeremy Taylor

O God, the Creator and Preserver of all mankind, we humbly beseech
thee for all sorts and conditions of men; that thou wouldest be pleased
to make thy ways known unto them, thy saving health unto all nations.
More especially we pray for the good estate of the Catholick Church;
that it may be so guided and governed by thy good Spirit, that all who
profess and call themselves Christians may be led into the way of truth,
and hold the faith in unity of spirit, in the bond of peace, and in righteousness of life.

Finally we commend to thy fatherly goodness all those who are any
ways afflicted or distressed in mind, body, or estate; that it may please
thee to comfort and relieve them, according to their sufferings, and a
happy issue out of all their afflictions. And this we beg for Jesus Christ
his sake.   Book of Common Prayer, Occasional Prayers

We bring before you, O Lord,
the troubles and perils of people and nations,
the sighing of prisoners and captives,
the sorrows of the bereaved,
the necessities of strangers,
the helplessness of the weak,
the despondency of the weary,
the failing powers of the aged.
O Lord, draw near to each;
for the sake of Jesus Christ our Lord.

Anselm

———————— ✝ ————————

Social justice

Strengthen us, O God, to relieve the oppressed, to hear the groans of poor prisoners, to reform the abuses of all professions; that many be made not poor to make a few rich; for Jesus Christ's sake.

Oliver Cromwell

Lord, make me an instrument of your peace.
Where there is hatred, let me sow love,
where there is injury, pardon,
where there is doubt, faith,
where there is despair, hope,
where there is darkness, light,
where there is sadness, joy.

O Divine Master, grant that we may not so much seek
to be consoled as to console,
not so much to be understood as to understand,
not so much to be loved as to love.
For it is in giving that we receive,
it is in pardoning that we are pardoned,
it is in dying that we are born to eternal life.

Attributed to St Francis of Assisi

✛

The poor and hungry

Dear Jesus, help me to spread your fragrance everywhere I go.
Flood my soul with your spirit and life.
Penetrate and possess my whole being so utterly that all my life may be
      only a radiance of yours.
Shine through me and be so in me that every soul we come into con-
      tact with may feel your presence in my soul.
Let them look up and see no longer me but only Jesus.

John Henry Newman, used daily by the Missionaries of Charity

✛

Refugees

O Brother Jesus, who as a child was carried into exile,
Remember all those who are deprived of their home or country,
Who groan under the burden of anguish and sorrow,
Enduring the burning heat of the sun,
The freezing cold of the sea, or the humid heat of the forest,
Searching for a place of refuge.
Cause these storms to cease, O Christ.
Move the hearts of those in power
That they may respect the men and women
Whom you have created in your own image;
That the grief of refugees may be turned into joy.

African Prayer for Refugees

———————— ✠ ————————

Rulers and governments

Almighty God, who rulest over all the kingdoms of the world, and dost order them according to thy good pleasure: We yield thee unfeigned thanks, for that thou wast pleased, as on this day, to set thy Servant our Sovereign Lady, Queen Elizabeth, upon the Throne of this Realm. Let thy wisdom be her guide, and let thine arm strengthen her; let truth and justice, holiness and righteousness, peace and charity, abound in her days; direct all her counsels and endeavours to thy glory, and the welfare of her subjects; give us grace to obey her cheerfully for conscience sake, and let her always possess the hearts of her people; let her reign be long and prosperous, and crown her with everlasting life in the world to come; through Jesus Christ our Lord. Amen.

Book of Common Prayer, Accession Service

O God, who providest for thy people by thy power, and rulest over them in love: Vouchsafe so to bless thy Servant our Queen, that under her this nation may be wisely governed, and thy Church may serve thee in all godly quietness; and grant that she being devoted to thee with her whole heart, and persevering in good works unto the end, may, by thy guidance, come to thine everlasting kingdom; through Jesus Christ thy Son our Lord, who liveth and reigneth with thee and the Holy Ghost, ever one God, world without end. Amen.

Book of Common Prayer, Accession Service

Almighty Father,
whose will is to restore all things in your beloved Son, the king of all:
govern the hearts and minds of those in authority,
and bring the families of the nations,
divided and torn apart by the ravages of sin,
to be subject to his just and gentle rule;
who is alive and reigns with you and the Holy Spirit,
one God, now and for ever.   *Alternative Service Book 1980*

Jesus shall reign where'er the sun
Does his successive journeys run:
His kingdom stretch from shore to shore
Till moons shall wax and wane no more. Isaac Watts

O God, almighty Father, King of kings and Lord of lords, grant that the
hearts and minds of all who go out as leaders before us, the statesmen,
the judges, the men of learning and the men of wealth, may be so filled
with the love of thy laws and of that which is righteous and life-giving,
that they may be worthy stewards of thy good and perfect gifts; through
Jesus Christ our Lord. Knights of the Garter prayer, fourteenth century

Almighty God, by whom alone kings reign and princes decree justice
and from whom alone cometh all wisdom and understanding: we thine
unworthy servants, here gathered together in thy name, do most humbly
beseech thee to send down thy heavenly wisdom from above, to direct
and guide us in all our consultations; and grant that, we having thy fear
always before our eyes and laying aside all private interests, prejudices
and partial affections, the result of all our counsels may be the glory of
thy blessed name, the maintenance of true religion and justice, the safety, honour and happiness of the Sovereign, the public welfare, peace and
tranquillity of the realm and the uniting and knitting together of the
hearts of all persons and estates within the same in true Christian love
and charity towards one another; through Jesus Christ our Lord.
Sir Christopher Yelverton, House of Commons prayer, composed about
1578, prayed at every sitting of the House of Commons

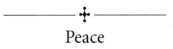

Peace

Drop your still dews of quietness
Till all our strivings cease:
Take from our lives the strain and stress,
And let our ordered lives confess
The beauty of your peace. J.G. Whittier

O God, who art Peace everlasting, whose chosen reward is the gift of peace, and who hast taught us that the peacemakers are thy children, pour thy sweet peace into our souls, that everything discordant may utterly vanish, and all that makes for peace be sweet to us forever.

Gelasian Sacramentary

Almighty God, from whom all thoughts of truth and peace proceed, kindle, we pray, in the hearts of all people the true love of peace, and guide with your pure and peaceable wisdom those who take counsel for the nations of the earth; that in tranquillity your kingdom may go forward, till the earth is filled with the knowledge of your love; through Jesus Christ our Lord.

Francis Paget

O God, who art the author of peace and lover of concord, in knowledge of whom standeth our eternal life, whose service is perfect freedom: defend us thy humble servants in all assaults of our enemies; that we, surely trusting in thy defence, may not fear the power of any adversities; through the might of Jesus Christ our Lord.

Book of Common Prayer, Morning Prayer, 1549

The less able

O God, who art the Father of lights, and with whom there is no darkness at all: we thank you for the good gift of sight which you have given us, and we pray that you will fill us with your own compassion for those who do not have it.

Direct and prosper the efforts that are made for their welfare. Reveal to them by your Spirit the things which eyes have not seen, and comfort them with the hope of the light everlasting, to which, of your great mercy, we ask you to bring us all; through Jesus Christ our Saviour.

A.W. Robinson

✤

Victims of war

Comfort, O Lord, we pray thee, all who are mourning the loss of those who laid down their lives in war. Be with them in their sorrow, support them in their loneliness. Give them faith to look beyond the troubles of this present time, and to know that neither life nor death can separate us from thy love which is in Christ Jesus our Lord.   Author unknown

In memory of those who made the supreme sacrifice, O God, make us better men and women, and give us peace in our time; through Jesus Christ our Lord.   Author unknown

✤

Animals and pets

O Lord Jesus Christ, who has taught us that without the knowledge of our Father in heaven no sparrow falls to the ground, help us to be very kind to all animals and our pets. May we remember that you will one day ask us if we have been good to them. Bless us as we take care of them; for your sake.   Author unknown

Chapter Seven

PRAYERS FOR HOME AND FAMILY

Unless the Lord builds the house,
those who build it labour in vain.

Psalm 127:1 NRSV

Truly we have learn a great lesson when we have learned that
'saying prayers' is not praying.

J.C. Ryle

✛

Our own home and family

Lord Jesus Christ, you welcomed the children who came to you, accept also from me, this evening prayer. Shelter me under the shadow of your wings, that in peace I may lie down and sleep. When you wake me up may I live for you, for you alone are full of mercy.

Eastern Orthodox Church

Bless my children with healthy bodies, with good minds, with the graces and gifts of your Spirit, with sweet dispositions and holy habits, and sanctify them throughout their bodies and souls and spirits, and keep them blameless until the coming of the Lord Jesus.   Jeremy Taylor

Lord God, who by the grace of your Holy Spirit has poured out your love into the hearts of your faithful people: Mercifully grant to those whom we love health of body and soul; that they may serve you with all their strength and gladly fulfil all your good pleasure; through Jesus Christ our Lord.   Gregorian Sacramentary

Lord, behold our family here assembled.
We thank you for this place in which we dwell,
for the love accorded us this day,
for the hope with which we expect the morrow;
for the health, the work, the food and the bright skies
that make our lives delightful;
for our friends in all parts of the earth.
Give us courage and gaiety and the quiet mind.
Spare us to our friends, soften us to our enemies.
Bless us, if it may be, in all our innocent endeavours;
if it may not, give us the strength to endure that which is to come
that we may be brave in peril, constant in tribulation,
temperate in wrath and in all changes of fortune
and down to the gates of death, loyal and loving to one another.
We beseech of you this help and mercy for Christ's sake.

R.L. Stevenson

—————— ☦ ——————

Friends

O God, you are present with your faithful people in every place, mercifully hear our prayers for those we love who are now separated from us.
Watch over them, we pray, and protect them in anxiety, danger and
temptations; and assure both them and us that you are always near and
that we are one with you for ever; through Jesus Christ our Lord.

B.F. Westcott

O blessed Lord, who has commanded us to love one another, grant us
grace that having received your undeserved bounty, we may love everyone in you and for you. We pray for your clemency for everyone; but
especially for the friends whom your love has give us. Love them, O
fountain of love, and make them love you with all their heart, that they
may will and speak and do those things only which are pleasing to you.

Anselm

Our neighbours

Lord, Thou hast taught us that all who come our way are our neighbours. But hear our prayer for those with whom we come in daily contact because they live close to us. Help us to be good neighbours to them. Give us the grace to ignore petty annoyances and to build on all that is positive in our relationship, that we may love them as we love ourselves, with genuine forbearance and kindness.   B.F. Westcott

✢

Marriage

Unless the Lord builds the house, those who build it labour in vain.
                                                            Psalm 127:1. NRSV

The Lord make you holy and bless you, the Lord pour the riches of his grace on you, that you may please him, and live together in holy love to your lives' end.   John Knox

May God be with you and bless you.
May you see your children's children.
May you be poor in misfortune, rich in blessings.
May you know nothing but happiness
From this day forward.   Old Wedding Blessing

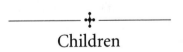

Death of a child

O God, to me who am left to mourn his departure, grant that I may not sorrow as one without hope for my beloved who sleeps in you; but, as always remembering his courage, and the love that united us on earth, I may begin again with new courage to serve you more fervently who are the only source of true love and true fortitude; that when I have passed a few more days in this valley of tears and this shadow of death, supported by your rod and staff, I may see him face to face, in those pastures and beside those waters of comfort where I believe he already walks with you. O Shepherd of the sheep, have pity on this darkened soul of mine.

E.W. Benson, on the death of his young son Martin

O God, you have dealt very mysteriously with us. We have been passing through deep waters; our feet were well-nigh gone, But though you slay us, yet we will trust in you ... You have reclaimed your lent jewels. Yet, O Lord, shall I not thank you now? I will thank you not only for the children you have left to us, but for those you have reclaimed. I thank you for the blessing of the last ten years, and for all the sweet memories of these lives ... I thank you for the full assurance that each has gone to the arms of the Good Shepherd, whom each loved according to the capacity of her years. I thank you for the bright hopes of a happy reunion, when we shall meet to part no more. O Lord, for Jesus Christ's sake, comfort our desolate hearts.

Campbell Tait, five of whose six children died of scarlet fever
in one month, in 1856

Children

Almighty God and heavenly Father, we thank you for the children which you have given us; give us also grace to train them in your faith, fear and love; that as they advance in years they may grow in grace, and may hereafter be found in the number of your elect children; through Jesus Christ our Lord.

John Cosin

Chapter Eight

PRAYERS FOR
TIMES OF LIFE

I am the vine, you are the branches. Those who abide in me and I in them bear much fruit, because apart from me you can do nothing.

John 15:5 NRSV

Prayer is ordained to this end: that we should confess our needs to God, and bare our hearts to him, as children lay their troubles in full confidence before their parents.

John Calvin

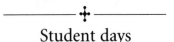

Student days

Almighty Father, grant that our universities and colleges may be houses of faith and fruitful study; and that their students may so learn truth as to bear its light along all their ways, and so learn Christ as to be found in him; who liveth and reigneth with thee and the Holy Spirit, one God, world without end. King's College, Cambridge

O God, our heavenly Father, by whose Spirit people are taught knowledge, who gives wisdom to all who ask you: Grant your blessing, we beseech you, on this school, and help us in the work you have given us to do. Enable us all to work diligently, not with eye-service, but in singleness of heart, remembering that without you we can do nothing, and that in your fear is the beginning of wisdom; through Jesus Christ our Lord. F.D. Maurice

Lord and Saviour, true and kind,
Be the master of my mind:
Bless and guide and strengthen still
All my powers of thought and will.

While I ply the scholar's task,
Jesus Christ, be near I ask:
Help the memory, clear the brain,
Knowledge still to seek and gain.   H.C.G. Moule

Give me grace, Lord, to be strong, prudent, just and wise in all things.
Give me an exact faith, generous love and unshakeable trust in you.
Fill me with the spirit of intelligence and wisdom. Let me always be con-
siderate about other people. O perfect and eternal Light, enlighten me.
                                                            Alcuin

Good Lord, you have refreshed our souls with the streams of knowledge;
lead in us at last to yourself, the source and spring of knowledge.
                                                            Alcuin

Grant, O Lord, to all students, to know what is worth knowing, to love
what is worth loving, to praise what delights you most, to value what is
precious in your sight and to reject what is evil in your eyes. Grant them
true discernment to distinguish between different things. Above all, may
they search out and do what is most pleasing to you; through Jesus
Christ our Lord.   Thomas à Kempis

Grant, O God, that we may wait patiently, as servants standing before
their Lord, to know your will; that we may welcome all truth, under
whatever outward forms it may be uttered; that we may bless every good
deed, by whomsoever it may be done; and that we may rise above all
party strife to the contemplation of the eternal Truth and Goodness;
through Jesus Christ our Lord.   Charles Kingsley

---- ✠ ----

Retirement

O God, who has ordained that whatever is to be desired should be sought by labour, and who, by your blessing, brings honest labour to good effect, look with mercy on my studies and endeavours. Grant me, O Lord, to design only what is lawful and right; and afford me calmness of mind and steadiness of purpose, that I may so do your will in this short life, as to obtain happiness in the world to come, for the sake of Jesus Christ our Lord.

Dr Johnson, written in his private register when he was 67 years old,
July 25, 1776

---- ✠ ----

Growing old

Grow old along with me!
The best is yet to be,
The last of life, for which the first was made:
Our times are in his hand
Who saith, 'A whole I planned,
Youth shows but half; trust God: see all, nor be afraid!'   Robert Browning

Lord, our God, we are in the shadow of your wings. Protect us and bear us up. You will care for us as if we were little children, even to our old age. When you are our strength we are strong, but when we are our own strength we are weak. Our good always lives in your presence, and we suffer when we turn our faces away from you. We now return to you, O Lord, that we may never turn away again.

Augustine, as he contemplated old age

Lord, thank you that in your love you have taken from me all earthly riches, and that you now clothe me and feed me through the kindness of others. Lord, thank you, that since you have taken from me my sight, you serve me now with the eyes of others.

Lord, thank you that since you have taken away the power of my hands and my heart, you serve me through the hands and hearts of others. Lord, I pray for them. Reward them for with your heavenly love, that they may faithfully serve and please you until they reach their happy end.

Mechthild of Magdeburg

Chapter Nine

PRAYERS OF DAILY LIFE

This is the day that the Lord has made;
let us rejoice and be glad in it.

Psalm 118:24 NRSV

Catherine of Siena made a cell in her heart. Afterwards, in a most busy life she could keep quite close to God and without the least distraction.

E.B. Pusey

Keep us, Lord, so awake in the duties of our callings that we may sleep in your peace and wake in your glory.   John Donne

O Lord Jesus Christ, our Watchman and Keeper, take us to thy care; grant that, our bodies sleeping, our minds may watch in thee, and be made merry by some sight of that celestial and heavenly life, wherein thou art the King and Prince, together with the Father and the Holy Spirit, where thy angels and holy souls be most happy citizens. Oh purify our souls, keep clean our bodies, that in both we may please thee, sleeping and waking, for ever.   *Christian Prayers*

Alone with none but you, my God,
I journey on my way.
What need I fear, when you are near
O king of night and day?
More safe am I within your hand
than if a host did round me stand.

Columba

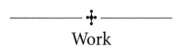

Birthdays and anniversaries

Happy birthday to you,
Happy birthday to you,
Happy birthday dear __ ,
God bless you today.

My Jesus, my King, my Life, my All; I again dedicate my whole self to Thee. Accept me, and grant, O gracious Father, that ere this year is gone I may finish my task. In Jesus' name I ask it. Amen, so let it be.

David Livingstone, *Last Journal*, 19 March 1872, his birthday

Work

O Lord, I do not pray for tasks equal to my strength: I ask for strength equal to my tasks.　　　　Phillips Brooks

O Lord, let us not live to be useless, for Christ's sake.　　　John Wesley

O God, who has commanded that no one should be idle, give us grace to employ our talents and faculties in the service appointed for us; that, whatever our hand finds to do, we may do it with our might.

James Martineau

Grant, O Father, that this day we may be doers of your Word, and not hearers only.　　　　Christopher Smart

Remember, Christian soul,
that thou hast this day,
and every day of thy life,
God to glorify,
Jesus to imitate,
a soul to save,
a body to mortify,
sins to repent of,
virtues to acquire,
hell to avoid,
heaven to gain,
eternity to prepare for,
time to profit by,
neighbours to edify,
the world to despise,
devils to combat,
passions to subdue,
death perhaps to suffer,
judgement to undergo.

Christopher Smart

O Lord, in whose hands are life and death, by whose power I am sustained, and by whose mercy I am spared, look down upon me with pity. Forgive me that I have until now so much neglected the duty which thou hast assigned to me, and suffered the days and hours of which I must give account to pass away without any endeavour to accomplish thy will. Make me to remember, O God, that every day is thy gift and ought to be used according to your command. Grant me, therefore, so to repent of my negligence, that I may obtain mercy from thee, and pass the time which thou shalt yet allow me in diligent performance of thy commands, through Jesus Christ.

Dr Johnson

Grant, O merciful God, that with malice towards none, with charity to all, with forgiveness in the right as you enable us to see the right, we may strive to finish the work we are engaged in; to bind up the nation's wounds, to care for ... the widow and orphan; to do all which may achieve a just and lasting peace among ourselves and with all nations.

After Abraham Lincoln

O God, give us work
    till our life shall end,
and give us life
    till our work is done.
Traditional

The things, good Lord, that we pray for, give us the grace to labour for.
Thomas More

Forth in your name, O Lord, I go,
My daily labour to pursue,
You, only you, resolved to know
In all I think, or speak or do.

The task your wisdom has assigned
O let me cheerfully fulfil,
In all my works your presence find,
And prove your good and perfect will.
Charles Wesley

O Lord, give your blessing, we pray, to our daily work, that we may do
    it in faith and heartily, as to the Lord and not to men.
All our powers of body and mind are yours, and we devote them to
    your service. Sanctify them, and the work in which we are
    engaged; and, Lord, so bless our efforts that they may bring
    forth in us the fruits of true wisdom.
Teach us to seek after truth and enable us to gain it; and grant that
    while we know earthly things, we may know you, and be
    known by you, through and in your Son Jesus Christ.
Thomas Arnold

O Lord, renew our spirits and draw our hearts to yourself, that our work
may not be to us a burden but a delight. Let us not serve you with the
spirit of bondage like slaves, but with freedom and gladness, delighting
in you and rejoicing in your work, for Jesus Christ's sake.
Benjamin Jenks

———— ✠ ————

Stress

Blessed Jesus, you are always near in times of stress.
Although we cannot feel your presence you are close.
You are always there to help and watch over us.
Nothing in heaven or on earth can separate you from us.

After Margery Kempe, fifteenth century

———— ✠ ————

Difficulties and trouble

Grant, we beseech thee, O Lord our God, that in whatever dangers we are placed we may call upon thy name, and that when deliverance is given us from on high we may never cease from thy praise; through Jesus Christ our Lord.

Leonine Sacramentary

In you, O Lord, I seek refuge;
    do not let me ever be put to shame;
    in your righteousness deliver me.
Incline your ear to me;
    rescue me speedily.
Be a rock of refuge for me,
    a strong fortress to save me.
...Into your hand I commit my spirit;
    you have redeemed me, O Lord, faithful God.

Psalm 31:1–2, 5 NRSV

Lord, Thou art life, though I be dead,
Love's fire Thou art, however cold I be;
Nor heaven have I, nor place to lay my head,
Nor home, but Thee.

Christina Rossetti

O Lord our God, teach us to ask aright for the right blessings. Guide the vessel of our life towards yourself, the tranquil haven of all storm-tossed souls. Show us the course we should take. Renew a willing spirit within us. Let your Spirit curb our wayward senses and guide and enable us to what is our true good, to keep your laws and in all our deeds always to rejoice in your glorious and gladdening presence. For yours is the glory and praise of all your saints for ever and ever.   Basil the Great

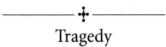

Tragedy

We humbly beseech thee, O Father, mercifully to look upon our infirmities; and for the glory of thy Name turn from us all those evils that we most righteously have deserved; and grant that in all our troubles we may put our whole trust and confidence in thy mercy, and evermore serve thee in holiness and pureness of living, to thy honour and glory; through our only Mediator and Advocate, Jesus Christ our Lord.

Book of Common Prayer, the Litany, 1549

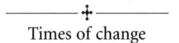

Times of change

O God, our Help in ages past,
Our Hope for years to come,
Our Shelter from the stormy blast,
And our eternal Home!

Beneath the shadow of Thy throne
Thy saints have dwelt secure;
Sufficient is Thine arm alone,
And our defence is sure.

Before the hills in order stood,
Or Earth received her frame,
From everlasting Thou art God,
To endless years the same.

Thy Word commands our flesh to dust:
'Return, ye sons of men!'
All nations rose from earth at first
And turn to earth again.

A thousand ages in Thy sight
Are like an evening gone;
Short as the watch that ends the night
Before the rising sun.

The busy tribes of flesh and blood,
With all their cares and fears,
Are carried downward by the flood,
And lost in following years.

Time, like an ever rolling stream,
Bears all its sons away;
They fly forgotten as a dream
Dies at the opening day.

Like flowery fields the nations stand,
Pleased with the morning light;
The flowers beneath the mower's hand
Lie withering ere 'tis night.

Our God our help in ages past,
Our hope for years to come,
Be Thou our guard while life shall last,
And our eternal Home.

Isaac Watts

Through all the changing scenes of life,
In trouble and in joy,
The praises of my God shall still
My heart and tongue employ.

Nahum Tate and Nicholas Brady

Now thank we all our God,
With heart and hand and voices,
Who wondrous things has done,
In whom his world rejoices;
Who from our mother's arms
Has blessed us on our way
With countless gifts of love
And still is ours today.

O may this bounteous God
Through all our life be near us,
With ever joyful hearts
And blessed peace to cheer us;
And keep us in his grace,
And guide us when perplexed,
And free us from all ills
In this world and the next.

Martin Rinkart, translated by Catherine Winkworth

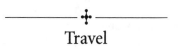

Travel

May the Lord keep our going out and our coming in from this time on
and for evermore.　　　　　　　　　　After Psalm 121:8 NRSV

Chapter Ten

PRAYERS FOR
THE SICK

*Are any among you sick? They should call for the elders of the
church and have them pray over them, anointing them with oil
in the name of the Lord. The prayer of faith will save the sick,
and the Lord will raise them up.*

James 5:14–15

*What a man is on his knees before God, that he is –
no more, no less.*

Robert Murray McCheyne

Over the door of a Christian hospital
O God, make the door of this house wide enough to receive all who need
human love and fellowship, and a heavenly Father's care; and narrow
enough to shut out all envy, pride and hate. Make its threshold smooth
enough to be no stumbling-block to children, nor to straying feet, but
rugged enough to turn back the tempter's power: make it a gateway to
thine eternal kingdom.

Thomas Ken

Lord, bless all means that are used for my recovery, and restore me to my
health in your good time; but if you have appointed that it should be
otherwise, your blessed will be done. Draw me away from an affection
for things below, and fill me with an ardent desire for heaven. Lord, fit
me your yourself, and then call me to those joys unspeakable and full of
glory, when it pleases you, and that for the sake of your only Son, Jesus,
my Saviour.

Thomas Ken

Asking for miraculous healing

Heal me, O Lord, and I shall be healed;
    save me, and I shall be saved;
        for you are my praise. Jeremiah 17:14 NRSV

O Lord and Master Jesus Christ, Word of the everlasting Father, who
hast borne our griefs and carried the burden of our infirmities: Renew
by thy Holy Spirit in thy Church, we beseech thee, thy gifts of healing,
and send forth thy disciples again to preach the gospel of thy kingdom,
and to cure the sick and relieve thy suffering children, to the praise and
glory of thy holy name. Liturgy of St Mark

O Lord God of our salvation, to whom no sickness is incurable, we pray
that in your compassion you will drive away from your servants, who
look for your heavenly medicine, all illness; show forth in them the
might of your healing power, and make them whole both in body and
soul; through Jesus Christ our Lord. Mozarabic Psalter

People caring for the sick

O Lord Jesus Christ, who went about doing good and healing all kinds
of sickness: give strength, wisdom and gentleness to all your ministering
servants, our doctors, surgeons and nurses; that always bearing your
presence with them, they may not only heal but bless, and shine as lamps
of hope in the darkest hours of distress and fear; who lives and reigns
with the Father and the Holy Spirit, ever one God world without end.

Church Missionary Society, 1899

Chapter Eleven

PRAYERS FOR FACING DEATH AND BEREAVEMENT

If for this life only we have hoped in Christ, we are of all people most to be pitied.

1 Corinthians 15:19 NRSV

Prayer unites the soul to God.

Julian of Norwich

✦

Contemplating death

My Redeemer and my Lord,
I beseech Thee, I entreat Thee,
Guide me in each act and word,
That hereafter I may meet Thee,
Watching, waiting, hoping, yearning,
With my lamp well trimmed and burning!

Interceding
With these bleeding
Wounds upon Thy hands and side,
For all who have lived and erred
Thou hast suffered, Thou hast died,
Scourged, and mocked, and crucified,
And in the grave hast Thou been buried!

If my feeble prayer can reach Thee,
O my Saviour, I beseech Thee,
Even as Thou has died for me,
More sincerely
Let me follow where Thou leadest,
Let me, bleeding as Thou bleedest,
Die, if dying I may give
Life to one who asks to live,
And more nearly,
Dying thus, resemble Thee!

H.W. Longfellow

Look, God, I have never spoken to you,
And now I want to say, 'How do you do?'
And see, God, they told me you did not exist,
And I, like a fool, believed all this.
Last night, from a shell-hole, I saw your sky,
I figured that they had told me a lie.
Had I taken time before to see things you had made,
I'd sure have known they weren't calling a spade a spade.

I wonder, God, if you would shake my poor hand?
Somehow I feel you would understand.
Strange I had to come to this hellish place
Before I had time to see your face.
Well, I guess, there isn't much more to say,
But I'm glad, God, that I met you today.
The zero hour will soon be here,
But I'm not afraid to know that you're near.

The signal has come – I shall soon have to go,
I like you lots – this I want you to know.
I am sure this will be a horrible fight;
Who knows? I may come to your house tonight.
Though I wasn't friendly to you before,
I wonder, God, if you'd wait at your door?
Look, I'm shedding tears – *me* shedding tears!
Oh! I wish I'd known you these long, long years.

Well, I have to go now, dear God. Good bye,
But now that I've met you I'm not scared to die.

Author unknown. Lines discovered on the dead body of an American soldier
killed in North Africa in the Second World War, 1944

O Lord, who thy dear life didst give
     For us in narrow grave to lie,
Teach us to die that we may live,
     To live that we may never die.

C.F. Alexander

O Lord Jesus Christ, Son of the living God, who at the ninth hour of the
day, with outstretched hands and bowed head, commended your spirit
to God the Father, and by your death unlocked the gates of paradise:
Mercifully grant that in the hour of our death our souls may come to the
true paradise, which is yourself; who lives and reigns God, world without end.

Office of None

From death to life: from sorrow to joy: from a vale of misery to a
        paradise of mercy.
I know that my Redeemer liveth, and that I shall be raised again in the
        last day.
I shall walk before the Lord in the land of the living.
In thee, O Lord, have I trusted: let me never be confounded.
Into thy hands I comment my spirit: for thou has redeemed me, O
        Lord, thou God of truth.
Thou art my helper and Redeemer: make no long tarrying, O my God.
Come, Lord Jesu, come quickly.
Lord Jesus, receive my sprit.

Meditations and Prayers, compiled by John Cosin

O my most blessed and glorious Creator, who has fed me all my life, and
redeemed me from all evil; seeing it is your merciful pleasure to take me
out of this frail body, and to wipe away all tears from my eyes, and all
sorrows from my heart, I do with all humility and willingness consent
and submit myself wholly to your sacred will.

186

My most loving Redeemer, into your saving and everlasting arms I comment my spirit; I am ready, my dear Lord, and earnestly expect and long for your good pleasure. Come quickly, and receive the soul of your servant who trusts in you.   Henry Vaughan

God that madest earth and heaven,
    Darkness and light,
Who the day for toil hast given,
    For rest the night;
Guard us waking, guard us sleeping,
    And when we die:
May we in thy mighty keeping
    All peaceful lie.   Reginald Heber

Finish, then, Thy new creation;
Pure and spotless let us be.
Let us see Thy great salvation
Perfectly restored in Thee;
Changed from glory into glory,
Till in heaven we take our place,
Till we cast our crowns before Thee,
Lost in wonder, love, and praise.   Charles Wesley

O Jesus, be mindful of your promise; think on us your servants; and when we leave this world, speak these loving words to our souls: 'Today you will be with me in joy.' O Lord Jesus Christ, remember us your servants to trust in you, when our tongue cannot speak, when our eyes cannot see and when our ears cannot hear. Let our soul always rejoice in you, and be joyful about your salvation, which you have bought for us through your death.   Miles Coverdale

O Who will show me those delights on high?
ECHO   *I.*
Thou Echo, thou art mortal, all men know.
ECHO   *No.*
Wert thou not born among the trees and leaves?
ECHO   *Leaves.*
And are there any leaves, that still abide?
ECHO   *Bide.*
What leaves are they? Impart the matter wholly.
ECHO   *Holy.*
And holy leaves the Echo then of bliss?
ECHO   *Yes.*
Then tell me, what is that supreme delight?
ECHO   *Light.*
Light to the mind: what shall the will enjoy?
ECHO   *Joy.*
But are there cares and business with the pleasure?
ECHO   *Leisure.*
Light, joy, and leisure; but shall they persever?
ECHO   *Ever.*

George Herbert, *The Temple*

O God, the protector of all that trust in thee, without whom nothing is strong, nothing is holy; Increase and multiply upon us thy mercy; that, thou being our ruler and guide, we may so pass through things temporal, that we finally lose not the things eternal: Grant this, O heavenly Father, for Jesus Christ's sake our Lord. Amen.

The Book of Common Prayer, Collect for the Fourth Sunday after Trinity

Lord Jesus Christ, true Man and God
Who borest anguish, scorn, the rod,
And didst at last upon the tree,
To bring thy Father's grace to me;
I pray thee, through that bitter woe,
Let me, a sinner, mercy know.

When comes the hour of failing breath,
And I must wrestle, Lord, with death,
Then come, Lord Jesus, come with speed,
And help me in my hour of need.
Lead me from this dark vale beneath,
And shorten then the pangs of death.

Joyful my resurrection be;
Thou in the judgment plead for me,
And hide my sins, Lord, from thy face,
And give me life, of thy dear grace.
I trust in Thee, O blessed Lord,
And claim the promise of thy Word.

Paul Eber, 1557, translated Catherine Winkworth, 1858

—————— ✝ ——————

Prayers for the dying

Abide with me; fast falls the eventide;
The darkness deepens; Lord, with me abide!
When other helpers fail, and comforts flee,
Help of the helpless, O abide with me.

Swift to its close ebbs out life's little day;
Earth's joys grow dim, its glories pass away;
Change and decay in all around I see;
O thou who changest not, abide with me.

I need thy presence every passing hour;
What but thy grace can foil the tempter's power?
Who like thyself my guide and stay can be?
Through cloud and sunshine, O abide with me.

I fear no foe with thee at hand to bless;
Ills have no weight, and tears no bitterness.
Where is death's sting? where, grave, thy victory?
I triumph still, if thou abide with me.

Hold thou thy cross before my closing eyes;
Shine through the gloom, and point me to the skies:
Heaven's morning breaks, and earth's vain shadows flee;
In life, in death, O Lord, abide with me!   H. F. Lyte

Bring us, O Lord God, at our last awakening into the house and gate of
heaven, to enter that gate and dwell in that house, where there shall be
no darkness nor dazzling, but one equal light; no noise nor silence, but
one equal music; no fears nor hopes, but one equal possession; no ends
nor beginnings, but one equal eternity; in the habitations of your glory
and dominion, world without end.   John Donne

Even such is time, that takes in trust
Our youth, our joys, our all we have,
And pays us but with earth and dust;
Who in the dark and silent grave,
When we have wandered all our ways
Shuts us the story of our days;
But from this earth, this grave, this dust,
My God shall raise me up, I trust.

Sir Walter Raleigh, written on the fly-leaf of his Bible the night before he was
executed at the Tower of London

------------ ✠ ------------

Prayers for the bereaved

The Lord gave, and the Lord has taken away; blessed be the name of
the Lord.   Job 1:21 NRSV

O Lord of all worlds, we bless your name for all those who have entered into their rest, and reached the promised land where you are seen face to face. Give us grace to follow in their footsteps, as they followed in the footsteps of your holy Son. Keep alive in us the memory of those dear to ourselves whom you have called to yourself; and grant that every remembrance which turns our hearts from things seen to things unseen may lead us always upwards to you, untill we come to our eternal rest; through Jesus Christ our Lord.   F.J.A. Hort

We give back to you, O God, those whom you gave to us. You did not lose them when you gave them to us, and we do not lose them by their return to you. Your dear Son has taught us that life is eternal and love cannot die, so death is only a horizon, and a horizon is only the limit of our sight. Open our eyes to see more clearly and draw us close to you that we may know that we are nearer to our loved ones, who are with you. You have told us that you are preparing a place for us: prepare us, that where you are we may be always, O dear Lord of life and death.
                                                                                    William Penn

God of all compassion, in your unending love and mercy for us your
            turn the darkness of death into the dawn of new life. Show
            compassion to your people in their sorrow.
Be our refuge and our strength to lift us from the darkness of this grief
            to the peace and light of your presence.
Your son, our Lord Jesus Christ, by dying for us, conquered death and
            by rising again, restored life.
May we then go forward eagerly to meet him, and after our life on
            earth be reunited with our brothers and sisters where every
            tear will be wiped away.   Author unknown

Almighty God, Father of all mercies and giver of all comfort, deal graciously, we pray, with those who mourn, that casting every care on you, they may know the consolation of your love; through Jesus Christ our Lord.   Author unknown

Eternal God, our heavenly Father, who loves us with an everlasting love: Help us now to wait on you with reverent and submissive hearts, that we, through patience and comfort of the Scriptures, may have hope, and be lifted above our distress into the light and peace of your presence; through Jesus Christ our Lord.   Author unknown

---------- ✜ ----------

Prayers of martyrs and others as they faced death

O Lord Jesu, who art the only health of all men living, and the everlasting life of those who die in thy faith: I give myself wholly unto thy will, being sure that the thing cannot perish whichis committed unto thy mercy.   Thomas Cromwell, before his execution

O eternal God and merciful Father, look down upon me in mercy; in the riches and fullness of all Thy mercies, look down upon me: but not till Thou hast nailed my sins to the Cross of Christ, not till Thou has bathed me in the Blood of Christ, not till I have hid myself in the wounds of Christ, that so the punishment due unto my sins may pass over me. And since Thou art pleased to try me to the utmost, I humbly beseech Thee, give me now, in this great instant, full patience, proportionable comfort, and a heart ready to die for Thine honour, the Kings's happiness, and the Church's preservation.

I am coming, O Lord, as quickly as I can. I know I must pass through death before I can come to see Thee. But it is only the mere shadow of death; a little darkness upon nature. Thou, by Thy merits, hast broken through the jaws of death. The Lord receive my soul, and have mercy upon me, and bless this kingdom with peace and plenty, and with brotherly love and charity, that there may not be this effusion of Christian blood among them: for Jesus Christ's sake, if it be Thy will.

Lord, receive my soul.

                    William Laud, martyred on Tower Hill, 10 January 1645

O Father of heaven, O Son of God, Redeemer of the world, O Holy Ghost, three persons and one God, have mercy upon me, most wretched caitiff and miserable sinner. I have offended both against heaven and earth more than my tongue can express. Whither, then, may I go, or whither shall I flee? To heaven I may be ashamed to lift up mine eyes, and in earth I find no place of refuge or succour. To thee, therefore, O Lord, do I run; to thee do I humble myself, saying, O Lord my God, my sins be great, but yet have mercy upon me for thy great mercy. The great mystery that God became man was not wrought for little or few offences. Thou didst not give thy Son, O heavenly Father, unto death for small sins only, but for all the greatest sins of the world, so that the sinner return to thee with his whole heart, as I do at this present. Wherefore have mercy on me, O God, whose property is always to have mercy; have mercy upon me, O Lord, for thy great mercy. I crave nothing for mine own merits, but for thy name's sake.

Thomas Cranmer, last words, before going to the stake, 21 March 1556

Father, make us more like Jesus. Help us to bear difficulty, pain, disappointment and sorrow, knowing that in your perfect working and design you can use such bitter experiences to mould our characters and make us more like our Lord. We look with hope to the day when we will be completely like Christ, because we will see him as he is ...

I am God's wheat. May I be grounded by the teeth of the wild beasts until I become the fine wheat bread that is Christ's. My passions are crucified, there is no heat in my flesh, a stream flows murmuring inside me; deep down in me it says: Come to the Father.

Ignatius, prior to his martyrdom

O Lord my God, I have hope in thee;
O my dear Jesus, set me free.
Though hard the chains that fasten me
And sore my lot, yet I long for thee.
I languish and groaning bend my knee,
Adoring, imploring, O set me free.

Mary Queen of Scots, on the eve of her execution

O my Lord, the hour I have so much longed for has surely come at last. The time has surely come that we will see one another. My Lord and Saviour, it is surely time for me to be taken out of this banishment and be for ever with you. The sacrifices of God are a broken spirit; a broken and a contrite heart, O God, you will not despise. Do not throw me out of your presence or take your Holy Spirit away from me. Create in me a clean heart, O God.

Teresa of Avila

O loving Christ, draw me, a weakling, after yourself; for if you do not draw me I cannot follow you. Give me a brave spirit that it may be ready alert. If the flesh is weak, may your grace go before me, come alongside me and follow me; for without you I cannot do anything, and especially, for your sake I cannot go to a cruel death. Grant me a ready spirit, a fearless heart, a right faith, a firm hope, and a perfect love, that for your sake I may lay down my life with patience and joy.

John Huss, as he lay chained in prison

Give me, good Lord, a full faith, a firm home and a fervent love, a love
for you incomparably above the love of myself.
Give me your grace, good Lord, to make death no stranger to me.
Lord, give me patience in tribulation and grace in everything to
conform my will to yours.
Give me, good Lord, a longing to be with you, not to avoid the
calamities of this wretched world, nor so much for the
attaining of the joys of heaven, as for a true love of you.
And give me, good Lord, your love and favour, which my love of you,
however great, could not deserve, were it not for your great
goodness.
These things, good Lord, that I pray for, give me your grace also to
work for.

Thomas More, after he had been condemned to death

Chapter Twelve

PRAYERS FOR YOUR LOCAL CHRISTIAN FELLOWSHIP

*I pray that you may have the power to comprehend, with all the
saints, what is the breadth and length and height and depth;
and to know the love of God that surpasses knowledge, so that
you may be filled with all the fullness of God.*

Ephesians 3:18–19 NRSV

*The best way to prevent wandering in prayer is not to let the
mind wander too much at other times; but to have God always
in our minds, in the whole course of our lives. Avoid, as much as
may be, multiplicity of business. Neither the innocency nor the
goodness of the employment will excuse us, if it possess our
hearts when we are praying to God. Make it a law to yourself to
meditate before you pray: as also to make certain pauses, to see
whether your heart goes along with your lips.*

Thomas Wilson

———— ✛ ————

As you start worship or a meeting

Heavenly Father, as we meet now in your presence,
we ask you to open our ears to hear your voice,
to open our lips to sing your praise,
and to open our hearts to love you more and more;
for Christ our Saviour's sake.   Author unknown

Sanctify, O Lord, our hearts and minds, and inspire our praise; and give
us grace to glorify you alike in our worship and in our work; through
Jesus Christ our Saviour.   Author unknown

Holy Spirit, you make alive; bless also this our gathering, the speaker and the hearer; fresh from the heart it shall come, by your aid, let it also go to the heart.

Søren Kierkegaard

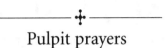

Pulpit prayers

Give us grace, O Lord, not only to hear your Word with our ears, but also to receive it into our hearts and to show it in our lives; for the glory of your great name.

Author unknown

O Lord, whom to know is to love, I beseech you to increase in me the knowledge of your truth. In the truth which I know, establish me; whatever I ought to know, teach me; in truths in which I waver, strengthen me; in things in which I am deceived, correct me; in things hard to understand, guide me; and from untruths deliver me. Send out your light and your truth, and let them lead me, until I know as I am known.

After Fulgentius Ruspensis, known as his 'Preacher's Prayer'

O Lord, uphold me, that I may uplift you; and may the words of my mouth, and the meditation of our hearts, be acceptable in your sight, O Lord, our strength and our redeemer.

Author unknown

O Lord, open to us your Word, and our hearts to your Word, that we may know you better and love you more; for your mercy and for your truth's sake.

Author unknown

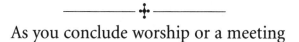

Offertory prayers

All things come from you, and of your own do we give you. Accept and bless, O God our Father, these our gifts, and pour out on us the spirit of your own abundant giving; that as we have freely received, so we may freely give, to the glory of your name; through Jesus Christ our Lord.

Author unknown

Grant, we beseech you, Almighty God, that these our gifts, being dedicated to your service, may be used for your glory and the good of your Church and people; through Jesus Christ our Lord.   Author unknown

As you conclude worship or a meeting

Be with us, Lord God, as we go back into the world.
May the lips which have sung your praises always speak the truth.
May the ears that have heard your Word be shut to what is evil.
May the feet that have brought us to your house always walk in your
        ways; through Jesus Christ our Lord.   Author unknown

May God give us light to guide us, courage to support us, and love to unite us, now and always.   Author unknown

Let your mighty outstretched arm, O Lord God, be our defence; your mercy and loving kindness in Jesus Christ, your dear Son, our salvation; your true word our instruction; the grace of your life-giving Spirit our comfort and consolation, to the end and in the end; through the same Jesus Christ our Lord.

John Knox, Book of Common Order, 1564

Heavenly Father, be pleased to accept and bless all that we have offered to you in this act of worship; and give us grace to show your praise not only with our lips, but in our lives; through Jesus Christ our Lord.

Author unknown

Sanctify, O Lord, both our coming in and our going out; and grant that when we leave your house we may not leave your presence, but may abide evermore in your love; through our Lord and Saviour Jesus Christ.

Author unknown

Grant, O Lord, that we may live in your fear,
die in your favour,
rest in your peace,
rise in your power,
reign in your glory;
for your own beloved Son's sake,
Jesus Christ our Lord.

William Laud

Grant, we beseech you, merciful Lord, that the words we have said and sung with our lips we may believe in our hearts and show in our lives, to your honour and glory; through Jesus Christ our Lord.

Author unknown

Accept, O Lord, the praise we bring to you; pardon the imperfections of our worship; write on our hearts your holy Word; and give us grace to love and serve and praise you all our days; through Jesus Christ our Lord.

Author unknown

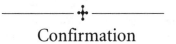

Baptism and thanksgiving for a birth

O almighty and eternal God, most merciful Father, as the just live by faith, and as it is impossible for anyone to please you without belief; we pray that you will grant to this child the gift of faith, in which you will seal and assure his heart in the Holy Spirit, according to the promise of your Son; that the inner regeneration of the Spirit may be truly represented by the outward baptism, and that the child may be buried with Christ into death, and be raised up from death by Christ, to the praise of your glory and the edifying of *his* neighbour.   Miles Coverdale

O Lord, holy Father, almighty, everlasting God, from whom all the light of truth comes: We pray that in your eternal and most tender goodness, you will bestow your blessing on this your servant, N., and enlighten *him* with the light of your knowledge. Purify and sanctify *him*, and give *him* true knowledge that he may be worthy to come to the grace of your baptism, that he may have a firm hope, true guidance, and holy teaching, and that he may so come to the grace of your baptism, through Christ our Lord.   Martin Luther

Almighty God, the Father of our Lord Jesus Christ, who has given you new birth through water and the Holy Spirit, and has forgiven you all your sin, strengthen you with his grace to life everlasting. Amen. Peace be with you.   Martin Luther, blessing after a baptism

Confirmation

Come, Holy Spirit, and daily increase in these your servants your many gifts of grace; the spirit of wisdom and understanding, the spirit of counsel and strength, the spirit of knowledge and true godliness; and fill them with the spirit of your holy fear, now and evermore.

Gelasian Sacramentary

O Jesus, thou hast promised
   To all who follow thee,
That where thou art in glory
   There shall thy servant be;
And, Jesus, I have promised
   To serve thee to the end;
O give me grace to follow,
   My Master and my Friend.

O let me see thy footmarks,
   And in them plant mine own:
My hope to follow duly
   Is in thy strength alone.
O guide me, call me, draw me,
   Uphold me to the end;
And then in heaven receive me,
   My Saviour and my Friend!   J.E. Bode

Defend, O Lord, this thy Child with thy heavenly grace, that *he* may continue thine for ever; and daily increase in thy Holy Spirit more and more, until *he* come unto thy everlasting kingdom.

Book of Common Prayer, Order of Confirmation

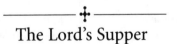

The Lord's Supper

O Thou, who didst manifest thyself in the breaking of bread to thy disciples at Emmaus: Grant us ever through the same blessed sacrament of thy presence to know thee, and to love thee more and more with all our hearts. Abide with us, O Lord, that we may ever abide in thee; for thy tender mercy's sake.   E.B. Pusey

We give you thanks, O heavenly Father, who has delivered us from the power of darkness and transferred us into the kingdom of your Son; grant, we pray, that as by his death he has recalled us to life, so by his presence abiding in us he may raise us to joys eternal; through the same Jesus Christ our Lord.   Mozarabic Sacramentary

A prayer for the evening before the Lord's Supper
As the night-watch looks for the morning, so do our eyes wait for you,
     O Christ.
As watchmen look for the morning, so do we look for you, O Christ;
       come with the dawning of the day, and make yourself known
       to us in the breaking of the bread; for you are our God for
       ever and ever.   Author unknown

Lord, I am indeed unworthy that you should come under my roof, but I need and long for your help and grace that I may walk in the right path. Therefore, I come to you, trusting only in the comforting words which I have heard, which you invite me with to your table and say to me, who is so unworthy, that I will receive forgiveness of my sins through your body and blood, if I eat and drink of this sacrament. Amen! Dear Lord, I do not doubt that your Word is true, and relying on this promise I eat and drink with you. Let it happen to me according to your will and Word.   Martin Luther

In this Holy Sacrifice,
may we be redeemed
by the precious Body and Blood
of our Saviour Jesus Christ:
may our lives be made new in him.

In this Holy Eucharist,
in humble thanksgiving
for the life, suffering and resurrection
of our Lord,
may we offer to him
ourselves, our souls and bodies.

In this Holy Communion,
may we be one in the mystical Body of Christ,
united in loving fellowship
with our Lord,
his saints in heaven,
and our fellow Christians everywhere.

In this Holy Communion,
may we be one with all humanity;
may we offer the joy and sorrow,
the good and evil
of all creation.

In this Holy Memorial of the Last Supper,
may we remember with penitence and joy
his great love for us sinners;
may we offer to him our sacrifice
of praise and thanksgiving.

In this Holy Mystery,
may we abide him
and he in us.

                                                              Peter Nott

Here, O my Lord, I see thee face to face;
Here would I touch and handle things unseen,
Here grasp with firmer hand the eternal grace,
And all my weariness upon thee lean.

Here would I feed upon the bread of God,
Here drink with thee the royal wine of heaven;
Here would I lay aside each earthly load,
Here taste afresh the calm of sin forgiven.

Mine is the sin, but thine the righteousness;
Mine is the guilt, but thine the cleansing blood;
Here is my robe, my refuge, and my peace –
Thy blood, thy righteousness, O Lord, my God.

                                                              Horatius Bonar

Prayer in preparation for the Lord's Supper
Glory be to Thee, O Lord, who makest Thine own Body and Blood to become our spiritual food, to strengthen and refresh our souls.

Glory be to Thee, O Lord, who by this heavenly food dost mystically unite us to Thyself; for nothing becomes one with our bodies more than the bodily food we eat, which turns into our very substance, and nothing makes us to become one with Thee more, than when Thou vouchsafest to become the very food of our souls!

Glory be to Thee, O Lord, who by this immortal food dost nourish our souls to live the life of grace here, and dost raise us up to life everlasting hereafter! Lord, do Thou evermore give us this bread! Amen, Amen.   Thomas Ken, *Manual for Winchester Scholars*

Almighty God, who has given your only Son to die for us: Grant that we who have been united in the communion of his most precious Body and Blood may be so cleansed from our past sins, and so strengthened to follow the example of his most holy life, that we may hereafter enjoy everlasting fellowship with you in heaven, through him who loved us and gave himself for us, the same Jesus Christ our Lord.   B.F. Westcott

Before Holy Communion
Almighty, everlasting God, I draw near to the sacrament of your only-
            begotten Son, our Lord Jesus Christ.
I who am sick approach the physician of life.
I who am unclean come to the fountain of mercy;
blind, to the light of eternal brightness;
poor and needy to the Lord of heaven and earth.
Therefore, I pray, that you will, in your endless mercy,
heal my sickness, cleanse my defilement,
enlighten my blindness, enrich my poverty,
and clothe my nakedness.
Then shall I dare to receive the bread of angels,
the King of kings and Lord of lords,
with reverence and humility, contrition and love,
purity and faith, with the purpose and intention necessary for the
            good of my soul...   Thomas Aquinas

A prayer just before receiving the bread and the wine
Jesus Christ, the Lamb, the Branch, the bright and Morning Star, the
Bread of life that came down from heaven, have mercy upon me. It is
Thy promise that whoever eateth Thy Flesh and drinketh Thy Blood
shall have eternal life in him, and Thou wilt raise him up at the last day.
Behold, O God, I am now coming to Thee, O Thou fountain of purga-
tion! Thou well of living waters, wash me clean.

Henry Vaughan, *The Mount of Olives*

Collect for Purity
Almighty God, unto whom all hearts be open, and all desires known,
and from whom no secrets are hid: cleanse the thoughts of our hearts,
by the inspiration of thy Holy Spirit: that we may perfectly love thee, and
worthily magnify thy holy name: through Christ our Lord.

Book of Common Prayer, 1549

Prayer of Humble Access
We do not presume to come to this thy table (O merciful Lord) trusting
in our own righteousness, but in thy manifold and great mercies: we be
not worthy so much as to gather up the crumbs under thy table: but
thou art the same Lord whose property is always to have mercy: Grant
us therefore (gracious Lord) so to eat the flesh of thy dear Son Jesus
Christ, and to drink his blood in these holy Mysteries, that we may continually dwell in him, and he in us, that our sinful bodies may be made
clean by his body, and our souls washed through his most precious
blood.   Book of Common Prayer, 1549

Welcome to the Table

> This is the feast of heav'nly wine,
>> And God invites to sup;
> The juices of the living vine
>> Were pressed, to fill the cup.
>
> Oh, bless the Saviour, ye that eat,
>> With royal dainties fed;
> Not heav'n affords a costlier treat,
>> For Jesus is the bread!
>
> The vile, the lost, he calls to them,
>> Ye trembling souls appear!
> The righteous, in their own esteem,
>> Have no acceptance here.
>
> Approach, ye poor, nor dare refuse
>> The banquet spread for you;
> Dear Saviour, this is welcome news,
>> That I may venture too.
>
> If guilt and sin afford a plea,
>> And may obtain a place;
> Surely the Lord will welcome me,
>> And I shall see his face!   William Cowper, *Olney Hymns*

We give thanks to you, almighty God, that you have refreshed us with this salutary gift; and we pray that in your mercy you will strengthen our faith in you, and in fervent love towards one another; through Jesus Christ, your dear Son, our Lord, who lives and reigns with you and the Holy Spirit, ever one God, world without end.   Martin Luther

We offer you immortal praise and thanks, heavenly Father, for the great blessing which you have conferred on us miserable sinners, in allowing us to partake of your Son Jesus Christ, whom was handed over to die for us, and now gives us the food of everlasting life. So we dedicate the rest of our lives to advance your glory and build up our neighbours, through the same Jesus Christ your Son, who, in the unity of the Holy Spirit, lives with you and reigns for ever. John Calvin

---

✛

Service and Witness

You are never tired, O Lord, of doing us good; let us never be weary of doing you service. But as you have pleasure in the well-being of your servants, let us take pleasure in the service of our Lord, and abound in your work and in your love and praise evermore. John Wesley

O God, the Father of the forsaken, who teaches us that love towards people is the bond of perfectness and the imitation of yourself: open our eyes and touch our hearts that we may see and do the things which belong to our peace.

Strengthen us in the work which we have undertaken; give us wisdom, perseverance, faith and zeal; and in your own time and according to your pleasure prosper our work; for the love of your Son Jesus Christ our Lord. Lord Shaftesbury

New Year

Give us the will, O God,
to pray to thee continually,
to learn to know thee rightfully,
to serve thee always holily,
to ask thee all things needfully,
to praise thee always worthily,
to love thee always steadfastly,
to ask thy mercy heartily,
to trust thee always faithfully,
to obey him always willingly,
to abide him always patiently,
to use thy neighbour honestly,
to live here always virtuously,
to help the poor in misery,
to thank thee ever gratefully,
to hope for heaven's felicity,
to have faith, hope and charity.

Thomas Tusser

O Lord God of time and eternity, who makes us creatures of time, that when time is over, we may attain your blessed eternity: With time, your gift, give us also wisdom to redeem the time, so our day of grace is not lost; for our Lord Jesus' sake.

Christina Rossetti

Father, let me dedicate
All this year to thee,
In whatever worldly state
Thou wilt have me be:
Not from sorrow, pain or care,
Freedom dare I claim;
This alone shall be my prayer,
'Glorify thy name.'

Lawrence Tuttiett

Chapter Thirteen

CHRISTIAN FESTIVALS

Therefore do not let anyone condemn you in matters of food and drink or of observing festivals, new moons, or sabbaths. These are only a shadow of what is to come, but the substance belongs to Christ.

Colossians 2:16–17 NRSV

Holy prayer is the column of all virtues; a ladder to God; the support of widows; the foundation of faith; the crown of religious; the sweetness of the married life.

Augustine of Hippo

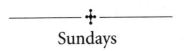

Sundays

Saturday, eve of Sunday

O Lord Jesus Christ, Son of the living God, who as on this day didst rest in the sepulchre, and didst thereby sanctify the grave to be a bed of hope to thy people: Make us so to abound in sorrow for our sins, which were the cause of thy passion, that when our bodies rest in the dust, our souls may live with thee; who livest and reignest with the Father and the Holy Spirit, one God, world without end.

Office of Compline

O God, who makes us glad with the weekly remembrance of the glorious resurrection of your Son our Lord; vouchsafe us this day such a blessing through your worship, that the days which follow it may be spent in your favour; through the same Jesus Christ our Lord. Amen.

William Bright

Shout joyfully to God, all the earth,
sing praise to his name,
proclaim his glorious praise.

Say to God: How tremendous your deeds are!
On account of your great strength
you enemies woo your favour.

Let the whole earth worship you,
singing praises, singing praises to your name.

Come and listen,
all you who fear God,
while I tell you what great things
he has done for me.

To him I cried aloud,
high praise was on my tongue.

From his holy temple
he heard my voice,
my entreaty reached his ears.

Bless our God, you peoples,
loudly proclaim his praise.

In him will every race
in the world be blessed;
all nations will proclaim his glory.

Blessed be the Lord, the God of Israel,
who alone does wondrous deeds.

Blessed forever be his glorious name;
may the whole world be filled with his glory.
Amen. Amen.

> Francis of Assisi. Prayer for Sundays and major feast days, to be said at
> nine o'clock in the morning (Terce)

O Lord Jesus Christ, who on the first day of the week rose again: Raise up our souls to serve the living God; and as you did also on this day send down on your apostles your most Holy Spirit, so take not the same Spirit from us, but grant that we may be daily renewed and plentifully enriched by his power; for your own mercy's sake, who lives and reigns with the Father and the Holy Spirit, ever one God, world without end.

Lancelot Andrewes

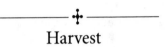

Harvest

We plough the fields and scatter
The good seed on the land.
But it is fed and watered
By God's almighty hand.
He sends the snow in winter,
The warmth to swell the grain,
The breezes and the sunshine,
And soft, refreshing rain:

All good gifts around us are sent from heaven above;
Then thank the Lord, O thank the Lord,
for all his love.

Matthias Claudius

Almighty God, Lord of heaven and earth, in whom we live and move and have our being; who does good unto all men, making your sun to rise on the evil and on the good, and sending rain on the just and on the unjust; favourably behold us your servants, who all on your name, and send us your blessing from heaven, in giving us fruitful seasons, and satisfying us with food and gladness; that both our hearts and mouths will be continually filled with your praise, giving thanks to you in your holy church; through Jesus Christ our Lord.

John Cosin

✛
All saints

O almighty God, who hast knit together thine elect in one communion and fellowship, in the mystical body of thy Son Jesus Christ our Lord: grant us grace so to follow thy blessed saints in all virtuous and godly living, that we may come to those unspeakable joys, which thou has prepared for them that unfeignedly love thee; through Jesus Christ our Lord.   Book of Common Prayer, 1549, Collect of All Saints' Day

Almighty and everlasting God, who dost kindle the flame of thy love in the hearts of the saints, grant unto us the same faith and power of love; that, as we rejoice in their triumphs, we may profit by their examples, through Jesus Christ our Lord.   Gothic missal

Thanks be to you, O God, for revealing yourself to humankind, and for
        sending your messengers in every generation.
Thanks be to you for the first apostles of Christ, sent into all the world
        to preach the gospel;
for those who brought the good news to our land;
for all who, in ages of darkness, kept alive the light, or in times of
        indifference were faithful to their Lord's command;
for all your followers in every age who have given their lives for the
        faith;
for those in our own day who have gone to the ends of the earth as
        heralds to your love;
for the innumerable company who now praise you from every race and
        nation and language.
With these and the whole company of heaven we worship you; through
        Jesus Christ our Lord.   Author Unknown

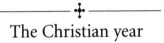

The Christian year

Advent

May the Lamb of God, who once came to take away the sins of the
world, take away from us every stain of sin. Amen.
And may he who came to redeem what was lost, at his second coming
not cast away what he has redeemed. Amen.
That, when he comes, we may have perpetual joy with him on whom
we have believed. Amen.   *Mozarabic Breviary*

Almighty God, give us grace that we may cast away the works of darkness, and put upon us the armour of light, now in the time of this mortal life in which thy Son Jesus Christ came to visit us in great humility;
that in the last day, when he shall come again in his glorious majesty to
judge both the quick and the dead, we may rise to the life immortal;
through him who liveth and reigneth with thee and the Holy Ghost, one
God, now and for ever. Amen.

Book of Common Prayer, First Sunday of Advent

We beseech you, O Lord, to purify our consciences by your daily visitation, that when your Son our Lord comes, he may find in us a mansion
prepared for himself; through the same Jesus Christ our Lord.

Gelasian Sacramentary

O Lord Jesu Christ, who at Thy first Coming didst send Thy messenger
to prepare Thy way before Thee; Grant that the ministers and stewards
of Thy mysteries may likewise so prepare and make ready Thy way, by
turning the hearts of the disobedient to the wisdom of the just, that at
Thy second Coming to judge the world we may be found an acceptable
people in Thy sight, Who livest and reignest with the Father and the
Holy Spirit, ever one God, world without end. Amen

Book of Common Prayer, 1661, Collect for the Third Sunday in Advent,
attributed to John Cosin.

Make us, we beseech you, O Lord our God, watchful and alert in waiting
for the coming of your Son Christ our Lord; that when he comes and
knocks, he will not find us sleeping in sin, but awake and rejoicing in his
praises; through the same Jesus Christ our Lord.   Gelasian Sacramentary

The Advent refrains on the Magnificat
Each may be followed by the response:
Even so, come Lord Jesus

O Wisdom, coming forth from the mouth of the Most High,
     and reaching mightily from one end of the earth
     to the other, ordering all things well:
Come and teach us the way of prudence.

O Adonai, and leader of the house of Israel,
     who appeared to Moses in the fire of the burning bush
     and gave him the law on Sinai:
Come and redeem us with an outstretched arm.

O Root of Jesse, standing as a sign to the people,
     before whom kings shall shut their mouths
     and the nations shall seek:
Come and deliver us and do not delay.

O Key of David, and sceptre of the house of Israel,
     who opens and no one can shut,
     who shuts and no one can open:
Come and bring the prisoners from the prison house,
     those who dwell in darkness and the shadow of death.

O Daystar, splendour of light eternal
     and sun of righteousness:
Come and enlighten those who dwell in darkness
     and the shadow of death.

O King of the nations, and their desire,
    the corner-stone making both one:
Come and save us, whom you formed from the dust.

O Emmanuel, our King and Lawgiver,
    the desire of all nations and their Saviour:
Come and save us, O Lord our God.   Author unknown, ninth century

Christmas

Christmas Eve

O Lord, we beseech Thee, incline Thine ear to our prayers, and lighten
the darkness of our hearts by Thy gracious visitation; through Jesus
Christ our Lord.   Gregorian Sacramentary

O God, who makes us glad with the yearly remembrance of the birth of
your only Son Jesus Christ. Grant that as we joyfully receive him for our
Redeemer, so we may with sure confidence behold him when he comes
to be our Judge; who lives and reigns with you and the Holy Spirit, ever
one God, world without end.   Gelasian Sacramentary

Almighty God, who hast given us thy only-begotten Son to take our
nature upon him, and as at this time to be born of a pure Virgin: Grant
that we, being regenerate and made thy children by adoption and grace,
may daily be renewed by thy Holy Spirit; through the same our Lord
Jesus Christ, who liveth and reigneth with thee and the same Spirit ever,
one God, world without end. Amen.   English reformers, 1549

Now the holly bears a berry
    as white as the milk.
And Mary bore Jesus,
    who was wrapped up in silk.

And Mary bore Jesus Christ
    our Saviour for to be,
And the first tree in the greenwood,
    it was the holly.

Now the holly bears a berry
    as black as the coal.
And Mary bore Jesus
    who died for us all.

Now the holly bears a berry
    as blood as it is red.
Then trust we our Saviour
    who rose from the dead.

Traditional Cornish carol

O holy Child of Bethlehem,
Descend to us, we pray;
Cast out our sin, and enter in:
Be born in us today.
We hear the Christmas angels
The great glad tidings tell:
O come to us, abide with us,
Our Lord Emmanuel.

Phillips Brooks

Merciful and most loving God, by whose will and bountiful gift Jesus Christ our Lord humbled himself that he might exalt humankind; and became flesh that he might restore in us the most celestial image; and was born of the Virgin that he might uplift the lowly: Grant us the inheritance of the meek, perfect in us your likeness, and bring us at last to rejoice in beholding your beauty, and with all your saints to glory your grace; through the same Jesus Christ our Lord.

Gallican Sacramentary

Lord Jesus Christ, who visited this world with the presence of your incarnation, and whose coming to judgment every Christian soul expects, justify us in the day of your coming with your wonted mercy, that we, who now celebrate the festival of your incarnation, may then be joined to the company of your saints; who with the Father and the Holy Spirit, lives and reigns, one God, world without end.   Mozarabic Sacramentary

Love came down at Christmas,
Love all lovely, love divine;
Love was born at Christmas,
Star and angels gave the sign.

Worship we the Godhead,
Love incarnate, love divine;
Worship we our Jesus:
But wherewith for sacred sign?

Love shall be our token,
Love shall be yours and love be mine,
Love to God and to all men,
Love for plea and gift and sign.   Christina Rossetti

O God, our loving Father, help us rightly to remember the birth of Jesus, that we may share in the song of the angels, the gladness of the shepherds and the worship of the wise men. May Christmas morning make us happy to be your children and Christmas evening bring us to our beds with grateful thoughts, forgiving and forgiven, for Jesus' sake.

R.L. Stevenson

Almighty God, who hast given us thy only-begotten Son to take our nature upon him, and as at this time to be born of a pure Virgin: Grant that we, being regenerate and made thy children by adoption and grace, may daily be renewed by thy Holy Spirit; through the same our Lord Jesus Christ, who liveth and reigneth with thee and the same Spirit ever, one God, world without end. Amen.

Book of Common Prayer, Collect for Christmas Day

Glory be to God in the highest, and on earth peace, goodwill towards men; for unto us is born this day a Saviour, who is Christ the Lord. We praise you, we bless you, we glorify you, we give thanks to you, for this your greatest mercy, Lord God, heavenly King, God the Father almighty.

Thomas Ken

The shepherds sing; and shall I silent be?
My God, no hymn for thee?
My soul's shepherd too; a flock it feeds
Of thoughts, and words, and deeds;
The pasture is thy word; the streams, thy grace
Enriching all the place.
Shepherd and flock shall sing, and all my powers
Out-sing the daylight hours.

George Herbert

O God, who makest us glad with the yearly remembrance of the birth of thine only Son Jesus Christ: grant that as we joyfully receive him for our Redeemer, so we may with sure confidence behold him when he shall come to be our judge; who liveth and reigneth with thee and the Holy Ghost world without end.

Book of Common Prayer, 1549, First Collect of Christmas

In the bleak mid-winter
    Frosty wind made moan,
Earth stood hard as iron,
    Water like a stone;
Snow had fallen, snow on snow,
    Snow on snow,
In the bleak mid-winter
    Long ago.

Our God, Heaven cannot hold Him,
    Nor earth sustain;
Heaven and earth shall flee away
    When He comes to reign:
In the bleak mid-winter
    A stable-place sufficed
The Lord God Almighty
    Jesus Christ.

Enough for Him whom cherubim
    Worship night and day,
A breastful of milk
    And a mangerful of hay;
Enough for Him whom angels
    Fall down before,
The ox and ass and camel
    Which adore.

Angels and archangels
    May have gathered there,
Cherubim and seraphim
    Throng'd the air,
But only His mother
    In her maiden bliss
Worshipped the Beloved
    With a kiss.

What can I give Him,
    Poor as I am?
If I were a shepherd
    I would bring a lamb,
If I were a wise man
    I would do my part,
Yet what I can I give Him –
    Give my heart.

Christina Rossetti

Nativity

Angels, from the realms of glory,
    Wing your flight o'er all the earth,
Ye who sang creation's story,
    Now proclaim Messiah's birth;
      Come and worship,
Worship Christ the newborn King.

Shepherds, in the field abiding,
    Watching o'er your flocks by night,
God with man is now residing,
    Yonder shines the infantlight;
      Come and worship,
Worship Christ the newborn King.

Sages, leave your contemplations,
    Brighter visions beam afar;
Seek the great Desire of nations;
    Ye have seen His natal star;
      Come and worship,
Worship Christ the newborn King.

Saints before the altar bending,
    Watching long in hope and fear,
Suddenly the Lord, descending,
    In His temple shall appear;
      Come and worship,
Worship Christ the newborn King.

Sinners, wrung with true repentance,
    Doom'd for guilt to endless pains,
Justice now revokes the sentence,
    Mercy calls you, break your chains
      Come and worship,
Worship Christ the newborn King.

James Montgomery

A Christmas dedication
Lord Jesus,
I give you my hands to do your work,
I give you my feet to go your way,
I give you my eyes to see as you do.
I give you my tongue to speak your words,
I give you my mind that you may think in me,
I give you my spirit that you may pray in me.

Above all, I give you my heart that you may love in me, your Father, and all mankind. I give you my whole self that you may grow in me, so that it is you, Lord Jesus, who live and work and pray in me.

I hand over to your care, Lord, my soul and body, my mind and thoughts, my prayers and hopes, my health and my work, my life and my death, my parents and my family, my friends and my neighbours, my country and all men. Today and always.

Lancelot Andrewes, *Private Prayers*

The worship of the wise men
O God, our loving Father, help us rightly to remember the birth of Jesus, that we may share in the songs of the angels, the gladness of the shepherds, and the worship of the wise men. May the Christmas morning make us happy to be Thy children, and the Christmas evening bring us to our beds with grateful thoughts, forgiving and forgiven, for Jesus' sake. R. L. Stevenson

The star of God's righteousness
Almighty and everlasting God, who hast made known the incarnation of thy Son by the bright shining of a star, which when the wise men beheld they adored thy majesty and presented costly gifts: Grant that the star of thy righteousness may always shine in our hearts, and that for our treasure we may give to thy service ourselves and all that we have; through the same Jesus Christ our Lord. Gelasian Sacramentary

The circumcision of Jesus

O God, who made the most glorious name of our Lord Jesus Christ, your one and only Son, to be exceeding sweet and supremely lovable to your faithful servants: Mercifully grant that all who devoutly venerate this name of Jesus on earth may in this life receive your holy comfort, and in the life to come receive your unending joy; through the same Jesus Christ our Lord. Sarum Missal

Epiphany

May our Lord Jesus Christ bless you, who of old on this day gloriously
appeared to the shepherds in the manger. Amen.
May he himself protect and defend us in all things, who for us mercifully took upon himself our human infancy. Amen.
And may he, who is our Lord and Saviour, graciously keep us until
eternity. Mozarabic Breviary

O God, whose blessed Son was manifested that he might destroy the works of the devil, and make us the sons of God, and heirs of eternal life; Grant us, we beseech thee, that, having this hope, we may purify ourselves, even as he is pure; that, when he shall appear again with power and great glory, we may be made like unto him in his eternal and glorious kingdom; where with thee, O Father, and thee, O Holy Ghost, he liveth and reigneth, ever one God, world without end.

Book of Common Prayer, 1662, Collect of the Sixth Sunday
after Epiphany

Ash Wednesday

Almighty and everlasting God, who hatest nothing that thou hast made and dost forgive the sins of all them that are penitent: Create and make in us new and contrite hearts, that we, worthily lamenting our sins, and acknowledging our wretchedness, may obtain of thee, the God of all mercy, perfect remission and forgiveness; through Jesus Christ our Lord. Amen. Book of Common Prayer, First day of Lent, Ash Wednesday

Lent

O Lord, which dost teach us that all our doings without charity are nothing worth: send thy Holy Ghost, and pour into our heart that most excellent gift of charity, the very bond of peace and all virtues, without the which, whosoever liveth is counted dead before thee: Grant this, for thy only son Jesus Christ's sake.

Book of Common Prayer, 1549, Collect for Quinquagesima

To Keep a True Lent
Is this a Fast, to keep
    The larder lean?
      And clean
From fat of veals and sheep?

Is it to quit the dish
    Of flesh, yet still
      To fill
The platter high with fish?

Is it a fast an hour,
    Or ragg'd to go,
      Or show
A down-cast look and sour?

No: 'tis a Fast to dole
    Thy sheaf of wheat
      And meat
Unto the hungry soul.

It is to fast from strife
    And old debate,
      And hate;
To circumcise thy life.

To show a heart grief-rent;
   To starve thy sin,
      Not bin;
And that's to keep thy Lent.

Robert Herrick

Palm Sunday

Almighty and everlasting God, who, of thy tender love towards mankind, hast sent thy Son, our Saviour Jesus Christ, to take upon him our flesh, and to suffer death upon the cross, that all mankind should follow the example of his great humility; Mercifully grant, that we may both follow the example of his patience, and also be made partakers of his resurrection; through the same Jesus Christ our Lord. Amen.

Book of Common Prayer, Palm Sunday

Ride on! ride on in majesty!
Hark! all the tribes 'Hosanna' cry:
O Saviour meek, pursue Thy road
With palms and scattered garments strowed.

Ride on! ride on in majesty!
In lowly pomp ride on to die:
O Christ, Thy triumphs now begin
O'er captive death and conquered sin.

Ride on! ride on in majesty!
The wingèd squadrons of the sky
Look down with sad and wondering eyes
To see the approaching sacrifice.

Ride on! ride on in majesty!
Thy last and fiercest strife is nigh;
The Father on His sapphire throne
Awaits His own anointed Son.

Ride on! ride on in majesty!
In lowly pomp ride on to die;
Bow thy meek head to mortal pain,
Then take, O God, Thy power and reign.   H. H. Milman

Maundy Thursday

Lord Jesus Christ, who when thou wast able to institute thy holy sacrament at the Last Supper, didst wash the feet of the apostles, and teach us by thy example the grace of humility: cleanse us, we beseech thee, from all stain of sin, that we may be worthy partakers of thy holy mysteries; who livest and reignest with the Father and the Holy Ghost, one God, world without end.

Office of the Royal Maundy in Westminster Abbey

Good Friday

My God, my God, why have you forsaken me?
    Why are you so far from helping me, from the words of my groaning?
O my God, I cry by day, but you do not anwser;
    and by night, but find no rest.
Yet you are holy,
    enthroned on the praises of Israel.
In you our ancestors trusted;
    they trusted, and you delivered them.
To you they cried, and were saved;
    in you they trusted, and were not put to shame.
But I am a worm, and not human;
    scorned by others, and despised by the people.
All who see me mock at me;
    they make mouths at me, they shake their heads;
'Commit your cause to the Lord; let him deliver –
    let him rescue the one in whom he delights!'
Yet it was you who took me from the womb;
    you kept me safe on my mother's breast.

On you I was cast from my birth,
　　and since my mother bore me you have been my God.
Do not be far from me,
　　for trouble is near
　　and there is no one to help.　　　　　　　　Psalm 22:1–11 NRSV

Fence me about, O Lord, with the power of your honourable and life-giving cross, and preserve me from every evil.　　Eastern Orthodox Church

Lord Jesus Christ, who for the redemption of the world ascended the wood of the cross, and the whole world was turned into darkness, grant us always that light, both in body and soul, whereby we may attain to everlasting life; who with the Father and the Holy Spirit live and reign, one God, world without end.　　　　　　　　　　Ambrosian Manual

May our dear Lord Jesus Christ show you his hands and his side, and with his love put joy into your hearts, and may you behold and hear only him until you find your joy in him.　　　　　　　　Martin Luther

O Cross that liftest up my head,
I dare not ask to fly from thee;
I lay in dust life's glory dead,
And from the ground there blossoms red
Life that shall endless be.　　　　　　　　George Matheson

There is a green hill far away
Outside a city wall,
Where the dear Lord was crucified,
Who died to save us all.

We may not know, we cannot tell
What pains he had to bear;
But we believe it was for us
He hung and suffered there.　　　　　　　　C.F. Alexander

The stations of the cross
First station: Jesus is condemned to death
O innocent Jesus, who with wonderful submission wast for our sakes condemned to die. Grant that we may bear in mind that our sins were the false-witnesses; our blasphemies, backbitings, and evil speakings were the cause of thy accepting with gladness the sentence of the impious judge. O may this thought touch our hearts and make us hate those sins which caused thy death.

Second station: Jesus receives his cross
O blessed Jesus, grant us by virtue of thy cross and bitter passion, cheerfully to submit to and willingly to embrace all the trials and difficulties of this our earthly pilgrimage, and may we be always ready to take up our cross daily and follow thee.

Third station: Jesus falls under the weight of the cross
O Jesus, who for our sins didst bear the heavy burden of the cross and didst fall under its weight, may the thought of thy sufferings, make us watchful against temptation, and do thou stretch out thy sacred hand to help us lest we fall into any grievous sin.

Fourth station: The cross is laid upon Simon of Cyrene
O Jesus! I thank thee, that thou has permitted me to suffer with thee, may it be my privilege to bear my cross may I glory in nothing else; by it may the world be crucified unto me, and I unto the world, may I never shrink from suffering, but rather rejoice, if I be counted worthy to suffer for thy name's sake.

Fifth station: Jesus speaks to the women of Jerusalem
O Lord Jesus, we mourn and will mourn both for thee and for ourselves; for thy sufferings, and for our sins which caused them. Oh, teach us so to mourn, that we may be comforted, and escape those dreadful judgments prepared for all those who reject or neglect them.

Sixth station: Jesus is stripped of his garments
O Lord Jesus! Thou didst suffer shame for our most shameful deeds. Take from us, we beseech thee, all false shame, conceit, and pride, and made us so to humble ourselves in this life, that we may escape everlasting shame in the life to come.

Seventh station: Jesus is nailed to the cross
O Jesus! Crucified for me, subdue my heart with thy holy fear and love, and since my sins were the cruel nails that pierced thee, grant that in sorrow for my past life I may pierce and nail to thy cross all that offends thee.

Eighth station: Jesus hangs on the cross
O Jesus! we do devoutly embrace that honoured cross, where thou didst love us even unto death. In thy death is all our hope. Henceforth let us live only unto thee, so that whether we live or die we may be thine.

Ninth station: Jesus is taken down from the cross
O Lord Jesus, grant that we may never refuse that cross, which thou hast laid upon us: who willed not to be taken down from the cross, until thou hadst accomplished the work which thou camest to do.

Tenth station: Jesus is laid in the sepulchre
O Jesus, most compassionate Lord, we adore thee dead and enclosed in the holy sepulchre. We desire to enclose thee within our hearts, that, united to thee, we may rise to newness of life, and by the gift of final perseverance die in thy grace.   *Treasury of Devotion*

His Saviour's Words, Going to the Cross
Have, have ye no regard, all ye
Who pass this way, to pity me
Who am a man of misery?

A man both bruis'd, and broke, and one
Who suffers not here for mine own
But for my friends' transgression?

Ah! Sion's Daughters, do not fear
The Cross, the Cords, the Nails, the Spear,
The Myrrh, the Gall, the Vinegar,

For Christ, your loving Saviour, hath
Drunk up the wine of God's fierce wrath;
Only, there's left a little froth,

Less for to taste, than for to shew
What bitter cups had been your due,
Had He not drank them up for you.

Robert Herrick

The Cross
The Cross, my seal in baptism, spread below
Doth by that form into an anchor grow,
Crosses grow anchors, bear as thou should'st do
Thy cross, and that cross grows an anchor too.
But he that makes our crosses anchors thus
Is Christ, Who there is crucified for us.

John Donne wrote these words to go with a signet ring that he gave to
Izaak Walton. On the ring was an engraving of Christ crucified, with
the cross in the shape of an anchor

The Dream of the Rood
Hear while I tell about the best of dreams
Which came to me the middle of one night
While humankind were sleeping in their beds.
It was as though I saw a wondrous tree
Towering in the sky suffused with light ...
... the best
Of woods began to speak these words to me:
'It was long past – I still remember it –
That I was cut down at the copse's end,
Moved from my roots. Strong enemies there took me,
Told me to hold aloft their criminals,
Made me a spectacle. Men carried me
Upon their shoulders, set me on a hill,
A host of enemies there fastened me.
And then I saw the Lord of all mankind
Hasten with eager zeal that He might mount
Upon me. I durst not against God's word
Bend down or break, when I saw tremble all
The surface of the earth. Although I might
Have struck down all the foes, yet stood I fast.
Then the young hero (who was God almighty)

Got ready, resolute and strong in heart.
He climbed onto the lofty gallows-tree,
Bold in the sight of many watching men,
When he intended to redeem mankind.
I trembled as the warrior embraced me.
But still I dared not bend down to the earth,
Fall to the ground. Upright I had to stand.
A rood I was raised up; and I held high
The noble King, the Lord of heaven above.
I dared not stoop. They pierced me with dark nails;
The scars can still be clearly seen on me,
The open wounds of malice. Yet might I
Not harm them. They reviled us both together.
I was made wet all over with the blood
Which poured out from His side, after He had
Sent forth His spirit. And I underwent
Full many a dire experience on that hill.
I saw the God of hosts stretched grimly out.
Darkness covered the Ruler's corpse with clouds,
His shining beauty; the shadows passed across,
Black in the darkness. All creation wept,
Bewailed the King's death; Christ was on the cross.
And yet I saw men coming from afar,
Hastening to the Prince. I watched it all.'

> This eighth century poem and meditation on the death of Christ is most
> unusually presented from the point of view of the rood (or cross) on which
> Christ was crucified.

The Sacrifice
O all ye, who pass by, whose eyes and mind
To worldly things are sharp, but to be blind;
To me, who took eyes that I might find you:
Was ever grief like mine?

… Mine own Apostle, who the bag did bear,
Though he had all I had, did not forbear
To sell me also, and to put me there:
Was ever grief like mine?

For thirty pence he did my death devise,
Who at three hundred did the ointment prize,
Not half so sweet as my sweet sacrifice:
Was ever grief like mine?

Therefore my soul melts, and my heart's dear treasure
Drops blood (the only beads) my words to measure:
'O let this cup pass, if it be thy pleasure:'
Was ever grief like mine?

These drops being temper'd with a sinner's tears,
A balsam are for both the Hemispheres,
Curing all wounds, but mine; all, but my fears:
Was ever grief like mine?

… Arise, arise, they come! Look how they run!
Alas! what haste they make to be undone!
How with their lanterns do they seek the sun:
Was ever grief like mine?

With clubs and staves they seek me, as a thief,
Who am the way of truth, the true relief,
Most true to those who are my greatest grief:
Was ever grief like mine?

Judas, dost thou betray me with a kiss?
Canst thou find hell about my lips? and miss
Of life, just at the gates of life and bliss?
Was ever grief like mine?

See, they lay hold on me, not with the hands
Of faith, but fury; yet at their commands
I suffer binding, who have loosed their bands:
Was ever grief like mine?

All my disciples fly, fear puts a bar
Betwixt my friends and me. They leave the star,
That brought the wise men of the East from far:
Was ever grief like mine?

... They bind, and lead me unto Herod: he
Sends me to Pilate. This makes them agree;
But yet friendship is my enmity:
Was ever grief like mine?

Herod and all his bands do set me light,
Who teach all hands to war, fingers to fight,
And only am the Lord of hosts and might:
Was ever grief like mine?

Herod in judgment sits, while I do stand;
Examines me with a censorious hand:
I him obey, who all things else command:
Was ever grief like mine?

The Jews accuse me with despitefulness;
And vying malice with my gentleness,
Pick quarrels with their only happiness:
Was ever grief like mine?

I answer nothing, but with patience prove
If stony hearts will melt with gentle love.
But who does hawk at eagles with a dove?
Was ever grief like mine?

... Hark how they cry aloud still, 'Crucify:
It is not fit he live a day', they cry,
Who cannot live less than eternally:
Was ever grief like mine?

Pilate a stranger holdeth off; but they,
Mine own dear people, cry, 'Away, away,'
With noises confused frighting the day:
Was ever grief like mine?

Yet still they shout, and cry, and stop their ears,
Putting my life among their sins and fears,
And therefore wish my blood on them and theirs:
Was ever grief like mine?

… They choose a murderer, and all agree
In him to do themselves a courtesy;
For it was their own cause who killed me:
Was ever grief like mine?

And a seditious murderer he was:
But I the Prince of Peace; peace that doth pass
All understanding, more than heaven doth glass:
Was ever grief like mine?

… Ah, how they scourge me! yet my tenderness
Doubles each lash: and yet their bitterness
Winds up my grief to a mysteriousness:
Was ever grief like mine?

They buffet me, and box me as they list,
Who grasp the earth and heaven with my fist,
And never yet, whom I would punish, miss'd:
Was ever grief like mine?

Behold, they spit on me in scornful wise;
Who with my spittle gave the blind man eyes,
Leaving his blindness to mine enemies:
Was ever grief like mine?

My face they cover, though it be divine.
As Moses' face was veiled, so is mine,
Lest on their double-dark souls either shine:
Was ever grief like mine?

Servants and abjects flout me; they are witty:
'Now prophesy who strikes thee,' is their ditty.
So they in me deny themselves all pity:
Was ever grief like mine?

And now I am deliver'd unto death,
Which each one calls for so with utmost breath,
That he before me well-nigh suffereth:
Was ever grief like mine?

Weep not, dear friends, since I for both have wept,
When all my tears were blood, the while you slept:
Your tears your own fortunes should be kept:
Was ever grief like mine?

The soldiers lead me to the common hall;
There they deride me, they abuse me all:
Yet for twelve heavenly legions I could call:
Was ever grief like mine?

Then the scarlet robe they me array;
Which shows my blood to be the only way,
And cordial left to repair man's decay:
Was ever grief like mine?

Then on my head a crown of thorns I wear;
For these are all the grapes Sion doth bear,
Though I my vine planted and water'd there:
Was ever grief like mine?

So sits the earth's great curse in Adam's fall
Upon my head; so I remove it all
From th' earth unto my brows, and bear the thrall:
Was ever grief like mine?

Then with the reed they gave to me before,
They strike my head, the rock from whence all store
Of heavenly blessings issue evermore:
Was ever grief like mine?

They bow their knees to me, and cry, 'Hail, King'
Whatever scoffs or scornfulness can bring,
I am the floor, the sink, where they it fling:
Was ever grief like mine?

Yet since man's sceptres are as frail as reeds,
And thorny all their crowns, bloody their weeds;
I, who am Truth, turn into truth their deeds:
Was ever grief like mine?

The soldiers also spit upon that face
Which angels did desire to have the grace,
And Prophets once to see, but found no place:
Was ever grief like mine?

Thus trimmed, forth they bring me to the rout,
Who 'Crucify him,' cry with one strong shout.
God holds his peace at man, and man cries out:
Was ever grief like mine?

They lead me in once more, and putting then
Mine own clothes on, they lead me out again.
Whom devils fly, thus is he toss'd of men:
Was ever grief like mine?

And now weary of sport, glad to engross
All spite in one, counting my life their loss,
They carried me to my most bitter cross:
Was ever grief like mine?

My cross I bear myself, until I faint:
Then Simon bears it for me by constraint,
The decreed burden of each mortal Saint:
Was ever grief like mine?

'O all ye how pass by, behold and see:'
Man stole the fruit, but I must climb the tree;
The tree of life to all, but only me:
Was ever grief like mine?

Lo, here I hang, charged with a world of sin,
The greater world o' the two; for that came in
By words, but this by sorrow I must win:
Was ever grief like mine?

Such sorrow, as if sinful man could feel,
Or feel his part, he would not cease to kneel,
Till all were melted, though he were all steel:
Was ever grief like mine?

But, 'O my God, my God!' why leav'st thou me,
The Son, in whom thou dost delight to be?
'My God, my God'
Never was grief like mine?

Shame tears my soul, my body many a wound;
Sharp nails pierce this, but sharper that confound;
Reproaches, which are free, while I am bound:
Was ever grief like mine?

Now heal thyself, Physician; now come down.
Alas! I did so, when I left my crown
And Father's smile for you, to feel his frown:
Was ever grief like mine?

In healing not myself, there doth consist
All that salvation, which ye now resist;
Your safety in my sickness doth subsist:
Was ever grief like mine?

Betwixt two thieves I spend my utmost breath,
As he that for some robbery suffereth.
Alas! what have I stolen from you? death:
Was ever grief like mine?

A king my title is, prefix'd on high;
Yet by my subjects I'm condemn'd to die
A servile death in servile company:
Was ever grief like mine?

They gave me vinegar mingled with gall,
But more with malice: yet, when they did call,
With Manna, Angels' food, I fed them all:
Was ever grief like mine?

They part my garments, and by lot dispose
My coat, the type of love, which once cured those
Who sought for help, never malicious foes:
Was ever grief like mine?

Nay, after death their spite shall farther go;
For they will pierce my side, I full well know;
That as sin came, so Sacraments might flow:
Was ever grief like mine?

But now I die; now all is finished.
My woe, man's weal: and now I bow my head:
Only let others say, when I am dead,
Never was grief like mine.

George Herbert, The Sacrifice

When I survey the wondrous Cross,
    On which the Prince of glory died,
My richest gain I count but loss,
    And pour contempt on all my pride.

Forbid it, Lord, that I should boast
    Save in the death of Christ my God;
All the vain things that charm me most,
    I sacrifice them to his blood.

See from his head, his hands, his feet,
    Sorrow and love flow mingled down;
Did e'er such love and sorrow meet,
    Or thorns compose so rich a crown?

His dying crimson like a robe,
    Spreads o'er his body on the Tree;
Then am I dead to all the globe,
    And all the globe is dead to me.

Were the whole realm of nature mine,
    That were a present far too small;
Love so amazing, so divine,
    Demands my soul, my life, my all.

Isaac Watts

Rex Tragicus
Put off thy robe of purple, then go on
To the sad place of execution:
Thine hour is come; and the tormentor stands
Ready, to pierce thy tender feet, and hands.
Long before this, the base, the dull, the rude,
Th' inconstant and unpurged multitude
Yawn for thy coming; some ere this time cry,
How he defers, how loath he is to die!
Amongst this scum, the soldier with his spear,
And that sour fellow, with his vinegar,
His sponge, and stick, do ask why thou dost stay?
So do the scurf and bran too: Go thy way,
Thy way, thou guiltless Man, and satisfy
By thine approach, each their beholding eye.
Not as a thief, shalt thou ascend the mount,
But like a person of some high account:
The cross shall be thy stage; and thou shalt there
The spacious field have for thy theatre.
Thou art that Roscius, and that marked-out man,
That must this day act the tragedian,
To wonder and affrightment: Thou art He,
Whom all the flux of nations comes to see;
Not those poor thieves that act their parts with Thee:
Those act without regard, when once a King,
And God, as thou art, comes to suffering.
No, no, this scene from thee takes life and sense,
And soul and spirit, plot and excellence.
Then begin, great King! ascend thy throne,
And thence proceed to act thy passion
To such a height, to such a period raised,
As hell, and earth, and heaven may stand amazed.
God, and good angels guide thee; and so bless
Thee in thy several parts of bitterness;
That those, who see thee nailed unto the tree,
May (though they scorn Thee) praise and pity Thee.
And we (Thy lovers) while we see Thee keep
The laws of action, will both sigh and weep;

And bring our spices, and embalm Thee dead;
That done, we'll see Thee sweetly buried.

Robert Herrick, 'Rex Tragicus', or 'Christ Going to his Cross'. The poet, as he
watches the scene in his imagination, addresses Christ.

The death of Christ
    O my chief good,
How shall I measure out thy blood?
How shall I count what thee befell,
    And each grief tell?

    Shall I thy woes
Number according to thy foes?
Or, since one star show'd thy first breath,
    Shall all thy death?

    Or shall each leaf
Which falls in Autumn, score a grief?
Or cannot leaves, but fruit, be sign
    Of the true vine?

    Then let each hour
Of my whole life one grief devour;
That thy distress through all may run,
    And be my sun.

    Or rather let
My several sins their sorrows get;
That, as each beast his cure doth know,
    Each sin may so ...

George Herbert, The Temple

O Lord Jesus Christ, Son of the living God, who at this evening hour didst rest in the sepulchre and didst thereby sanctify the grave to be a bed of hope to thy people: make us so to abound in sorrow for our sins, which were the cause of thy passion, that when our bodies lie in the dust, our souls may live with thee; who livest and reignest with the Father and the Holy Spirit, one God, world without end.   Office of Compline

It is a thing most wonderful

It is a thing most wonderful,
Almost too wonderful to be,
That God's own Son should come from heaven,
And die to save a child like me.

And yet I know that it is true:
He chose a poor and humble lot,
And wept, and toiled, and mourned, and died
For love of those who loved him not.

But even could I see him die,
I could but see a little part
Of that great love, which, like a fire,
Is always burning in his heart.

It is most wonderful to know
His love for me so free and sure;
But 'tis more wonderful to see
My love for him so faint and poor.

And yet I want to love thee, Lord;
O light the flame within my heart,
And I will love thee more and more,
Until I see thee as thou art.   W. W. How

O Christ, give us patience and faith and hope as we kneel at the foot of thy Cross, and hold fast to it. Teach us by thy Cross that however ill the world may be, the Father so loved us that he spared not thee.

Charles Kingsley

My song is love unknown,
My Saviour's love to me,
Love to the loveless shown,
That they might lovely be.
O, who am I,
That for my sake
My Lord should take
Frail flesh, and die?

He came from his blest throne,
Salvation to bestow:
But men made strange, and none
The longed-for Christ would know.
But O, my Friend,
My Friend indeed,
Who at my need
His life did spend!

Sometimes they strew his way,
and his sweet praises sing;
Resounding all the day
hosannas to their King;
Then 'Crucify!'
is all their breath,
And for his death
they thirst and cry.

Why, what hath my Lord done?
What makes this rage and spite?
He made the lame to run,
he gave the blind their sight.
Sweet injuries!
Yet they at these
Themselves displease,
and 'gainst him rise.

They rise, and needs will have
my dear Lord made away;
A murderer they save,
the Prince of Life they slay.
Yet cheerful he to suffering goes,
That he his foes
from thence might free.

Here might I stay and sing,
No story so divine;
Never was love, dear King,
Never was grief like thine!
This is my Friend,
In whose sweet praise
I all my days
Could gladly spend.

Samuel Crossman

Rock of ages, cleft for me,
Let me hide myself in Thee!
Let the water and the blood,
From Thy riven side which flowed,
Be of sin the double cure;
Cleanse me from its guilt and pow'r.

Not the labours of my hands
Can fulfil Thy law's demands:
Could my zeal no respite know,
Could my tears for ever flow,
All for sin could not atone:
Thou must save, and Thou alone!

Nothing in my hand I bring,
Simply to Thy Cross I cling;
Naked, come to Thee for dress;
Helpless, look to Thee for grace;
Foul, I to the fountain fly:
Wash me, Saviour, or I die!

While I draw this fleeting breath –
When my eye-strings break in death –
When I soar through tracts unknown –
See Thee on Thy judgement-throne –
Rock of ages, cleft for me,
Let me hide myself in Thee.

A. M. Toplady

Dying, let me still abide
Jesu, grant me this, I pray,
Ever in thy heart to stay;
Let me evermore abide
Hidden in thy wounded side.

If the evil one prepare,
Or the world, a tempting snare,
I am safe when I abide
In thy heart and wounded side.

If the flesh, more dangerous still,
Tempt my soul to deeds of ill,
Naught I fear when I abide
In thy heart and wounded side.

Death will come one day to me;
Jesu, cast me not from thee:
Dying let me still abide
In thy heart and wounded side.

Latin, seventeenth century, translated by H. W. Baker

O Lord Jesus, forasmuch as your life was despised by the world, grant us so to imitate you, even though the world despises us, that with your image always before our eyes, we may learn that only the servants of the cross can find the way of genuine happiness and true light. Hear us and save us, Lord Jesus.

Thomas à Kempis

O my Saviour, lifted
From the earth for me,
Draw me in thy mercy
Nearer unto thee.

Lift my earth-bound longings,
Fix them, Lord, above;
Draw me with the magnet
Of thy mighty love.

And I come, Lord Jesus,
Dare I turn away?
No, thy love hath conquered,
And I come today.   W. W. How

O Lord, in your great mercy, keep us from forgetting what you have suffered for us in body and soul. May we never be drawn by the cares of this
life from Jesus our Friend and Saviour, but daily may live nearer to his
cross.   Captain Hedley Vicars, killed in action at Sebastopol

Easter

May the Lord Jesus Christ, who, dying for the salvation of the whole
          world, rose this day from the dead, mortify you from your
          sins by his resurrection. Amen.
And may he, who, by the gibbet of the cross destroyed the rule of
          death, grant you a portion in the life of blessedness. Amen.
So that you, who celebrate this day of his resurrection with joy in this
          world, may attain the company of the saints in the heavenly
          kingdom. Amen.
Through the aid of his mercy, who with God the Father and the Holy
          Spirit lives and reigns one God, world without end. Amen.
                                        Mozarabic Sacramentary

O God, who by your One and only Son has overcome death and opened to us the gate of everlasting life; grant, we pray, that those who have been redeemed by his passion may rejoice in his resurrection, through the same Christ our Lord.   Gelasian Sacramentary

Almighty God, who through the death of your Son has destroyed sin and death, and by his resurrection has restored innocence and everlasting life, that we may be delivered from the dominion of the devil, and our mortal bodies raised up from the dead: Grant that we may confidently and whole-heartedly believe this, and, finally, with your saints, share in the joyful resurrection of the just; through the same Jesus Christ, your Son, our Lord.   Martin Luther

Love's redeeming work is done;
Fought the fight, the battle won:
Lo, our Sun's eclipse is o'er!
Lo, he sets in blood no more.

Vain the stone, the watch, the seal,
Christ has burst the gates of hell;
Death in vain forbids his rise;
Christ has opened Paradise.

Lives again our glorious King;
Where, O death, is now thy sting?
Dying once, he all doth save;
Where thy victory, O grave?   Charles Wesley

My Dancing Day
Tomorrow shall be my dancing day:
    I would my true love did so chance
to see the legend of my play,
    To call my true love to my dance:

Sing O my love, O my love, my love, my love;
This have I done for my true love.

Then was I born of a virgin pure,
    Of her I took fleshly substance;
Thus was I knit to man's nature,
    To call my true love to my dance:
Sing O my love …

In a manger laid and wrapped I was,
    So very poor, this was my chance,
Betwixt an ox and a silly poor ass,
    To call my true love to my dance:
Sing O my love …

Then afterwards baptised I was;
    The Holy Ghost on me did glance,
My Father's voice heard from above,
    To call my true love to my dance:
Sing O my love …

Into the desert I was led,
    Where I fasted without substance;
The devil bade me make stones my bread,
    To call my true love to my dance:
Sing O my love …

For thirty pence Judas me sold,
    His covetousness for to advance;
'Mark whom I kiss, the same do hold,'
    The same is he shall lead the dance.
Sing O my love …

Before Pilate the Jews me brought,
    Where Barabbas had deliverance;
They scourged me and set me at nought,
    Judged me to die to lead the dance:
Sing O my love …

Then on the cross hanged I was,
    Where a spear to my heart did glance;
There issued forth both water and blood,
    To call my true love to my dance:
Sing O my love …

Then down to hell I took my way
    For my true love's deliverance,
And rose again on the third day,
    Up to my true love and the dance:
Sing O my love …

Then up to heaven I did ascend,
    Where now I dwell in sure substance,
On the right hand of God, that man
    May come unto the general dance:
Sing O my love …   Author unknown, fifteenth century

Jesus Christ is risen today, Alleluya!
Jesus Christ is risen to-day, Alleluya!
Our triumphant holy day, Alleluya!
Who did once, upon the Cross, Alleluya!
Suffer to redeem our loss. Alleluya!

Hymns of praise then let us sing, Alleluya!
Unto Christ, our heavenly King, Alleluya!
Who endured the Cross and grave, Alleluya!
Sinners to redeem and save. Alleluya!

But the pains that he endured, Alleluya!
Our salvation have procured; Alleluya!
Now above the sky he's King, Alleluya!
Where the angels ever sing. Alleluya!

'Lyra Davidica', 1708, translated from a fourteenth century manuscript

Easter Wings
Lord, who createdst man in wealth and store,
    Though foolishly he lost the same,
        Decaying more and more,
           Till he became
            Most poor:

            With thee
          Oh let me rise
       As larks, harmoniously,
    And sing this day thy victories:
Then shall the fall farther the flight in me.

My tender age in sorrow did begin:
    And still with sickness and shame
        Thou did'st so punish sin,
           That I became
            Most thin

            With thee
         Let me combine,
      And feel this day the victory,
    For, if I imp my wing on thine,
Affliction shall advance the flight in me.

George Herbert, *The Temple*

I have no wit, no words, no tears;
    My heart within me like a stone
Is numbed too much for hopes or fears;
    Look right, look left, I dwell alone;
I lift mine eyes, but dimmed with grief
    No everlasting hills I see;
My life is in the falling leaf:
    O Jesus, quicken me.

My life is like a faded leaf,
My harvest dwindled to a husk;
    Truly my life is void and brief
        And tedious in the barren dusk;
My life is like a frozen thing,
    No bud nor greenness can I see:
Yet rise it shall – the sap of Spring;
    O Jesus, rise in me.

My life is like a broken bowl,
    A broken bowl that cannot hold
One drop of water for my soul
Or cordial in the searching cold;
    Cast in the fire the perished thing,
        Melt and remould it, till it be
A royal cup for Him my King:
    O Jesus, drink of me.

Christina Rossetti

Rise, heart; thy Lord is risen. Sing his praise
    Without delays,
Who takes thee by the hand, that thou likewise
    With him may'st rise:
That, as his death calcinèd thee to dust,
His life may make thee gold, and much more, Just.

Awake, my lute, and struggle for thy part
        With all thy art.
The cross taught all wood to resound his name
        Who bore the same.
His stretchèd sinews taught all strings, what key
Is best to celebrate this most high day.

Consort both heart and lute, and twist a song
        Pleasant and long:
Or since all music is but three parts vied,
        And multiplied;
O let thy blessed Spirit bear a part,
And make up our defects with his sweet art.   George Herbert, *The Temple*

I got me flowers to strew thy way;
I get me boughs off many a tree:
but thou wast up by break of day,
And brought'st thy sweets along with thee.

The Sun arising in the East,
Though he give light, and th' East perfume;
If they should offer to contest
With thy arising, they presume.

Can there be any day but this,
Though many suns to shine endeavour?
We count three hundred, but we miss:
There is but one, and that one ever.   George Herbert, *The Temple*

   Easter Monday
Out in the rain a world is growing green,
    On half the trees quick buds are seen
        Where glued-up buds have been.
Out in the rain God's Acre stretches green,
    Its harvest quick tho' still unseen:
        For there the Life hath been.

If Christ hath died His brethren well may die,
    Sing in the gate of death, lay by
        This life without a sigh:
For Christ hath died and good it is to die;
    To sleep when so He lays us by,
        Then wake without a sigh.

Yea, Christ hath died, yea, Christ is risen again:
    Wherefore both life and death grow plain
        To us who wax and wane;
For Christ Who rose shall die no more again:
    Amen: till He makes all things plain
        Let us wax on and wane.

Christina Rossetti

Most glorious Lord of Life, that on this day
Didst make thy triumph over death and sin;
And, having harrowed hell, didst bring away
Captivity, thence captive, us to win:
This joyous day, dear Lord, with joy begin;
And grant that we, for whom thou didst die,
Being with thy dear blood clean washed from sin,
May live for ever in felicity.
And that thy love, we weighing worthily,
May likewise love thee for the same again;
And for thy sake, that all like dear didst buy,
With love may one another entertain!
    So let us love, dear Lord, like as we ought.
    – Love is the lesson which the Lord us taught.

Edmund Spenser

Almighty God, which dost make the minds of all faithful men to be of one will: grant unto thy people, that they may love the thing, which thou commandest, and desire that which thou dost promise, that among the sundry and manifold changes of the world, our hearts may surely there be fixed, whereas true joys are to be found: through Jesus Christ our Lord.

Book of Common Prayer, 1549, Collect for the fourth Sunday
after Easter

Lord, from whom all good things do come; grant us thy humble servants, that by thy holy inspiration we may think those things that be good, and by thy merciful guiding may perform the same: through our Lord Jesus Christ.

Book of Common Prayer, 1549, Collect for the fifth Sunday after Easter

Ascension

Grant, we beseech thee, Almighty God, that like as we do believe thy only-begotten Son our Lord Jesus Christ to have ascended into the heavens; so we may also in heart and mind thither ascend, and with him continually dwell, who liveth and reigneth with thee and the Holy Ghost, one God, world without end. Amen. Book of Common Prayer, Ascension Day

Almighty and merciful God, into whose gracious presence we ascend, not by the frailty of the flesh but by the activity of the soul: Make us always by your inspiration to seek after the courts of the heavenly city, where our Saviour Christ has ascended, and by your mercy confidently to enter them, both now and hereafter; through the same Jesus Christ our Lord. Leonine Sacramentary

O Christ, the King of Glory, who through the everlasting gates didst ascend to thy Father's throne, and open the kingdom of heaven to all believers: Grant that, while you reign in heaven, we may not be bowed down to the things of earth, but that our hearts may be lifted up where you, our redemption, have gone ahead; who with the Father and the Holy Spirit lives and reigns, ever one God, world without end.

Mozarabic Sacramentary

The coming of the Holy Spirit

A temple of the Spirit's dwelling

Grant, we beseech thee, almighty and merciful God, that the Holy Ghost may come upon us, and by his gracious in-dwelling, may make us a temple of his glory; through Jesus Christ our Lord. Amen.

Treasury of Devotion

Almighty God, eternal Father of our Lord Jesus Christ, creator of heaven and earth and mankind, one with your Son and the Holy Spirit, have mercy on us. Justify us through your Son, Jesus Christ, and sanctify us with your Holy Spirit. Establish, guard and guide your church, O God.

Philipp Melanchthon

Send thy Holy Ghost

O Lord, who hast taught us that all our doings without love are nothing worth; send thy Holy Ghost, and pour into our hearts that most excellent gift of love, the very bond of peace and all virtues, without which whosoever liveth is counted dead before thee; grant us this for thy Son Jesus Christ's sake.   *Book of Common Prayer, 1549, Thomas Cranmer*

Trinity

Praise be to thee, O God the Father, who didst create all things by thy
    power and wisdom, and didst so love the world as to give thy
    Son to be our Saviour.
Praise be to thee, O God the Son, who wast made man like unto us in
    all things, sin except, and wast delivered for our offences and
    raised again for our justification.
Praise be to thee, O God the Holy Spirit, who dost lead us into all
    truth, and dost shed abroad the love of God in our hearts.
All praise and glory be to thee, O God, Father, Son, and Holy Spirit, for
    ever and ever.   *Author unknown*

God the Father bless me, Christ guard me, the Holy Spirit enlighten
　　　me, all the days of my life! The Lord be the defender and
　　　guardian of my soul and my body, now and always, world
　　　without end. Amen.
The right hand of the Lord preserve me always to old age!
The grace of Christ perpetually defend me from the enemy!
Direct, Lord, my heart into the way of peace.
Lord God, deliver and help me.　　　　　　　　　　　*Book of Cerne*

Almighty and everlasting God, who hast given unto us thy servants
grace, by the confession of a true faith to acknowledge the glory of
the eternal Trinity, and in the power of thy Divine Majesty to worship
the Unity; We beseech thee, that thou wouldst keep us steadfast in this
faith, and evermore defend us from all adversities, who livest and
reignest, one God, world without end. Amen.

Book of Common Prayer, collect for Trinity Sunday

May God the Father bless you, who created all things in the beginning.
　　　Amen.
May the Son bless you, who for our salvation came down from his
　　　throne on high. Amen.
May the Holy Spirit bless you, who rested as a dove on the Christ in
　　　Jordan. Amen.
May he sanctify you in the Trinity and unity whose coming to judg-
　　　ment all nations look for. Amen.
Which may he deign to grant, the Father, the Son, and the Holy Spirit,
　　　one God, world without end. Amen.　　　Gallican Sacramentary

A Litany
    Father of Heaven, and Him, by whom
It, and us for it, and all else for us
    Thou mad'st, and govern'st ever, come
And re-create me, now grown ruinous:
        My heart is by dejection, clay,
        And by self-murder, red.
From this red earth, O Father, purge away
All vicious tinctures, that new fashionèd
I may rise up from death, before I'm dead.

    The Son
    O Son of God, who seeing two things,
Sin and death, crept in, which were never made,
    By bearing one, tried'st with what stings
The other could Thine heritage invade;
        O be Thou nail'd unto my heart,
        And crucified again.
Part not from it, though it from Thee would part,
But let it be, by applying so Thy pain,
Drown'd in Thy blood, and in Thy passion slain.

    The Holy Ghost
    O Holy Ghost, whose temple I
Am, but of mud walls, and condensèd dust,
    And being sacrilegiously
Half wasted with youth's fires, of pride and lust,
        Must with new storms be weather-beat;
        Double in my heart Thy flame,
Which let devout sad tears intend; and let
(Though this glass lanthorn, flesh, do suffer main)
Fire, Sacrifice, Priest, Altar be the same.

John Donne, from *A Litanie*

Chapter Fourteen

SHORT PRAYERS

Grace be with you.

2 Timothy 4:22

A short prayer finds its way to heaven.

William Langland

Glory to God for all things.

Chrysostom

Pray God, keep us simple.

W.M. Thackeray

Teach us to pray often, that we may pray oftener.

Jeremy Taylor

O God, give me strength.

Gladys Aylward

Teach me to pray. Pray yourself in me.

Fénelon

Lord, make me see your glory in every place.

Michelangelo

Protect me, dear Lord;
My boat is so small,
And your sea is so big.

Breton fisherman's prayer

O God, make us children of quietness and heirs of peace.

Clement of Alexandria

Lord, let your glory be my goal, your word my rule, and then your will
be done. Charles I

You have made us for yourself and our hearts are restless until they
find their rest in you. Augustine

O Lord, thou knowest how busy I must be this day. If I forget thee, do
not thou forget me.

General Lord Astley, before the battle of Edgehill

Lord, give me what you are requiring of me. Augustine

O Lord, never allow us to think we can stand by ourselves and not
need you, our greatest need. John Donne

Lord, make your will our will in all things. Charles Vaughan

Let this day, O Lord, add some knowledge or good deed to yesterday.
Lancelot Andrewes

O Lord, let us not live to be useless, for Christ's sake. John Wesley

Jesus, strengthen my desire to work and speak and think for you.
John Wesley

Let our chief goal, O God, be your glory, and to enjoy you for ever.
John Calvin

I ask not to see; I ask not to know; I ask only to be used. J.H. Newman

Lord, make me according to your heart.   Brother Lawrence

Lord Jesus Christ, Son of God, have mercy on me, a sinner.
>   The *Jesus Prayer*. The Eastern Orthodox Church teaches that this prayer is to
>   be said many times regularly during the day.

O God, help us not to despise or oppose what we do not understand.
                                                    William Penn

Lord, give us faith that right makes might.   Abraham Lincoln

My God and My All!   The Meditation Prayer of St Francis of Assisi

The things, good Lord, that we pray for, give us the grace to labour for.
                                                    Thomas More

--------------- ✦ ---------------

Short Bible prayers

Speak, for your servant is listening.   1 Samuel 3:10 NRSV

Let the words of my mouth and the meditation of my heart be
acceptable to you, O Lord, my rock and my redeemer.
                                                    Psalm 19:14 NRSV

Wait for the Lord;
>
> be strong, and let your heart take courage,
> wait for the Lord!   Psalm 27:14 NRSV

O send out your light and your truth;
>
> let them lead me;

let them bring me to your holy hill
>
> and to your dwelling.   Psalm 43:3 NRSV

O God, you know my folly;
>
> the wrongs I have done are not hidden from you.

Psalm 69:5 NRSV

Be pleased, O God, to deliver me.
>
> O Lord, make haste to help me!   Psalm 70:1 NRSV

Will you not revive us again,
>
> so that your people may rejoice in you?   Psalm 85:6 NRSV

Bless the Lord, O my soul,
>
> and all that is within me,
> bless his holy name.   Psalm 103:1 NRSV

Lord save me!   Matthew 14:30

Lord, help me.   Matthew 15:25

I believe, help my unbelief!   Mark 9:24

Here am I, the servant of the Lord; let it be with me according to your
word.   Luke 1:38 NRSV

God, be merciful to me, a sinner!   Luke 18:13

Jesus, remember me when you come into your kingdom.   Luke 23:42

My Lord and my God!   John 20:28

Come, Lord Jesus!   Revelation 22:20

The grace of the Lord Jesus be with all the saints. Amen.
                                                  Revelation 22:21 NRSV

✝

Short reflections and arrow prayers

Have some arrow prayers to pray during the day, or a psalm.

A good watchmaker is one who makes watches and prays: a good
housemaid is one who sweeps and prays.
Prayer may be equally with words or without: it may be 'Jesu, my
God and my all.'   E.B. Pusey

Remember your mercies, Lord.

Be gracious to me, O God.

In you I hope all day long.

In your love remember me.

In you I place all my trust.

Awake, O my soul, awake!

God is worthy of our praise.

Create a clean heart in me.

Have mercy on me, O God.

Holy is the Lamb of God.

Jesus is the Lamb of God.

Glory to the Lamb of God.

Holy, holy, holy Lord.

My cup is overflowing.

Joy cometh in the morning.

I have been given mercy.

Taste and see that the Lord is good.

You are my strength and my song.

I will never forget you.

His eye is on the sparrow.

The Lord keeps the little ones.

How good is the Lord to all.

Fill me with joy and gladness.

Let the healing waters flow.

Oh, that we might know the Lord!

I have grasped you by the hand.

His love is everlasting.

I have called you by your name.

My peace is my gift to you.

Let go and let God.

Chapter Fifteen

BIBLE PRAYERS

Pray in the Holy Spirit.

Jude 20 NRSV

To pray in the Spirit is the inward principle of prayer. It comprehends both the spirit of the person praying, and the Spirit of God by which our spirits are fitted for, and acted in, prayer.

William Gurnall

✤

Old Testament prayers

I will sing to the Lord, for he has triumphed gloriously;
    horse and rider he has thrown into the sea.
The Lord is my strength and my might,
    and he has become my salvation;
this is my God, and I will exalt him...
Who is like you, O Lord, among the gods?
Who is like you, majestic in holiness,
awesome in splendour, doing wonders?

Moses, Exodus 15:1–2, 11 NRSV

Blessed are you, O Lord, the God of our ancestor Israel, for ever and
      ever.
Yours, O Lord, are the greatness, the power, the glory, the victory, and
      the majesty;
for all that is in the heavens and on the earth is yours;
yours is the kingdom, O Lord, and you are exalted as head above all.

David, 1 Chronicles 29:10–11 NRSV

My heart exults in the Lord;
  my strength is exalted in my God.
My mouth derides my enemies,
  because I rejoice in my victory.
There is no Holy One like the Lord;
  no one besides you;
  there is no Rock like our God.
... The barren has borne seven,
  but she who has many children is forlorn.
... The Lord will judge the ends of the earth;
  he will give strength to his king,
  and exalt the power of his anointed.

                    Hannah's prayer, 1 Samuel 2:1–2, 5, 10 NRSV

You are great, O Lord God; for there is no one like you, and there is no
      God besides you, according to all that we have heard with our
      ears.   David's prayer, 2 Samuel 7:22

The Lord is my rock, my fortress, and my deliverer,
  my God, my rock, in whom I take refuge,
my shield and the horn of my salvation,
  my stronghold and my refuge,
  my saviour; you save me from violence.

                              David, 2 Samuel 22:1 NRSV

The spirit of the Lord speaks through me,
  his word is upon my tongue.
The God of Israel has spoken,
  the Rock of Israel has said to me:
One who rules over people justly,
  ruling in the fear of God,
is like the light of morning,
  like the sun rising on a cloudless morning,
gleaming from the rain on the grassy land.

                            David, 2 Samuel 23:2–4 NRSV

But will God indeed dwell on the earth? Even heaven and the highest heaven cannot contain you, much less this house that I have built! Have regard to your servant's prayer and his plea, O Lord my God, heading the cry and the prayer that your servant prays to you today; that your eyes may be open night and day towards this house, the place of which you said, 'My name shall be there', that you may heed the prayer that your servant prays towards this place. Hear the plea of your servant and of your people Israel when they pray towards this place; O hear in heaven your dwelling-place; heed and forgive.

Solomon, at the dedication of the temple, 1 Kings 8:27–30 NRSV

Prayers from the Psalms

You show me the path of life.
In your presence there is fullness of joy;
in your right hand are pleasures for evermore.   Psalm 16:11 NRSV

I love you, O Lord, my strength.   Psalm 18:1 NRSV

The Lord is my shepherd, I shall not want.
He makes me lie down in green pastures;
he leads me beside still waters;
he restores my soul.
He leads me in right paths
for his name's sake.

Even though I walk through the darkest valley,
I fear no evil;
for you are with me;
your rod and your staff –
they comfort me.

You prepare a table before me
in the presence of my enemies;
you anoint my head with oil;
my cup overflows.

Surely goodness and mercy shall follow me
    all the days of my life,
and I shall dwell in the house of the Lord
    my whole life long.   Psalm 23 NRSV

To you, O Lord, I lift up my soul.
... Make me to know your ways, O Lord;
    teach me your paths.
Lead me in your truth, and teach me,
    for you are the God of my salvation;
    for you I wait all day long.
Be mindful of your mercy, O Lord, and of your steadfast love,
    for they have been from of old.   Psalm 25:1–6 NRSV

The Lord is my light and my salvation;
    whom shall I fear?
The Lord is the stronghold of my life;
    of whom shall I be afraid?
... I believe that I shall see the goodness of the Lord
    in the land of the living.
Wait for the Lord;
    be strong, and let your heart take courage;
    wait for the Lord!   Psalm 27:1, 13–14 NRSV

For with you is the fountain of life;
    in your light we see light.   Psalm 36:9 NRSV

Why are you cast down, O my soul,
    and why are you disquieted within me?
Hope in God; for I shall again praise him,
    my help and my God.

                           Psalm 42:11 NRSV

Be still and know that I am God. Psalm 46:10 NRSV

Be merciful to me, O God, be merciful to me,
    for in you my soul takes refuge;
in the shadow of your wings I will take refuge,
    until the destroying storms pass by. Psalm 57:1 NRSV

Hear my cry, O God;
    listen to my prayer.
From the end of the earth I call to you,
    when my heart is faint.

Lead me to the rock
    that is higher than I;
for you are my refuge,
    a strong tower against the enemy. Psalm 61:1–3 NRSV

O God, you are my God, I seek you,
    my soul thirsts for you;
my flesh faints for you,
    as in a dry and weary land where there is no water.
Psalm 63:1 NRSV

God be merciful unto us, and bless us : and shew us the light of his
    countenance, and be merciful unto us;
That thy way may be known upon earth : thy saving health among all
    nations.
Let the peoples praise thee, O God : yea, let all the peoples praise thee.
O let the nations rejoice and be glad : for thou shalt judge the folk
    righteously, and govern the nations upon earth.
Let the people praise thee, O God : yea, let all the people praise thee.
Then shall the earth bring forth her increase : and God, even our own
    God, shall give us his blessing.
God shall bless us : and all the ends of the world shall fear him.
Deus misereatur, Psalm 67, Book of Common Prayer

How lovely is your dwelling-place,
　　O Lord of hosts!
My soul longs, indeed it faints
　　for the courts of the Lord;
my heart and my flesh sing for joy
　　to the living God.

Even the sparrow finds a home,
　　and the swallow a nest for herself,
　　where she may lay her young,
at your altars, O Lord of hosts,
　　my King and my God.
Happy are those who love in your house,
　　ever singing your praise.

Happy are those whose strength is in you,
　　in whose heart are the highways of Zion.
As they go through the valley of Baca
　　they make it a place of springs;
　　the early rain also covers it with pools.
They go from strength to strength;
　　the God of gods will be seen in Zion.　　　　　Psalm 84:1–7 NRSV

O sing unto the Lord a new song : for he hath done marvellous things.
With his own right hand, and with his holy arm : hath he gotten
　　　　himself the victory.
The Lord declared his salvation : his righteousness hath he openly
　　　　showed in the sight of the heathen.
He hath remembered his mercy and truth toward the house of Israel :
　　　　and all the ends of the world have seen the salvation of our
　　　　God.
Show yourselves joyful unto the Lord, all ye lands : sing, rejoice, and
　　　　give thanks.
Praise the Lord upon the harp : sing to the harp with a psalm of
　　　　thanksgiving.
With trumpets also and shawms : O shew yourselves joyful before the
　　　　Lord the King.

Let the sea make a noise, and all that therein is : the round world, and
      that dwell therein.
Let the floods clap their hands, and let the hills be joyful together
      before the Lord : for he cometh to judge the earth.
With righteousness shall he judge the world : and the peoples with
      equity.   Cantate Domino, Psalm 98, Book of Common Prayer

O come, let us sing unto the Lord : let us heartily rejoice in the
      strength of our salvation.
Let us come before his presence with thanksgiving : and show
      ourselves glad in him with Psalms.
For the Lord is a great God : and a great King above all gods.
In his hand are all the corners of the earth : and the strength of the
      hills is his also.
The sea is his, and he made it : and his hands prepared the dry land.
O come, let us worship and fall down : and kneel before the Lord our
      Maker.
For he is the Lord our God : and we are the people of his pasture, and
      the sheep of his hand.
To day if ye will hear his voice, harden not your hearts : as in the
      provocation, and as in the day of temptation in the
      wilderness;
When your fathers tempted me : proved me, and saw my works.
Forty years long was I grieved with this generation, and said : It is a
      people that do err in their heart, and they have not known my
      ways.
Unto whom I sware in my wrath that they should not enter into my
      rest.
Glory be to the Father, and to the Son : and to the Holy Ghost;
As it was in the beginning, is now, and ever shall be : world without
      end. Amen.   Psalm 95, Book of Common Prayer

O be joyful in the Lord, all ye lands : serve the Lord with gladness, and
      come before his presence with a song.
Be ye sure that the Lord he is God; it is he that hath made us, and not
      we ourselves : we are his people, and the sheep of his pasture.

O go your way into his gates with thanksgiving, and into his courts
       with praise : be thankful unto him, and speak good of his
       Name.
For the Lord is gracious, his mercy is everlasting : and his truth
       endureth from generation to generation.

       Jubilate Deo, Psalm 100, Book of Common Prayer

Though the fig tree does not blossom,
    and no fruit is on the vines;
though the produce of the olive fails
    and the fields yield no food;
though the flock is cut off from the fold
    and there is no herd in the stalls,
yet I will rejoice in the Lord;
    I will exult in the God of my salvation.   Habakkuk 3:17–18 NRSV

Incline your ear, O my God, and hear. Open your eyes and look at our
desolation and the city that bears your name. We do not present our
supplication before you on the ground of your great mercies. O Lord,
hear; O Lord, forgive; O Lord, listen and act and do not delay! For your
own sake, O my God, because your city and your people bear your
name!   Daniel 9:18–19 NRSV

———— ✟ ————

New Testament prayers

Glory to God in the highest heaven,
    and on earth peace among those whom he favours!

    Luke 2:14 NRSV

Prayers of Jesus

Our Father in heaven,
    hallowed be your name.
    Your kingdom come.
    Your will be done,
        on earth as it is in heaven.

Give us this day our daily bread.
And forgive us our debts,
    as we also have forgiven our debtors.
And do not bring us to the time of trial,
    but rescue us from the evil one.   Matthew 6:9–13 NRSV

My soul doth magnify the Lord : and my spirit hath rejoiced in God
    my Saviour.
For he hath regarded : the lowliness of his handmaiden.
For behold, from henceforth : all generations shall call me blessed.
For he that is mighty hath magnified me : and holy is his Name.
And his mercy is on them that fear him : throughout all generations.
He hath showed strength with his arm : he hath scattered the proud in
    the imagination of their hearts.
He hath put down the mighty from their seat : and hath exalted the
    humble and meek.
He hath filled the hungry with good things : and the rich he hath sent
    empty away.
He remembering his mercy hath holpen his servant Israel : as he
    promised to our forefathers, Abraham and his seed, for ever.
                    Magnificat, Luke 1:46–55, Book of Common Prayer

Blessed the Lord God of Israel : for he hath visited and redeemed his
    people;
And hath raised up a mighty salvation for us : in the house of his ser-
    vant David;
As he spake by the mouth of his holy Prophets : which have been since
    the world began;
That we should be saved from our enemies : and from the hand of all
    that hate us.
To perform the mercy promised to our forefathers : and to remember
    his holy Covenant;
To perform the oath which he sware to our forefather Abraham : that
    he would give us;
That we being delivered out of the hand of our enemies : might serve
    him without fear;
In holiness and righteousness before him : all the days of our life.

And thou, Child, shalt be called the Prophet of the Highest : for thou
        shalt go before the face of the Lord to prepare his ways;
To give knowledge of salvation unto his people : for the remission of
        their sins,
Through the tender mercy of our God : whereby the day-spring from
        on high hath visited us;
To give light to them that sit in darkness, and in the shadow of death :
        and to guide our feet into the way of peace.
Glory be to the Father, and to the Son : and to the Holy Ghost;
As it was in the beginning, is now, and ever shall be : world without
        end. Amen.

Benedictus, Luke 1:68–79, The Book of Common Prayer

Lord, now lettest thou thy servant depart in peace : according to thy
        word.
For mine eyes have seen : thy salvation,
Which thou hast prepared : before the face of all people;
To be a light to lighten the Gentiles : and to be the glory of thy people
        Israel.   *Nunc dimittis, Luke 2:29–32, Book of Common Prayer*

I thank you, Father, Lord of heaven and earth, because you have hidden
these things from the wise and the intelligent and have revealed them to
infants; yes, Father, for such was your gracious will.   *Luke 10:21 NRSV*

Father, I thank you for having heard me. I knew that you always hear me,
but I have said this for the sake of the crowd standing here, so that they
may believe that you sent me.   *John 11:41–42 NRSV*

Father, if you are willing, remove this cup from me; yet, not my will but
yours be done.   *Luke 22:42 NRSV*

Father, glorify your name.   *John 12:28 NRSV*

Prayers of Jesus on the cross

Father, forgive them; for they know not what they do.   Luke 23:34 AV

My God, my God, why hast thou forsaken me?   Matthew 27:46 AV

It is finished.   John 19:30 AV

Father, into thy hands I commend my spirit.   Luke 23:46 AV

And now, Lord, look at their threats, and grant to your servants to speak your word with all boldness, while you stretch out your hand to heal, and signs and wonders are performed through the name of your holy servant Jesus.   Acts 4:29–30 NRSV

Lord Jesus, receive my spirit ... Lord, do not hold this sin against them.
Stephen, as he was being martyred. Acts 7:59–60 NRSV

Prayers of Paul

What am I to do, Lord?   Acts 22:10 NRSV

O the depth of the riches and wisdom and knowledge of God! How
        unsearchable are his judgements and how inscrutable his
        ways!
    'For who has known the mind of the Lord? Or who has been his
        counsellor?'
    'Or who has given a gift to him,
        to receive a gift in return?'
For from him and through him and to him are all things. To him be
        the glory for ever. Amen.   Romans 11:33–36 NRSV

May the God of hope fill you with all joy and peace in believing, so that you may abound in hope by the power of the Holy Spirit.

Romans 15:13 NRSV

Blessed be the God and Father of our Lord Jesus Christ, the Father of mercies and the God of all consolation, who consoles us in all our affliction, so that we may be able to console those who are in any affliction with the consolation with which we ourselves are consoled by God.

2 Corinthians 1:3–4 NRSV

The grace of the Lord Jesus Christ, the love of God, and the communion of the Holy Spirit be with all of you.   2 Corinthians 13:13 NRSV

Grace to you and peace from God our Father and the Lord Jesus Christ, who gave himself for our sins to set us free from the present evil age, according to the will of our God and Father, to whom be the glory for ever and ever. Amen.   Galatians 1:3–4 NRSV

Blessed be the God and Father of our Lord Jesus Christ, who has blessed us in Christ with every spiritual blessing in the heavenly places, just as he chose us in Christ before the foundation of the world to be holy and blameless before him in love.   Ephesians 1:3–4 NRSVs

Now may our God and Father himself and our Lord Jesus direct our way to you.   1 Thessalonians 3:11

May the God of peace himself sanctify you entirely; and may your spirit and soul and body be kept sound and blameless at the coming of our Lord Jesus Christ.   1 Thessalonians 5:23 NRSV

Now may our Lord Jesus Christ himself and God our Father, who loved us and through grace gave us eternal comfort and good hope, comfort your hearts and strengthen them in every good work and word.

2 Thessalonians 2:16–17 NRSV

Other New Testament prayers

Now may the God of peace, who brought back from the dead our Lord Jesus, the great shepherd of the sheep, by the blood of the eternal covenant, make you complete in everything good so that you may do his will, working among us that which is pleasing in his sight, through Jesus Christ, to whom be the glory for ever and ever. Amen.

Hebrews 13:20–21 NRSV

Blessed be the God and Father of our Lord Jesus Christ! By his great mercy we have been born anew to a living hope through the resurrection of Jesus Christ from the dead, and to an inheritance which is imperishable, undefiled, and unfading, kept in heaven for you, who by God's power are guarded through faith for a salvation ready to be revealed in the last time.

1 Peter 1:3–5 NRSV

Now to him who is able to keep you from falling, and to make you stand without blemish in the presence of his glory with rejoicing, to the only God our Saviour, through Jesus Christ our Lord, be glory, majesty, power, and authority, before all time and now and for ever. Amen.

Jude 24–25 NRSV

To him who loves us and freed us from our sins by his blood, and made us to be a kingdom, priests serving his God and Father, to him be glory and dominion for ever and ever. Amen.

Revelation 1:5–6 NRSV

You are worthy, our Lord and God,
> to receive glory and honour and power,
for you created all things,
> and by your will they existed and were created.

> > Revelation 4:11 NRSV

Amen! Blessing and glory and wisdom
and thanksgiving and honour
and power and might
be to our God for ever and ever! Amen.   Revelation 7:12 NRSV

Great and amazing are your deeds,
> Lord God the Almighty!
Just and true are your ways,
> King of the nations!
Lord, who will not fear
> and glorify your name?
For you alone are holy.
> All nations will come
> and worship before you.
for your judgements have been revealed.   Revelation 15:3–4 NRSV

Chapter Sixteen

BLESSINGS

*People were bringing little children to him [Jesus] in order that
he might touch them; and the disciples spoke to them. But when
Jesus saw this, he was indignant and said to them, 'Let the
children come to me; do not stop them; for it is to such as these
that the kingdom of God belongs. Truly I tell you, whoever does
not receive the kingdom of God as a little child will never enter
it.' And he took them up in his arms, laid his hands on them,
and blessed them.*

Mark 10:13–16 NRSV

*When we speak with God, our power of addressing him, of
holding communion with him, and listening to his still small
voice, depends on our will being one and the same with his.*

Florence Nightingale

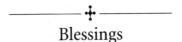

Blessings

May God the Father bless us, may Christ take care of us; the Holy Spirit
enlighten us all the days of our life. The Lord our defender and keeper of
body and soul, both now and for ever, to the ages of ages.   Aedelwald

The everlasting Father bless us with his blessing everlasting.

Primer, 1559

God bless all those that I love;
God bless all those that love me.
God bless all those that love those that I love
And all those that love those that love me.

From an old New England sampler

To the Holy Spirit who sanctifies us, with the Father who made and created us, and the Son who redeemed us, be given all honour and glory, world without end.

Thomas Cranmer

Bless all who worship thee,
From the rising of the sun
Unto the going down of the same.
Of thy goodness, give us;
With thy love, inspire us;
By thy spirit, guide us;
By thy power, protect us;
In thy mercy, receive us,
Now and always.

Fifth century

Unto God's gracious mercy and protection we commit you. The Lord bless you and keep you. The Lord make his face shine upon you, and be gracious to you. The Lord lift his countenance upon you, and give you peace.

Aaronic blessing, Numbers 6:24–26

May the grace of our Lord Jesus Christ,
and the love of God,
and the fellowship of the Holy Spirit,
be with you all.

2 Corinthians 13:13

Now may the God of peace who brought again from the dead our Lord Jesus, the great shepherd of the sheep, by the blood of the eternal covenant, equip you with everything good that you may do his will, working in you that which is pleasing in his sight, through Jesus Christ; to whom be glory for ever and ever. Amen.

Hebrews 13:20–21 RSV

May the grace of Christ our Saviour,
And the Father's boundless love,
With the Holy Spirit's favour,
Rest upon us from above.

John Newton

Son of God, Lord Jesus Christ, crucified on a cross for us and raised up from the grave, to you we pray. Receive us into your eternal church and keep us always. In the light of your Word, with your Holy Spirit, guide us.   Philipp Melanchthon

May God, the Lord, bless us with all heavenly benediction, and make
     us pure and holy in his sight.
May the riches of his glory abound in us.
May he instruct us with the word of truth, inform us with the gospel
     of salvation and enrich us with his love, through Jesus Christ,
     our Lord.   Gelasian Sacramentary

The grace of God the Father and the peace of our Lord Jesus Christ, through the fellowship of the Holy Spirit, dwell with us for ever.
                                                                                                                John Calvin

May the eternal God bless and keep us, guard our bodies, save our souls, direct our thoughts, and bring us safe to the heavenly country, our eternal home, where Father, Son and Holy Spirit ever reign, one God for ever and ever.   Sarum Missal

The almighty God, Father of our Lord and Saviour, Jesus Christ,
     mercifully protect you, strengthen you, and guide you.
                                                                                        Philipp Melanchthon

May the love of the Lord Jesus draw us to himself;
may the power of the Lord Jesus strengthen us in his service;
may the joy of the Lord Jesus fill our souls.
May the blessing of God almighty, the Father, the Son, and the Holy
     Spirit, be among you and remain with you always.
                                                                                    After William Temple

The great Bishop of our souls, Jesus our Lord, so strengthen and assist
       your troubled hearts with the mighty comfort of the Holy
       Spirit, that neither earthly tyrants, nor worldly torments, may
       have power to drive you from the hope and expectation of
       that kingdom, which for the elect was prepared from the
       beginning, by our heavenly Father, to whom be all praise and
       honour, now and ever.   John Knox

May the almighty God, Father of our Saviour Jesus Christ, who
       through his gospel is gathering an eternal church among men
       and women, strengthen you in body and soul, and graciously
       keep and guide you, world without end.   Philipp Melanchthon

May the Almighty Lord, who bore the reproach of the cross, bless all
       this family present here. Amen.
May he, who hung on the tree, himself lead us to the heavenly
       kingdom. Amen.
May he place us at the right hand of the Father, who was made the
       cause of our peace. Amen.
Through the mercy of our God, who is blessed and reigns, and governs
       all things, world without end.   Mozarabic Breviary

The blessing of the Lord rest and remain upon all his people,
in every land and of every tongue;
the Lord meet in mercy all who seek him;
the Lord comfort all who suffer and mourn;
the Lord hasten his coming,
and give us his people peace by all means.   H.C.G. Moule

The peace of God, which passeth all understanding, keep your hearts
and minds in the knowledge and love of God, and of his Son Jesus Christ
our Lord: and the blessing of God Almighty, the Father, the Son, and the
Holy Ghost, be amongst you and remain with you always.
              Book of Common Prayer, Order for Holy Communion

God the Father bless me;
Jesus Christ defend and keep me;
the power of the Holy Spirit enlighten me and sanctify me,
this night and for ever.

Treasury of Devotion

The mighty God of Jacob be with you to defeat his enemies, and give
you the favour of Joseph.

The wisdom and spirit of Stephen be with your heart and with your
mouth, and teach your lips what to say, and how to answer all
things.

He is our God, if we despair in ourselves and trust in him; and his is
the glory.
William Tyndale

The Lord bless you and keep you.
May he show his face to you and have mercy on you.
May he turn his countenance to you and give you peace.
The Lord bless you, Brother Leo.

Francis of Assisi, blessing to Brother Leo, which Brother Leo always
carried with him.

Blessing and honour, thanksgiving and praise
more than we can utter unto thee,
O most adorable Trinity, Father, Son and Holy Ghost,
by all angels, all men, all creatures
for ever and ever. Amen and Amen.
Thomas Ken

May the blessing of God Almighty, the Father, the Son, and the Holy
Spirit, rest on us and on all our work and worship done in his name.
May he give us light to guide us, courage to support us, and love to unite
us, now and for evermore.
Author unknown

Go in peace; and may the blessing of God the Father, the Son, and the Holy Spirit rest on you and remain with you, this day (*night*) and for evermore.   Author unknown

May the road rise to meet you,
may the wind be always at your back,
may the sun shine warm upon your face,
may the rain fall softly on your fields,
may God hold you in the hollow of his hand.   Traditional Gaelic prayer

May the love of the Father enfold us,
the wisdom of the Son enlighten us,
the fire of the Spirit inflame us;
and may the blessing of the triune God rest on us,
and abide with us,
now and evermore.   Author unknown

——————— ✠ ———————
Doxologies

To God the Father, who has made us and all the world;
to God the Son, who has redeemed us and all mankind;
to God the Holy Spirit, who sanctifies us and all the elect people of
          God;
to the one living and true God be all glory for ever and ever.
                                                        Author unknown

Bless us, O God the Father, who has created us.
Bless us, O God the Son, who has redeemed us.
Bless us, O God the Holy Spirit, who sanctifies us.
O Blessed Trinity, keep us in body, soul, and spirit to everlasting life.
                                                        Author unknown

To God the Father, who first loved us, and made us accepted in the
　　　　Beloved;
to God the Son, who loved us, and washed us from our sins in his own
　　　　blood;
to God the Holy Ghost, who sheds the love of God abroad in our hearts:
to the one true God be all love and all glory, for time and eternity.

Thomas Ken

Praise God, from whom all blessings flow;
Praise him, all creatures here below;
Praise him above ye heavenly host;
Praise Father, Son and Holy Ghost.　　　　　　Thomas Ken

Chapter Seventeen

PRAYERS OF THE FAMOUS

Lord, give us faith that right makes might.

Abraham Lincoln

Lord, make me see your glory in every place.

Michelangelo

O Lord my God, I have hope in thee;
O my dear Jesus, set me free.
Though hard the chains that fasten me
And sore my lot, yet I long for thee.
I languish and groaning bend my knee,
Adoring, imploring, O set me free.

Mary Queen of Scots, on the eve of her execution

Strengthen us, O God, to relieve the oppressed, to hear the groans of poor prisoners, to reform the abuses of all professions; that many be made not poor to make a few rich; for Jesus Christ's sake.

Oliver Cromwell

Go with each of us to rest; if any awake, temper them the dark hours of watching; and when the day returns, return to us, our sun and comforter, and call us up with morning faces and with morning hearts, eager to labour, eager to be happy, if happiness should be our portion, and if the day be marked for sorrow, strong to endure it.

R.L. Stevenson, written on the eve of his unexpected death

Make me remember, O God, that every day is Thy gift and ought to be used according to Thy command, through Jesus Christ our Lord.

Samuel Johnson

O Lord God, grant us always, whatever the world may say, to content ourselves with what you say, and to care only for your approval, which will outweigh all worlds; for Jesus Christ's sake.

General Charles Gordon

O Lord God, when Thou givest to Thy servants to endeavour any great matter, grant us also to know that it is not the beginning, but the continuing of the same to the end, until it be thoroughly finished, which yieldeth the true glory; through Him who for the finishing of Thy work laid down His life, our Redeemer, Jesus Christ.

Source unknown, based on a saying of Sir Francis Drake

Take from us, O God, all pride and vanity, all boasting and self-assertiveness, and give us the true courage that shows itself by gentleness; the true wisdom that shows itself by simplicity; and the true power that shows itself by modesty; through Jesus Christ our Lord.

Charles Kingsley

Grant, O Lord, that we may keep a constant guard on our thoughts and passions, that they may never lead us into sin; that we may live in perfect love with all humankind, in affection to those who love us, and in forgiveness to those, if any there are, who hate us. Give us good and virtuous friends. In the name of our blessed Lord and Saviour Jesus Christ.

Warren Hastings

O my sweet Saviour Christ, who in your undeserved love towards humankind so kindly suffered the painful death of the cross, do not allow me to be cold or lukewarm in love again towards you.

Thomas More

O Saviour, pour upon me thy Spirit of meekness and love,
annihilate the selfhood in me, be thou all my life.   William Blake

O merciful God, fill our hearts, we pray, with the graces of your Holy
       Spirit; with love, joy, peace, patience, gentleness, goodness,
       faithfulness, humility and self-control.
O Lord, in confidence of your great mercy and goodness to all who
       truly repent and resolve to do better, I most humbly implore
       the grace and assistance of the Holy Spirit to enable me to
       become every day better.
Grant me the wisdom and understanding to know my duty, and the
       heart and will to do it.
Endue me, O Lord, with the true fear and love of you, and with a
       prudent zeal for your glory.
Increase in me the graces of charity and meekness, of truth and justice,
       of humility and patience, and a firmness of spirit to bear
       every condition with constancy of mind.   King William III

I beseech Thee, good Jesus, that as Thou hast graciously granted to me
here on earth sweetly to partake of the words of Thy wisdom and knowledge, so Thou wilt vouchsafe that I may some time come to Thee, the
fountain of all wisdom, and always appear before Thy face; who livest
and reignest, world without end.   Bede

Merciful God, be thou now unto me a strong tower of defence. Give me
grace to await thy leisure, and patiently to bear what you doest unto me,
nothing doubting or mistrusting thy goodness towards me. Therefore
do with me in all things as thou wilt: Only arm me, I beseech thee, with
thy armour, that I may stand fast; above all things taking to me the shield
of faith, praying always that I may refer myself wholly to thy will, being
assuredly persuaded that all thou doest cannot but be well. And unto
thee be all honour and glory.   Lady Jane Grey, before her execution

The Passionate Man's Pilgrimage
Give me my scallop-shell of quiet,
My staff of faith to walk upon,
My scrip of joy, immortal diet,
My bottle of salvation,
My gown of glory, hope's true gage;
And thus I'll take my pilgrimage.

Blood must be my body's balmer;
No other balm will there be given;
Whilst my soul, like quiet palmer,
Travelleth towards the land of heaven;
    Over the silver mountains,
    Where spring the nectar fountains:
    There will I kiss
    The bowl of bliss,
And drink mine everlasting fill
Upon every milken hill.
My soul will be a-dry before;
But, after, it will thirst no more.

From thence to heaven's Bribeless hall
Where no corrupted voices brawl,
No Conscience molten into gold,
Nor forged accusers bought and sold,
No cause deferred, nor vain spent journey,
For there Christ is the King's Attorney:
Who pleads for all without degrees,
And he hath Angels, but no fees.

When the grand twelve million Jury,
Of our sins with dreadful fury,
'Gainst our souls black verdicts give,
Christ pleads his death, and then we live,
Be thou my speaker, taintless pleader,
Unblotted Lawyer, true proceeder,
Thou movest salvation even for alms:
Not with a bribed Lawyer's palms.

And this is my eternal plea,
To him that made Heaven, Earth and Sea,
Seeing my flesh must die so soon,
And want a head to dine next noon,
Just at the stroke when my veins start and spread
Set on my soul an everlasting head.
Then am I ready like a palmer fit,
To tread those blest paths which before I writ.

> Sir Walter Raleigh, written when he was a prisoner in the Tower of London, awaiting execution. The scallop-shell was a symbol of pilgrimage in the Middle Ages.

Almighty God, the Protector of all who trust in you, without whose grace nothing is strong, nothing is holy, increase and multiply on us your mercy, that through your holy inspiration we may think the things that are right and by your power may carry them out, through Jesus Christ our Lord.

Martin Luther

Almighty and most merciful Father, look down on us your unworthy servants through the mediation and merits of Jesus Christ, in whom only are you well pleased. Purify our hearts by your Holy Spirit, and as you add days to our lives, so good Lord, add repentance to our days; that when we have passed this mortal life we may be partakers of your everlasting kingdom; through the merits of Jesus Christ our Lord.

King Charles I

Lord God Almighty, shaper and ruler of all creatures, we pray that by your great mercy and by the token of the holy cross you will guide us to your will. Make our minds steadfast, strengthen us against temptation, and keep us from all unrighteousness. Shield us against our enemies, seen and unseen. Teach us to inwardly love you before all things with a clean mind and a clean body. For you are our Maker and Redeemer, our help and comfort, our trust and hope, for ever.

King Alfred the Great

O Lord Jesus Christ, you have made me and redeemed me and brought me to where I now am: you know what you wish to do with me; do with me according to your will, for your tender mercies' sake.

King Henry VI

Our Father, here I am, at your disposal, your child,
to use me to continue your loving the world,
by giving Jesus to me and through me,
to each other and to the world.
Let us pray for each other that we allow Jesus to love in us
and through us with the love with which his Father loves us.

Mother Teresa

Jesus, your light is shining within us,
let not my doubts and my darkness speak to me;
Jesus, your light is shining within us,
let my heart always welcome your love.

Brother Roger

Teach me, my Lord Jesus, instruct me, that I may learn from you what I ought to teach about you.

William Laud

O Lord, I am yours. Do what seems good in your sight,
and give me complete resignation to your will.

David Livingstone

In my Redeemer's name,
I give myself to thee;
And, all unworthy as I am,
My God will cherish me.

Anne Brontë

Give us grace, almighty Father, to address you with all our hearts as well as with our lips.
You are present everywhere: from you no secrets can be hidden.
Teach us to fix our thoughts on you, reverently and with love, so that
our prayers are not in vain, but are acceptable to you, now
and always, through Jesus Christ our Lord.   Jane Austen

O almighty God, the searcher of all hearts, who has declared that who draw near to you with their lips when their hearts are far from you are an abomination to you: cleanse, we beseech you, the thoughts of our hearts by the inspiration of your Holy Spirit, that no wandering, vain, or idle thoughts may put out of our minds that reverence and godly fear that becomes all those who come into your presence.   Jonathan Swift

───── ✟ *Chapter Eighteen* ✟ ─────

FAMOUS PRAYERS

The peace of God, which passeth all understanding, keep your hearts and minds in the knowledge and love of God, and of his Son Jesus Christ our Lord: and the blessing of God Almighty, the Father, the Son, and the Holy Ghost, be amongst you and remain with you always.

Book of Common Prayer, Order for Holy Communion

The grace of the Lord Jesus Christ, the love of God, and the communion of the Holy Spirit be with all of you. 2 Corinthians 13:13 NRSV

Father, if you are willing, remove this cup from me; yet, not my will but yours be done. Luke 22:42 NRSV

My soul doth magnify the Lord : and my spirit hath rejoiced in God
    my Saviour.
For he hath regarded : the lowliness of his handmaiden.
For behold, from henceforth : all generations shall call me blessed.
For he that is mighty hath magnified me : and holy is his Name.
And his mercy is on them that fear him : throughout all generations.
He hath showed strength with his arm : he hath scattered the proud in
    the imagination of their hearts.
He hath put down the mighty from their seat : and hath exalted the
    humble and meek.
He hath filled the hungry with good things : and the rich he hath sent
    empty away.
He remembering his mercy hath holpen his servant Israel : as he
    promised to our forefathers, Abraham and his seed, for ever.

Magnificat, Luke 1:46-55, Book of Common Prayer

The Lord is my shepherd, I shall not want.
    He makes me lie down in green pastures;
he leads me beside still waters;
    he restores my soul.
He leads me in right paths
    for his name's sake.

Even though I walk through the darkest valley,
    I fear no evil;
for you are with me;
    your rod and your staff –
    they comfort me.

You prepare a table before me
    in the presence of my enemies;
you anoint my head with oil;
    my cup overflows.

Surely goodness and mercy shall follow me
    all the days of my life,
and I shall dwell in the house of the Lord
    my whole life long.
                                  Psalm 23 NRSV

Lord Jesus Christ, Son of God, have mercy on me, a sinner.

                                  The *Jesus Prayer*

Easter Wings
Lord, who createdst man in wealth and store,
    Though foolishly he lost the same,
        Decaying more and more,
           Till he became
             Most poor:

             With thee
           O let me rise
        As larks, harmoniously,
      And sing this day thy victories:
Then shall the fall farther the flight in me.

My tender age in sorrow did begin:
   And still with sickness and shame
      Thou did'st so punish sin,
        That I became
         Most thin

        With thee
      Let me combine,
    And feel this day the victory,
  For, if I imp my wing on thine,
Affliction shall advance the flight in me.   George Herbert, *The Temple*

Lord, make me an instrument of your peace.
Where there is hatred, let me sow love,
where there is injury, pardon,
where there is doubt, faith,
where there is despair, hope,
where there is darkness, light,
where there is sadness, joy.

O Divine Master, grant that we may not so much seek
to be consoled as to console,
not so much to be understood as to understand,
not so much to be loved as to love.
For it is in giving that we receive,
it is in pardoning that we are pardoned,
it is in dying that we are born to eternal life.

                    Attributed to St Francis of Assisi

We beg you, Lord, to help and defend us.
Deliver the oppressed,
have compassion on the despised,
raise the fallen,
reveal yourself to the needy,
heal the sick,
bring back those who have strayed from you,
feed the hungry,

lift up the weak,
remove the prisoners' chains.
May every nation come to know that you are God alone,
that Jesus is your Son,
that we are your people, the sheep of your pasture.   Clement of Rome

O Lord, convert the world – and begin with me.

Chinese student's prayer

Be present, O merciful God, and protect us through the silent hours of
this night, so that we who are wearied by the changes and chances of this
fleeting world, may repose on your eternal changelessness; through Jesus
Christ our Lord.   Office of Compline, Roman Breviary

Save us, Lord, while waking, and guard us while sleeping, that awake we
may watch with Christ, and asleep we may rest in peace.

Office of Compline, Roman Breviary

O God, from whom all holy desires, all good counsels, and all just works
do proceed: Give unto thy servants that peace which the world cannot
give; that both our hearts may be set to obey thy commandments, and
also that by thee we, being defended from the fear of our enemies, may
pass our time in rest and quietness; through the merits of Jesu Christ
our Saviour.   Book of Common Prayer, 1549, Evensong, Second Collect

My dearest Lord,
be thou a bright flame before me,
be thou a guiding star above me,
be thou a smooth path beneath me,
be thou a kindly shepherd behind me,
today – tonight – and forever.   Columba

O Lord, support us all the day long, until the shadows lengthen, and the evening comes, and the busy world is hushed, and the fever of life is over, and our work is done. Then, Lord, in your mercy grant us a safe lodging, and a holy rest, and peace at the last; through Jesus Christ our Lord.

Used by J.H. Newman, based on a sixteenth-century prayer

O Lord, forgive what I have been, sanctify what I am, and order what I shall be.   *Author unknown*

Our Father,
which art in heaven,
Hallowed be thy Name.
Thy kingdom come.
Thy will be done in earth,
As it is in heaven.
Give us this day our daily bread.
And forgive us our trespasses,
As we forgive them that trespass against us.
And lead us not into temptation,
But deliver us from evil.
For thine is the kingdom,
The power, and the glory,
For ever and ever. Amen.   *Book of Common Prayer*

Grant to us your servants: to our God – a heart of flame; to our fellow men – a heart of love; to ourselves – a heart of steel.   *Augustine*

God, give us the serenity to accept what cannot be changed;
give us the courage to change what should be changed;
give us the wisdom to distinguish one from the other.

Attributed to Reinhold Niebuhr, also known as 'The Serenity Prayer'

Let nothing disturb you
nothing frighten you,
all things are passing;
patient endurance
attains all things.
One whom God possesses
lacks nothing,
for God alone suffices.   Teresa of Avila

I asked God for strength, that I might achieve,
I was made weak, that I might learn humbly to obey.
I asked for health, that I might do greater things,
I was given infirmity, that I might do better things.
I asked for riches, that I might be happy,
I was given poverty, that I might be wise.
I asked for power, that I might have the praise of men,
I was given weakness, that I might feel the need of God.
I asked for all things, that I might enjoy life,
I was given life, that I might enjoy all things.
I got nothing that I asked for
but everything that I had hoped for,
almost despite myself, my unspoken prayers were answered.
I am among all men most richly blessed.
'A Soldier's Prayer', written by an anonymous confederate soldier in the US civil war

Dearest Lord, teach me to be generous;
teach me to serve you as you deserve;
to give and not to count the cost,
to fight and not to heed the wounds,
to toil and not to see for rest,
to labour and not to seek reward,
except to know that I do your will.   Ignatius Loyola

Almighty God, in whom we live and move and have our being, you have made us for yourself and our hearts are restless until they find their rest in you. Grant us purity of heart and strength of purpose, that no selfish passion may hinder us from knowing your will, no weakness from doing it; but that in your light we may see light clearly, and in your service we may find our perfect freedom; through Jesus Christ our Lord.

Augustine

Grant me, I beseech thee, almighty and merciful God, fervently to desire, wisely to search out, truly to acknowledge, and perfectly to fulfil, all that is well-pleasing to thee. Order thou my worldly condition to the honour and glory of thy name; and of all that thou requirest me to do, grant me the knowledge, the desire, and the ability, that I may so fulfil it as I ought, and as is expedient for the welfare of my soul. *Thomas Aquinas*

O Lord, thou knowest how busy I must be this day. If I forget thee, do not thou forget me. *General Lord Astley, before the battle of Edgehill*

Thanks be to you, my Lord Jesus Christ,
for all the benefits you have won for me.
For all the pains and insults you have borne for me.
O most merciful Redeemer, Friend, and Brother,
may I know you more clearly,
love you more dearly,
and follow you more nearly,
day by day. *Richard of Chichester*

Father,
give us wisdom to perceive you,
intellect to understand you,
diligence to seek you,
patience to wait for you,
eyes to behold you,
a heart to meditate on you

and a life to proclaim you,
through the power of the Spirit
of our Lord Jesus Christ.   Benedict

O Lord, remember not only the men and women of good will, but also those of ill will. But do not remember all the suffering they have inflicted on us; remember the fruits we have brought, thanks to this suffering – our comradeship, our loyalty, our courage, our generosity, the greatness of heart which has grown out of all this, and when they come to judgment let all the fruits which we have borne be their forgiveness.

Prayer found near the body of a dead child in the
Ravensbruck concentration camp

Blessing and honour, thanksgiving and praise
        more than we can utter,
        more than we can conceive,
be unto you, O most holy and glorious Trinity,
        Father, Son and Holy Spirit,
by all angels, all people, all creatures
        for ever and ever. Amen and Amen.   Lancelot Andrewes

I bind to myself the name,
the strong name of the Trinity;
by invocation of the same,
The Three in One, and One in Three.
Of whom all nature has creation;
eternal Father, Spirit, Word:
Praise to the Lord of my salvation,
Salvation is of Christ the Lord.   St Patrick

Christ be with me, Christ within me,
Christ behind me, Christ before me,
Christ beside me, Christ to win me,
Christ to comfort and restore me,
Christ beneath me, Christ above me,
Christ in quiet, Christ in danger,
Christ in hearts of all that love me,
Christ in mouth of friend and stranger.   Breastplate of St Patrick

Lord Jesus Christ, you said that you are the Way, the Truth, and the
       Life.
Help us not to stray from you, for you are the Way;
nor to distrust you, for you are the Truth;
nor to rest on any other than you, as you are the Life.
You have taught us what to believe, what to do, what to hope, and
       where to take our rest.
Give us grace to follow you, the Way, to learn from you, the Truth, and
       live in you, the Life.   Desiderius Erasmus

Soul of Christ, sanctify me.
Body of Christ, save me.
Blood of Christ, inebriate me.
Water from the side of Christ, wash me.
Passion of Christ, strengthen me.
O good Jesus, hear me.
Hide me within your wounds
and never allow me to be separated from you.
From the wicked enemy defend me.
In the hour of my death call me,
and bid me come to you,
so that with your saints I may praise you
for ever and ever.   *Anima Christi,* fourteenth century

God be in my head,
and in my understanding;
God be in my eyes,
and in my looking;
God be in my mouth,
and in my speaking;
God be in my heart,
and in my thinking;
God be at my end,
and at my departing.

Book of Hours, 1514

We praise thee, O God : we acknowledge thee to be the Lord.
All the earth doth worship thee : the Father everlasting.
To thee all Angels cry aloud : the Heavens, and all the Powers therein.
To thee Cherubim and Seraphim : continually do cry,
Holy, Holy, Holy : Lord God of Sabaoth;
Heaven and earth are full of the Majesty : of thy glory.
The glorious company of the Apostles : praise thee.
The goodly fellowship of the Prophets : praise thee.
The noble army of Martyrs : praise thee.
The holy Church throughout all the world : doth acknowledge thee;
The Father : of an infinite Majesty;
Thine honourable, true : and only Son;
Also the Holy Ghost : the Comforter.
Thou art the King of Glory : O Christ.
Thou art the everlasting Son : of the Father.
When thou tookest upon thee to deliver man : thou didst not abhor
     the Virgin's womb.
When thou hadst overcome the sharpness of death : thou didst open
     the Kingdom of Heaven to all believers.
Thou sittest at the right hand of God : in the glory of the Father.
We believe that thou shalt come : to be our Judge.
We therefore pray thee, help thy servants : whom thou hast redeemed
     with thy precious blood.
Make them to be numbered with thy Saints : in glory everlasting.
O Lord, save thy people : and bless thine heritage.
Govern them : and lift them up for ever.
Day by day : we magnify thee;

And we worship thy Name : ever world without end.

Vouchsafe, O Lord : to keep us this day without sin.

O Lord, have mercy upon us : have mercy upon us.

O Lord, let thy mercy lighten upon us : as our trust is in thee.

O Lord, in thee have I trusted : let me never be confounded.

Te Deum Laudamus, fifth century, Book of Common Prayer

I rise today with the power of God to guide me,

the might of God to uphold me,

the wisdom of God to teach me,

the eye of God to watch over me,

the ear of God to hear me,

the word of God to give me speech,

the hand of God to protect me,

the path of God to lie before me,

the shield of God to shelter me,

the host of God to defend me

    against the snares of the devil and the temptations of the world,

    against every man who meditates injury to me,

    whether far or near.   *Breastplate of St Patrick*

Almighty God, who hast given us grace at this time with one accord to make our common supplications unto thee; and dost promise, that when two or three are gathered together in thy Name thou wilt grant their requests; Fulfil now, O Lord, the desires and petitions of thy servants, as may be most expedient for them; granting us in this world knowledge of thy truth, and in the world to come life everlasting. Amen.

John Chrysostom

Father, into thy hands I commend my spirit.   *Luke 23:46 AV*

INDEX OF
FIRST LINES

INDEX OF SUBJECTS

INDEX OF AUTHORS
AND SOURCES OF
PRAYERS

Aedelwald, c. 908–84, known for a collection of 74 prayers and hymns called the *Prayer Book of Aedelwald the Bishop*, and the *Book of Cerne* 276

Alcuin, c. 737–804, English scholar and theologian 51, 68, 95, 106, 146, 171

Alexander, Cecil Francis, 1823–95, hymn writer 186, 225

Alford, Henry, 1810–71, Dean of Canterbury 109

Alfred the Great, 849–99, King of Wessex 78, 287

Alternative Service Book 1980 88, 162

Ambrose, c. 339–97, Bishop of Milan 58, 60

Ambrosian Manual 104, 225

Andrewes, Lancelot, 1555–1626, Bishop of Chichester and then Winchester, one of the translators of the Authorized Version of the Bible 10, 45, 65, 71, 73, 76, 77, 100, 130, 131, 132, 136–7, 138, 151, 210, 220, 256, 297

Anima Christi, fourteenth century 34, 298

Anselm, 1033–1109, Archbishop of Canterbury 21, 38, 56, 66, 101, 117, 125, 160, 167

Aquinas, Thomas, 1225–74, Italian Dominican monk, theologian and philosopher 56, 71, 74, 84, 203, 296

Arndt, Johann, 1555–1621, German Lutheran 115

Arnold, Thomas, 1795–1842, Headmaster of Rugby School 177

Astley, General Lord Jacob, 1579–1652, soldier 67, 256, 296

Augustine, 354–430, Bishop of Hippo in North Africa, very influential theologian 26, 27, 56–7, 57, 59, 63, 72, 74, 82, 84, 88, 95, 109, 115, 134, 172, 256, 294, 296

Austen, Jane, 1775–1817, English novelist 64, 103, 289

Aylward, Gladys, 1902-70, missionary to China 255

Niebuhr, Reinhold, 1892–1971, American theologian 107, 294
Nott, Peter, Bishop of Norwich, b. 1933 45–7, 85, 201–2

Office of None, in the monastic ritual, one of the daily religious
    services, originally recited at 3 p.m. 186
Office of the Royal Maundy in Westminster Abbey 224

Paget, Francis, 1851–1911, Bishop of Oxford 117, 164
Palmer, Ray, 1808–87 130
Paterson, Alexander, prison reformer 114
Patrick, c. 385–461, English missionary to Ireland 5, 38, 45, 297, 300
Penn, William, 1644–1718, English Quaker, founded Pennsylvania 191,
    257
Pierpoint, Folliott Sandford, 1835–1917, hymn writer 6
Polycarp, c. 69–155, Bishop of Smyrna, knew the apostle John, burnt to
    death for his faith 80, 122
Primer, 1557 18
Primer, 1559 75, 276
Private Devotions 53
Pusey, Edward Bouverie, 1800–82, Tractarian leader 38, 62, 84, 110,
    114, 118, 200, 259

Raleigh, Sir Walter, 1552–1618, English courtier, writer and adventurer
    86–7, 190, 286–7
Ravensbruck concentration camp 55, 297
Reynolds, Edward, Bishop of Norwich 14
Richard of Chichester, 1197–1253, Bishop of Chichester 67, 296
Ridley, Nicholas, c. 1500–55, Protestant reformer and Bishop of
    London, martyred under Queen Mary 92, 104
Rinkart, Martin, 1586–1649, German minister and poet 181
Robinson, Arthur W., 1856–1928, Canon of Canterbury 164
Roger, Brother, Roger Schutz, b. 1915, founder of Taizé 105, 116, 122, 288
Rolle, Richard, 1290–1349, Yorkshire hermit and spiritual writer 50,
    55, 57
Roman Breviary, contains psalms and Bible readings for daily services
    28, 147, 293
Rossetti, Christina, 1830–94, British poet 9, 11, 29, 31, 41, 48, 55, 65,
    73, 76, 78, 96, 103, 105, 106, 112, 121, 133, 178, 207, 216, 217–18,
    248, 249–50

INDEX OF BIBLE REFERENCES AND BIBLE PRAYERS

ACKNOWLEDGEMENTS

Extracts from the Alternative Service Book 1980 are copyright © The Central Board of Finance of the Church of England 1980 and are reproduced by permission.

Extracts from the Book of Common Prayer, the rights of which are vested in the Crown, are reproduced by permission of the Crown's Patentee, Cambridge University Press.

Extracts from *More Everyday Prayers* and *Further Everyday Prayers* appear by permission of the National Christian Education Council.

Extracts from *Parish Prayers* appear by permission of Hodder & Stoughton.

The publishers are grateful to Peter Nott, former Bishop of Norwich, for permission to reproduce four of his prayers.